RESOURCE*LINES*

7/8

PEARSON

Prentice Hall

Toronto

Canadian Cataloguing in Publication Data
Main entry under title:
Prentice Hall language ResourceLines 7/8
Includes Bibliographical references and index.
ISBN 0-13-12918-6

1. English language - Juvenile literature. 2. English language -
Grammar - Juvenile literature.

PE1112.P73 1999 428 C99-930146-2

Prentice-Hall, Inc., Upper Saddle River, New Jersey
Prentice-Hall International, Inc., London
Prentice-Hall of Australia, Pty., Ltd., Sydney
Prentice Hall of India Pvt., Ltd., New Delhi
Prentice-Hall of Japan, Inc., Tokyo
Prentice-Hall of Southeast Asia (PTE) Ltd., Singapore
Editora Prentice-Hall do Brasil Ltda., Rio de Janeiro
Prentice-Hall Hispanoamericana, S.A., Mexico

ISBN 0-13-012918-6

Publisher: Carol Stokes
Project Manager: Helen Mason
Contributing Editor: Elma Schemenauer
Development Editors: Janet Shorten, Helen Mason
Director of Secondary Publishing: MaryLynne Meschino
Copy Editors: Susan Lawrence, Carol Grant, Isobel Stevenson
Production Co-ordinator: Sharon Houston
Permissions: Michaele Sinko
Interior Design: Zena Denchik
Cover Design: Alex Li
Cover Image: ©Anson Liaw 1999
Chapter Opening Illustrations: © Anson Liaw 1999
Ilustrations: VictoR GAD, elephant works inc.

Printed and bound in Canada
9   10   FP   07

Prentice Hall Canada wishes to thank the following:
Content Consultants: Wendy Mathieu, Susan Tywoniuk
Equity Reviewer: Nora Allingham
Aboriginal Content: Rocky Landon
Reviewers: Barbara Wohleber, ON; Susan Dunlop, ON; Leigh Morris,
ON; Don Quilliams, AB; Nancy Horton, AB; Stuart Bent, BC; Melody
Sawkins, BC; Dale Loveridge, NF; Janet L. Hiscott, NS; Dorene
Alexander, NB; Wendy Mathieu, AB; Susan Tywoniuk, AB; Joan
Penny Lorintt, BC.

Contents

Chapter Three: Speaking and Listening

Chapter Four: Viewing

Welcome to ResourceLines

ResourceLines 7/8 language arts resource textbook is an integral part of the *SightLines* Program. This easy-to-use "how-to" book for students covers all aspects of the six language arts strands:

❋ Reading

❋ Writing

❋ Listening

❋ Speaking

❋ Viewing

❋ Representing

Tightly integrated into the *SightLines* program, *ResourceLines* is designed for teacher-directed instruction and independent student work (individually and in groups).

❋ Teacher-directed instruction: For every selection, Teacher's Guide activities reference the relevant language skills in *ResourceLines*; teachers can then refer the students to ResourceLines as they do the activities.

❋ Independent student work: If students need help while doing any language arts assignment, they can simply turn to the relevant section of *ResourceLines* for guidance, processes, and models.

ResourceLines 7/8 offers the following features:

❋ Seven chapters providing comprehensive coverage of all six language arts strands, and more:

1. Reading
2. Writing
3. Listening and Speaking
4. Viewing
5. Representing
6. Researching
7. Handbook (Grammar, Usage, Style, Spelling)

❋ Coverage of all curriculum outcomes for grades 7 and 8

❋ A wide range of models (e.g., letters, posters, graphic organizers) for students.

❋ Technology is integrated throughout, especially in the chapters on writing, researching, viewing, and representing.

▪ Each main section is accompanied by a short list of outcomes in student-accessible language, which help to focus students' learning and thinking.

▪ Each main section provides a short set of activities that reinforce the skills and information in the section.

▪ Each chapter ends with a student self-evaluation checklist called "Measure Your Growth."

how Learners Learn

CONTENTS

Language Arts Learning

Focus Your Learning
- Retell from different points of view
- Address information gaps
- Distinguish between fact and opinion

Think about some of the things you have learned: at least one language, how to play games, how to use a calculator or a computer, and lots more. Now take time to think about *how* you learn. This will help you grasp new things more easily.

You'll learn language arts better if you know what they are. There are several language arts. People don't always list them the same way, but here is one list:

- ★ Reading

- ★ Writing

- ★ Researching

- ★ Speaking and listening

- ★ Viewing

- ★ Representing (expressing ideas through drawing and other means that aren't mainly writing)

You'll also learn language arts better if you apply the following principles of language arts learning.

1. All language arts are related to each other, like cousins.

2. Language arts are also related to science, history, mathematics, and other content areas.

3. Language arts learning involves the emotions as well as the brain.

Horses have three gaits—walk, trot, canter. The trot is the hardest to learn because...

Sherilee tape-records herself talking about her topic. Then she plays back the tape, takes notes, and turns them into a report.

Let's Practise

In which language arts area do you have a special talent? How can you use that talent to help you learn?

Personal Learning Styles

Focus Your Learning
- Assume various roles
- Create original text in various forms
- Reflect on personal growth
- Obtain information from various sources

Did you learn to ride a bike the same way you learned to multiply and divide? Of course not. That's because people learn in different ways. The same person might learn one thing one way, and another thing another way.

Let's Practise

Which learning style best matches your own? What other ones can you adapt for your own use?

Processing Information

Focus Your Learning
- Assess and evaluate research process
- Evaluate information
- Use comprehension strategies
- Activate and use prior knowledge
- Listen to identify main ideas
- Develop outlines and graphic organizers
- Map concepts
- Summarize
- Ask questions to elicit additional information

In school and elsewhere, you need to handle or process information in different ways to meet different expectations. You have to absorb new ideas, recall them, and use them. This kind of learning may sometimes seem difficult, but you *can* make it happen. Try out the following strategies for processing information, and keep track of which ones work best for you. You will soon become an expert on your own information processing style.

Making Notes

Think about the best way to learn from an information presentation like a speech, CD-ROM, video, or TV program. You should begin by mentally preparing to watch and listen *actively*. For example, as the presentation proceeds, you can compare new information with what you already know. You can also keep focussed by making notes. Following these steps will make it easier.

1. **Get your mind ready for the topic.** Suppose a speaker says, "Today we'll talk about how Mayan society worked." Write a heading that captures that idea: *Mayan society*.

2. **Listen for the order of ideas.** An informational video, for example, usually follows a plan for presenting information in an organized way. Your notes can mirror that plan. You hear this: "The first important thing is …. Second, …." You might write this: *Important things: 1., 2.*

3. **Summarize information in your own words — or using charts, graphs, diagrams, or drawings.** The idea is to use words or pictures that will help you think about what you're hearing, not to get it down word for word.

   Mayan society
   1 000 years ago
   System of government
   Agriculture

4. **Copy down information that is displayed.** For instance, a speaker may write key points on a board, show information on an overhead projector, or give a multimedia presentation with slides and sound effects. Write down the main ideas of such displays. Also, be sure to get a copy of any handouts.

5. **Add your own remarks.** These might be questions to yourself; points you agree or disagree with; associated ideas; or things you find surprising, confusing, or interesting.

6. **Review your notes afterward.** First, mentally turn your headings into questions: *How did Mayan society work?* Then circle or highlight any information that answers the questions. Also, if the speaker is available, you might ask some follow-up questions based on your notes.

Let's Practise

Use two information processing strategies from this section to help you process some information you find hard to grasp—maybe a section of a mathematics text, an instructional video on cameras, or an Internet article about icebergs.

Time Management

Focus Your Learning

- Develop timelines
- Make notes for different purposes and situations
- Create instructions
- Plan to gather, access, and record information
- Use the steps in the writing process

Do you know people who always get a lot done? They clean the fish tank, fold their laundry, do their homework, and even find time for hobbies. Such people are usually well organized. They know how to make short-range and long-range plans, and how to manage their time to accomplish their goals. If you'd like to be better organized, try some time management techniques. They'll turn you into someone who can finish homework and everyday chores, and still have free time to do other enjoyable things.

Log It, Schedule It

Keeping track of the assignments and chores you have to do will help you become a successful time manager. One tried-and-true method is to write them down in a pocket-size notebook. Another way is to log them on a pocket calendar or computerized organizer. Whichever way you choose, try the following strategies. (These strategies apply to school assignments, but you can also adapt them to such chores as lawn mowing and dog walking.)

1. **Log in** the assignment as soon as possible after you get it. For each entry, note the date you get the assignment, what subject or class it's for, and when it's due.

2. **Write down** any special requirements such as length, format, use of ink or pencil, and so on. Make a "mind-video" of yourself doing each assignment. This mind-video will help you think of problems or questions ahead of time, and get them cleared up in advance.

3. **Read over** the day's assignments before you leave school so that you'll remember to take home any books or other resources you'll need.

4. **Survey** the day's assignments again as you prepare to do your homework. Decide which ones can be done easily and which will need more effort.

5. **Plan a schedule** for doing your homework and decide how you'll divide your time. Will it be easier to do the hard assignments first, while you're more alert, or to work from the simplest to the most complex?

Do I have everything I need?

6. **Highlight** (using a marker or a symbol) long-range assignments like studying for a test, writing a book report, or completing a research project. You'll want to break these assignments into smaller steps and schedule them over a period of time.

7. **Check off** each assignment as you complete it.

Get More Done: Concentrate

Is this a familiar scene? Krystal is sitting at her desk, staring at an open book. She's been working on this assignment for two hours, and she isn't even half done. What's the problem? Krystal has made a work schedule, but she isn't using her scheduled time wisely. She really only *appears* to be working. Her mind has wandered off the subject at least ten times since she began.

If you share Krystal's problem, don't despair. With practice, you can learn to concentrate better and get more work done in less time.

Decide where, when, and how. Figure out when and where you do your best work. Do you need to be in your room, at your desk, with familiar things around you? Or do you find a quiet library atmosphere more helpful? Do you like lots of books and papers piled around? Or do you want only a computer and the book you're consulting at the moment? It's important to learn what's most comfortable for you and stick to a routine—a regular place and time for studying.

Collect a penny for your thoughts. To make yourself aware of the moments your mind drifts away from your studies, put a penny in a dish each time you catch yourself daydreaming. Focus on improving your concentration; try to cut your costs and become a more efficient—and richer—learner. **Need help reading in content areas? See pages 21–35.**

Take a break. Set short-term goals. For example, tell yourself that you'll read five pages of a chapter, or draft the answer to one essay question. When you reach that goal, reward yourself with a few minutes off. Stand up, stretch, eat a few grapes, and then get back to work. Taking breaks this way will help keep your mind fresh and give your ideas a chance to settle down. You might suddenly think of a better way to arrange your essay or solve a math problem.

Set Long-Term Goals

Pierre is trying to save enough money to buy a jacket. Midori is planning a surprise birthday party for a friend. Coach Saldanha is getting her team ready for the first game of the season. What do all three have in common? They are setting long-term goals.

There are two basic things you can do to reach a long-term goal. First, figure out what steps are needed to reach the goal. Second, set aside enough time to complete each step. The following schedule shows how one student planned to arrive at her goal.

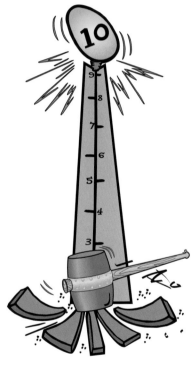

GOAL
Present an oral science report on February 8.

10   D-DAY! Feb. 8.

9   Put oral and visual elements together and practise presentation Feb. 5–6.

8   Fine-tune artwork Feb. 3–4.

7   Begin to practise oral part of report Feb. 1–2.

6   Revise draft Jan. 25–30.

5   Write first draft and gather visual display materials Jan. 18–22.

4   Make working outline by Jan. 16.

3   Collect information Jan. 9–15.

2   Get topic approved by Mr. Ramos on Jan. 8.

1   Choose topic; may need to do research at library Jan. 4–7.

P.S. Checking off each step after it's done can be very satisfying!

Let's Practise

From this section, choose at least three time management suggestions that you think will be especially useful to you. Write them down, and then apply them. Start today!

Exercising Your Memory

Many people think they are born with a bad memory. But you can exercise your memory, much the same way as you can exercise your body. Over time, people have developed all kinds of methods to connect new information with what they already know. Here are some you can try.

Link It Up. You can connect items on a list by creating mental images that are powerful, silly, or shocking.

Use Letter Strategies. You can use the letters of the alphabet to help recall terms. One way is to create acronyms—new words that use the first letters of the words you want to remember. For example, the acronym *HOMES* can represent the names of the Great Lakes (Huron, Ontario, Michigan, Erie, Superior). Another strategy is to create a sentence using words that begin with the first letters of the terms you're memorizing.

Develop Rhymes and Rhythms. "Thirty days hath September, April, June, and November." Rhymes and rhythmic patterns are powerful memory aids. Try chanting, tapping, or making up songs to help you remember information.

Use Categories. Twenty facts are hard to remember. But if you group the facts into categories—by meaning, size, sound, or any other grouping—you'll remember them more easily. For example, if you have to describe the work of twenty people, put the names in small groups—seven national leaders, four scientists, four explorers, and five writers.

Focus Your Learning
- Use prior knowledge to understand new ideas and information
- Rehearse mentally
- Read, recite, and review
- Map concepts

Bring permission slip, running shoes, and gym shorts.

PERM

Humorous mental images will boost your memory.

Let's Practise

Choose something you have trouble remembering. Use one or more memory aids from this section to help you remember.

Test-Taking Tips

Tests are important in school, and in life in general. People use test-taking skills throughout their lives. Many jobs require licences that can be obtained only by passing a test. Some promotions are based on test scores. You would be surprised how often people don't follow test directions. The following pointers are useful:

❄ Prepare yourself well. Find out what will be included in the test. Develop a study schedule and follow it.

❄ Make up study notes that include the most important terms and ideas you need to remember.

❄ Find out how the test will be scored. Some tests penalize you for guessing; others don't.

❄ Take time to read each set of directions as slowly as you need to. Reread them to make sure that you're doing what is asked.

❄ Study any examples provided.

❄ Decide on an order for answering the questions. Do the easier ones first.

❄ Don't get hung up on a question. If you can't think of an answer, move on and come back to it later.

❄ For multiple-choice questions, rule out those answers you know are wrong. Then choose from the remaining answers.

❄ For questions that require longer answers, take time to outline and draft your responses.

❄ When you have finished writing the test, proofread your answers for correct spelling, punctuation, and usage.

Let's Practise

Ask your teacher for a sample test to practise on. Use the test-taking tips in this section to answer some or all of the questions. Discuss your strategies and answers with a group or with the class.

Measure Your Growth

Focus Your Learning

• Reflect on personal growth to set goals

Write the numbers 1–10 in your notebook. Beside each, rate yourself according to the following scale:

A Excellent

B Good

C Fair

D Needs a lot of work

1. I know and apply principles of language arts learning.

2. I recognize my personal learning styles and use them to gain new knowledge and skills.

3. I adapt my learning strategies to suit various situations.

4. During information presentations, I can take notes that are useful in helping me grasp and remember information.

5. I manage my time, including keeping track of and scheduling tasks.

6. When I do homework or study, I know and apply strategies to help me concentrate.

8. I can set and reach long-term goals.

9. I can use memory aids to help me remember important information.

10. I know and apply effective test-taking strategies.

CHAPTER *one*

Reading

CONTENTS

The Reading Process

Focus Your Learning

- Determine purpose for reading
- Skim
- Scan
- Read closely
- Reread
- Use textual and non-textual clues
- Understand use of organizational features
- Identify opinions and points of view
- Reflect
- Interpret and justify point of view

Reading can entertain you, make you smarter, help you plan a vacation—even show you how to tune up your bike. To get the most from your reading, READ ON.

Set a Purpose for Reading

You read better if you know why you're doing it. Different situations in life lead you to different reading purposes. In turn, different purposes call for different kinds of reading materials. The chart below shows some sample situations, purposes, and reading materials.

What reading purpose might you set if you were learning to sew or wanted to find the area of a triangle? What if you were choosing a video to rent or feeling sad after your best friend moved away?

Situations	Purposes	Reading Material
wanting to find out more about Mars, mathematics equations, or musical scales	gain information in content areas such as science, mathematics, music, history, geography	textbooks, factual books, encyclopedias, web sites, CD-ROMs
relaxing or waiting in a bus depot	be entertained	short stories, novels, magazines, comic books
deciding which shoes to buy or which candidate to vote for in a student election	make a choice between several alternatives	advertisements, labels, catalogues, posters, campaign literature, newspaper articles, web sites
looking for encouragement or meaning in life	be inspired	poetry, biographies of inspiring people, religious writings, self-help books

Sometimes people read for two or more purposes at once. For example, suppose you read a short story taking place in India. You may read mainly for entertainment, but also to gain information about India. Suppose you read a biography of a Canadian hero such as Terry Fox. You may read mainly for inspiration, but also to gain information and be entertained.

Skim, Scan, and Read

Suppose you want specific facts on the history of Canadian forts. Do you read every word of the information on forts that you see on the Internet and library shelves? Probably not. When your reading purpose is to gain information, it's often best to read quickly first, then slowly.

1. Quickly scan materials first to see which are most useful to you. When you scan you look at overall things such as titles and tables of contents to get an idea of what information is there.

2. Once you've chosen materials, quickly skim the most promising sections. **For more on previewing, scanning, and skimming, see pages 23 and 24.**

3. When you find the specific information you want, slow down and read it word by word. You may read it several times, especially if it gives directions on where to find something such as the crumbling remains of an old fur-trading fort.

Similarly, when your purpose is to make a choice between several alternatives, it's often best to read quickly at first. If you're choosing a breakfast cereal, you don't want to stand at the grocery shelf all day. You probably scan the cereal pictures and names. If you find a cereal that interests you, you may slow down and read most of what's on the box.

When you're reading to be entertained or inspired, speed is up to you. Suspense in a story may prompt you to read quickly to find out what happened to the Green Slime or the lost child. Description may prompt you to read slowly, picturing in your mind the mysterious dungeon or castle. Beautiful language in a poem may prompt you to read slowly, savouring every word.

Notice Design and Layout

Rivka was flipping through an atlas. She noticed that pages about North America had red edges. Pages about Asia had green edges. How might this design aspect help Rivka find a map of the Philippines?

Grant was reading a magazine article about a singer. He couldn't find out where she was born. Then he noticed that the article's layout included long captions under most photographs. How might this layout aspect help Grant find the information he wanted?

As you read, watch for other design and layout aspects. How might each of the following help you?

★ Text boxes giving in-depth information on aspects of a general topic being discussed.

★ Marginal notes giving extra bits of information.

★ Symbols. In a history book, for example, all information about explorers may have a globe beside it. All information about politics may have a flag.

★ Icons leading to related information.

Make It Personal

Some people think reading is like a one-way lecture—all you have to do is sit there and take it all in. But reading is more like a discussion; you become an active participant in a two-way process.

Reading comes alive when you bring in your personal experiences and feelings. For example, you may be reading an article about a sled-dog trainer in the Yukon. Even if you've never been to the Yukon, you probably know what it's like to be cold or to care about an animal. Your experiences and thoughts help you understand what you read.

Notice how this happens spontaneously when you read.

★ You think about your reactions: "I guess I don't like this character. I'm not rooting for him."

★ You make comparisons: "This character reminds me of my sister. They're both strong-willed."

★ You form opinions: "That baby-sitter has to work hard, even harder than I did when I baby-sat for that family. He earns every cent he's paid."

Notice how you react as you read. What are you feeling? What images does this give you? What surprises you the most? Does this remind you of anything? Anyone? Anywhere?

Your reactions are very personal. Other people's reactions may be similar or very different from yours.

To make reading more personal, you might ask yourself:

Could anything like this ever happen to me?

What would I do if I were in the same situation?

What do I hope will happen to this character?

What would I ask the writer if I had the chance?

> What would I do if I were in a similar situation?

Bright Ideas

for Making It Personal

❋ **Use pencils, pastels, or paints:** Sketch the feelings you have, illustrate your favourite section, or design costumes, props, and sets for the story.

❋ **Use your voice:** Improvise a conversation between characters, or read aloud the funniest, scariest, or most beautiful passages. **To perform a Readers' Theatre presentation, see page 163.**

❋ **Use a pen:** Write a letter to a character, create a diary entry as if you were a character, or write an alternative conclusion.

Responses to Reading

Look for ways to express your responses to what you read. Get them down on paper. Tell them to a friend who has read the same thing, and then … listen. He or she may have a totally different reaction or an interesting insight. You can learn a great deal—and have quite a bit of fun—by sharing your ideas.

Use a Reading Log

Make a reading log. Use it to record some or all of the reading you do this year. How do you think your log will help you improve as a reader? How will it help you understand yourself better?

Date	Purpose for Reading	Title and Author of Material Read	Kind of Reading Material	Comments

Use a Response Journal

You can use a notebook to record your thoughts about what you read. Fill the pages with your feelings, opinions, questions, answers, and discoveries. Focus on exploring how you feel about the people and the events you're reading about.

Experiment with different forms of note-taking. For example, write down quotes, facts, images, feelings and responses, interesting or well-written phrases. Arrange these in two columns.

Here's an example of one student's response to a story she read:

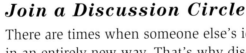

> The story "Frankenstein" is probably the favourite thing I've read so far. I'm amazed at how different the story is from the film, and I actually think it's scarier to read than to watch. I love the passage "The dull yellow eye of my creature opened!"

Join a Discussion Circle

There are times when someone else's idea helps you see an issue in an entirely new way. That's why discussion circles can be so interesting. People who have read the same thing talk about their responses and listen to each other's ideas. You don't always agree, but that's O.K. There isn't one right answer to the kinds of things you talk about: whether you did or didn't like the book or what you would do in the same situation. Discussion circles work best when each member of the group makes a list of questions and ideas ahead of time. **For more on group discussion, see page 125.**

For more on group discussion, see page 125.

Compile a Future Book List

One good book can often lead you to another. The jacket flap or the back cover of a favourite book may list other books written by the same author. You can ask your friends which books they recommend. Make a list of people and subjects that really interest you, and then search in the library for books on those subjects.

You can also try "shelf shopping" while you're in the library. Just scan the book titles on the shelves and look more closely at those that seem interesting.

Sell a Book

Imagine you're a salesperson and you want to sell the book you've just read. To convince your customers to read the book, you have to let them know what you like about it. You might describe a likable character, draw a poster of an intriguing setting, or compose an advertising jingle describing the story. Don't give away any surprises, though. If you do, your customers won't buy the book. **For more on persuasive speaking, see page 143.**

Talk to the World

In a dialogue journal, you share ideas with another person—a friend, teacher, relative, or anyone you wish—about what you're reading. The writing is informal and friendly, just like writing a note to a friend. An electronic dialogue uses computers instead of paper. You can discuss what you're reading with people all over the world through computer networks. **For more on journals, see page 68.**

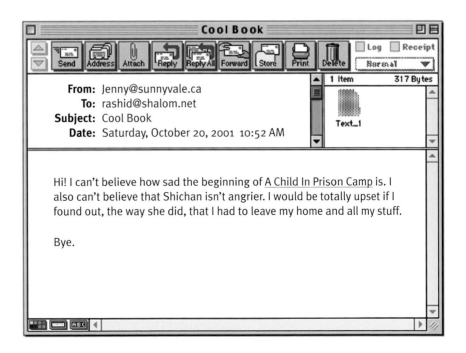

Cool Book

From: Jenny@sunnyvale.ca
To: rashid@shalom.net
Subject: Cool Book
Date: Saturday, October 20, 2001 10:52 AM

1 Item   317 Bytes

Text_1

Hi! I can't believe how sad the beginning of A Child In Prison Camp is. I also can't believe that Shichan isn't angrier. I would be totally upset if I found out, the way she did, that I had to leave my home and all my stuff.

Bye.

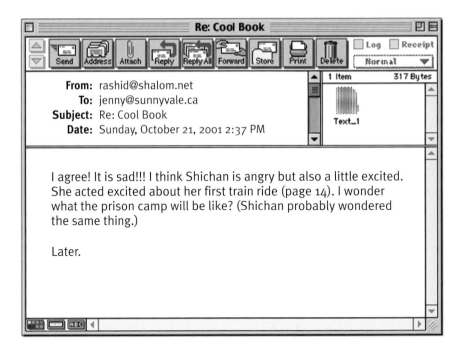

Re: Cool Book

From: rashid@shalom.net
To: jenny@sunnyvale.ca
Subject: Re: Cool Book
Date: Sunday, October 21, 2001 2:37 PM

1 Item   317 Bytes

Text_1

I agree! It is sad!!! I think Shichan is angry but also a little excited. She acted excited about her first train ride (page 14). I wonder what the prison camp will be like? (Shichan probably wondered the same thing.)

Later.

Let's Practise

1. Choose three pieces of writing you've recently read. They could include a personal letter, a web site, an encyclopedia entry, an article, a story, a book, or some other piece of writing. In your notebook make a log like the one on page 17. Fill it in for your three pieces of writing.

2. Choose a piece of writing you've read recently. Write two or three sentences explaining how you used one of the following in reading it: suitable reading speeds, design and layout, questions to make it personal.

Reading in Content Areas

Focus Your Learning

- Use prereading strategies
- Evaluate effectiveness and limitations of various writing forms
- Evaluate usefulness of information
- Read, recite, and review
- Preview/review
- Use structural features
- Use footnotes and hypertext
- Summarize
- Map concepts
- Identify main idea from two or more texts and explain how details support main idea
- Identify main patterns of organization

Written information is everywhere: in textbooks, magazines, and newspapers. Information also includes the on-screen instructions for a video game and the steps in a recipe.

What have astronomers recently learned about the solar system? To answer science questions like this and questions in other content areas, you need information. Where do you find information? Stories have some, but when your purpose is finding facts and information quickly, you'll probably choose nonfiction sources.

The way you read is important, too. You might let the words flow past you when you read for entertainment. But when you read for information, you actively seek the knowledge you need.

You can get more information speedily by using a reading plan. Let's take a look at three plans: the KWL Plan, the Think-Write Plan, and the SQ3R Plan. Don't let the titles scare you—these plans are easy.

The KWL Plan

The letters *KWL* stand for What I Already *K*now, What I *W*ant to Know, and What I *L*earned. Before you read about a subject, label three columns *K, W,* and *L* on notebook paper. To fill in the K column, think about what you already know. Next, think of what else you want to know, and list your questions in the W column. After reading the material carefully, write answers to your questions in the L column. Here's an example:

What I Already *K*now	What I *W*ant to Know	What I *L*earned
There are two main kinds of camels.	• What are the two kinds? • What do they look like? • Where do they live?	The two kinds are Arabian and Bactrian. Arabian camel has one hump; Bactrian has two. Arabian is native to north Africa, India, and the Near East. Bactrian lives in central Asia. Camels can go several days without food and water.

The Think-Write Plan

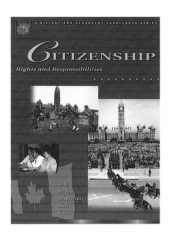

When you think-write, you make notes on what's going through your mind while you read. You write on self-stick removable notes. Or you write directly on the pages if it's material you're allowed to write on. Material you can write on may include a photocopy, a magazine or book you own, a letter, or an e-mail. Think-writing can make you more aware of the reading strategies you use: previewing, questioning, guessing, making links, summarizing, evaluating, and so on.

Read Sarita's think-writing on the following e-mail printout. If you had received the e-mail, what might you have written?

Why is Marlis up so early?

06:00 AM 10/3/02

To: sbraha@sundbo.net
From: Marlis Peal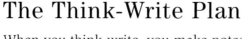
Subject: liff   *Looks like a spelling mistake but M. doesn't make many. I guess it's a joke. Liff must mean life.*
Cc:
Bcc:
X-Attachments:

Hi Sarita,   *I think I saw Adams on TV.*

Do you know the book *The Meaning of Liff* by Douglas Adams? With your sense of humour, you might like it and his dozen or so other science fiction spoofs. I couldn't sleep so I was reading it in bed.

Wonder if it's about that Noah's ark thing again.

Life goes on much the same except Mom's in Turkey on a field trip. She's due back Saturday.

Dad and I took a walk on the beach. I bet you didn't know we have a long beach right in downtown Toronto. We usually don't tell noisy, nosy tourists, but I'll show you when you come in July.

It's not nice of M. to say that about tourists.

Write soon,

Marlis Peal, Toronto, ON, Canada

The SQ3R Reading Plan

The letters of this plan stand for *Survey*, *Question*, *Read*, *Recite*, and *Review*. Let's look at the plan briefly before examining it in depth. SQ3R means:

1. **Survey.** To get an overview, scan the pages to read titles, headings and subheadings, illustrations, and captions.

2. **Question.** Before you read and as you read, ask yourself questions. Then, while you are reading, answer your questions, either to yourself or by jotting down notes.

3. **Read.** Focus on what you are reading. Look up difficult vocabulary. Reread difficult passages.

4. **Recite.** Talk about what you've read to make sure you really understand it.

5. **Review.** Write brief summaries of what you read. Review the answers to your questions.

"Outside of a dog, a book is a man's best friend. Inside of a dog, it's too dark to read."

—Groucho Marx

Survey, or Preview

Reading material is easier to understand if you preview it before reading it. As you preview the selection, your mind prepares a mental outline of the main ideas. Then, as you read in depth, it fills in the details.

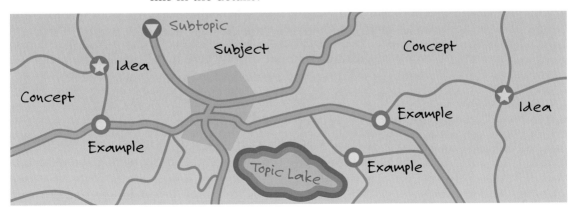

As you do your preview, note the following:

1. **Headings and subheadings.** Flip through the pages to find them. A mental outline begins to form as you read them. If you see the heading *Your Mouse and You* with the subheading *White Mice as Pets*, your mind begins to fill in the outline with a certain kind of detail. If the subheading is *Secrets of Computer Control*, a completely different set of details begins to form.

2. **Illustrations including pictures, graphs, and charts.** Look them over before you read. Writers often use illustrations to help explain important or difficult ideas.

3. **First paragraph.** Read it carefully. Writers often use it to give their special slant on the information.

4. **Questions or summaries at the end of the selection.** Read them before you read the selection itself. They'll help you focus on key ideas as you read.

5. **Words or sections that are highlighted, underlined, or printed in bold or italic type.** Skim them before you read the selection. Writers often use them to signal important words and ideas. **For more on underlining and italics, see page 340.**

Question

You'll be better able to understand what you read if you ask yourself questions *before* you read and *as* you read.

Ask yourself:

Questions raised by the headings. If you see the heading *Continents Drift,* you might ask: "How do continents drift? Why do continents drift? Which continents drift?" Find answers to your questions as you read—and you'll probably find the most important points.

Why might this be important? Where is this leading? Playing detective will keep you awake and focus your attention. Think of the *who, what, when, where, why,* and *how* of events and ideas.

What did I just read? Rephrase ideas, orally or in writing, every few paragraphs or so. Use your own words. If you can rephrase these ideas now, you'll probably be able to remember them later, when you need them.

Read in Depth

By slowing down your reading speed and carefully thinking about what you're reading, you're more likely to understand information the first time you read it.

By visualizing what you read, you can make any subject more meaningful, more interesting, and easier to understand. For example, it's one thing to read about the Yukon Territory before the 1898 gold rush. But turn on your theatre-of-the-mind, and imagine you're there. You see a tired prospector, alone in a vast, frozen wasteland. He stoops to fill his canteen from a stream of spring run-off. He sees a yellow gleam ....

Use Writers' Conventions as Guideposts

Here are more writers' conventions, or customs. Watch for and use these conventions as you read in depth.

1. **Punctuation:** commas, colons, semicolons, periods, question marks, exclamation marks, parentheses, and so on. A colon is sometimes used to introduce listed items such as the following: molasses, codfish, potatoes, blueberries, and soda bread. Parentheses are often used to set off added information.

    My friend (the one who turns cartwheels) is going to act in a stage play.

    For more on punctuation, see pages 336–342.

2. **Glossary:** a list defining key words and terms, usually at the back of a book. As you read, if you're in doubt about a word or term, try looking it up in the glossary. Example:

    Look up the term *SQ3R* in the glossary at the back of this book. Since glossaries are alphabetical, will *SQ3R* come before or after *summarize?*

3. **Footnote:** note at the bottom of a page about something on that page. It may, for example, give the source of material quoted from another writer. Or it may give extra information such as:

    Pewter is an alloy, or mixture, of tin with other metals, often copper or lead.

4. **Endnote:** note at the end of a chapter, article, or other piece of writing. It's like a footnote except for its placement. Endnotes are often numbered. Numbers within the piece of writing show what the endnotes relate to. Example:

An article may have a sentence like this with a number after it:

Darlene Peal found fragments of gopher wood on Mount Ararat (5).

Looking at endnote 5, you might see something like this:

5. Mount Ararat, in Turkey, is where Noah's ark is believed to have come to rest.

5. **Hypertext:** highlighted words in a computer web site, database, CD-ROM, or other technological resource. Clicking on the hypertext shows you what else the resource has on those words. Example:

Several <u>Edmonton</u> organizations promote <u>Chinese</u> <u>culture</u>.

Clicking on the hypertext might lead you to further information about Edmonton or Chinese culture.

Here's How to

Read Directions

Suppose you spend a whole weekend putting together a shelving unit for your magazines. Then on Monday morning you discover you started with the wrong piece and the unit won't stand up. Reading directions can save you more time than it takes.

1. **Read the directions, all of them, all the way through.**

2. **Make sure you understand what you're expected to do.** If you're unsure, ask questions before you plunge in!

3. **Visualize each step in the directions.**

4. **Gather any supplies you'll need.**

5. **Go back to the beginning and complete the directions, one step at a time.** If the directions are long or complicated (as in a recipe), review them once in a while to make sure you're on target.

Let's Practise

Choose a reading selection in a content area such as science, history, or mathematics. As you read it, stop once in a while to give yourself a sort of mental nudge. Answer the following questions to see how you're doing.

1. What are the main ideas I've read so far? (Put them in my own words.)

2. What are some connections between the ideas I've read so far?

3. What is the meaning of words in **boldface** or *italic* type?

4. How do the illustrations relate to the text?

5. What conclusions can I draw about what I just read?

Recite, or Speak to Learn

Telling someone about something forces you to clarify your thinking. Your brain does a quick dash to organize the information and pick out the most important points. What happens when you tell a second person about the same story or film? Since your mind has already had a rehearsal, it's a lot easier, isn't it? Using the mind-to-mouth connection can help you understand and remember what you read.

Review and Summarize

Review what you have read.

Terms. Check important terms that are in **boldface** or *italic* type.

Main Points. For each paragraph, ask yourself, "What is the most important thing I learned in this paragraph?" Then write that idea in your own words.

Connections. Read the beginning and closing paragraphs, headings, and subheadings to find key points. What are the connections between main ideas?

Simplify. Substitute a general term (such as *sports*) for a list of specific terms.

You can remember important points by summarizing them. Writing a summary will help you find the main ideas and see how the details support them. To write a summary, choose only the most important ideas in a chapter or article, and rewrite those ideas in your own words. Of course, your summary should be much shorter than the original.

Points	Text

Summarize this main point by using your own words. ············

When Europeans first invaded the Americas, they set in motion an exchange that has dramatically changed the way in which people live worldwide. The exchange involved both plants and animals.

Spanish conquistadors arriving in the Americas brought with them strange creatures—horses! Horses had long been extinct in the Americas, and so the Aboriginal people of the Plains had never seen these strange animals before. But within one generation, these people became expert at capturing, training, and riding the horses. Horses became a great aid in hunting bison.

Substitute a general term, vegetables, for this list. ········

Just as horses were strange creatures to the people of the Plains, so the tomatoes, squash, corn, and potatoes that grew in the Americas were strange vegetables to Europeans. However, these new plants became an important source of their nutrition.

These details are interesting, but for a summary, think of the point they make. ········

Potatoes, in particular, became an essential part of the diet of the people in Ireland. Potatoes grew well, could last through a winter, and provided good nourishment. The Irish became so dependent on potatoes that when a terrible blight struck the potato crop, famine followed. From 1845 to 1848, at least one million people died in Ireland. More than that number immigrated to North America, changing the face of that continent's population.

Student Summary

Since their first contact, Europeans and the Aboriginal people of the Americas have exchanged plants and animals. Aboriginal people received horses from Spain, which changed the way they followed bison. Foods from the Americas went to Europe. The Irish grew to depend on potatoes so much that crop failure led to deaths and forced many to move to North America.

Here's How to

Summarize Ideas from Several Sources

1. Set your sources side by side.
2. Read what each has to say about a topic.

Source A: Travel Book

Brazilian soccer teams have repeatedly won the World Cup competition. Rio de Janeiro's huge Maracana soccer stadium seats 200 000 eager spectators. They celebrate or weep, depending on whether their team wins or loses. Soccer is truly Brazil's best-loved sport.

Source B: Web Site

Nothing excites Brazilian sports-lovers as much as *futebol* (soccer). Every town and school has its own team, and many professional *futebol* players become national heroes.

Source C: Encyclopedia

Soccer is by far the top favourite sport of Brazilians. Soccer stars such as Pelé are national heroes. The Maracana soccer stadium in Rio de Janeiro is the world's largest stadium, seating more than 180 000.

3. In each selection, try to find a sentence that sums up the main idea. Examples: *Source A—last sentence, Source B—first sentence, Source C—first sentence.*
4. Compare all the main-idea sentences. In your own words, briefly note the one idea on which all agree. Example: *Soccer is Brazil's favourite sport.* **For more information on main ideas, see page 30.**

Patterns in Information

On the following pages you'll find a strategy you can use with any reading plan: Find out how information is organized. Once you identify the pattern of organization, you can better understand what you're reading.

Patterns of Organization

Information is often organized into these patterns:

Main Ideas and Supporting Details

Definition and Examples

Description

Classification and Lists

Problems and Solutions

Causes and Effects

Comparisons and Contrasts

Turning the pattern into a drawing, map, or diagram will help you see how one piece of information relates to another. Let's take a closer look at some of these patterns.

Main Ideas and Supporting Details

In this pattern of organization, one sentence tells the main idea of a paragraph or group of paragraphs. Sentences and phrases give details and examples that support that main idea.

Phrases such as *most remarkable, central concern, key idea,* and *main point* are clues to main ideas. Phrases such as *for example, for instance,* and *not only* are clues to supporting details. These phrases are highlighted in bold in the following quotation to help you organize your thoughts as you read.

When most people think of loons, they think of the bird's haunting cry, a sort of echoing, wailing laughter. The loon's **most remarkable** feature, however, is its rugged strength. **For example,** when a loon flies, its wings pump steadily 260 times per minute, minute after minute, hour after hour. With a strong tail wind, loons in flight can attain speeds of more than 160 kilometres per hour. Loons are powerful **not only** in the air, **but also** in the water. Loons diving for fish can stay underwater for five minutes and can dive to depths of 30 metres and more.

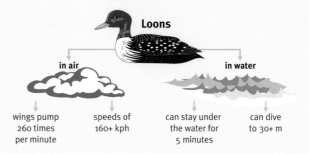

Definition and Examples

This pattern is similar to Main Ideas and Supporting Details. The central idea is a definition, and the supporting details are examples. Following is an example:

Each player has a joystick, **which is** a box-shaped device with a movable stick. The joystick controls the speed and direction of each player's Galactic Explorer on the computer screen. **For example,** to make a character dodge Space Blob Devourers approaching from the left, move the joystick rapidly to the right.

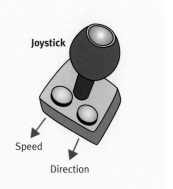

Phrases such as *which is, that is,* and *called* are clues to definitions. Phrases such as *for example, such as, for instance, like,* and *including* are clues to examples.

Description

In paragraphs or passages of description, the author tells what something looks like, feels like, or smells like. You can target the most important aspect of a description by illustrating it with your own diagram.

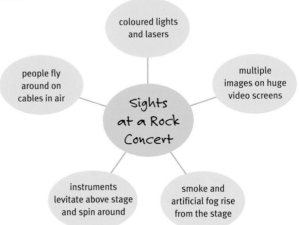

Classification and Lists

Classification names the smaller categories that make up a large category, and groups things according to these smaller categories.

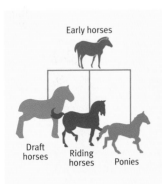

The first horses, tiny creatures only 25 to 51 centimetres in height, evolved into several **kinds of** much larger animals. Workhorses, such as the Belgian draft horse, can attain 190 centimetres in height and weigh an impressive 1000 kilograms. Riding horses, such as the Morgan, the Arabian, and the Tennessee walking horse, are average in height for modern horses, about 140 to 160 centimetres. Ponies, such as the Shetland pony, are the shortest horses at 120 centimetres.

If you've ever gone shopping or have given someone how-to instructions for making, building, or doing something, you've made a list. Lists are useful for stating the parts of something or explaining steps in a process. Lists might—or might not—be numbered.

Phrases such as *kinds of, types of,* or *categories of* are clues to classifications. Numerals, and words such as *first, next, then, materials, supplies,* and *contents,* are often clues to lists.

Problems and Solutions

You might encounter problem-and-solution patterns in social studies or science books, magazine and newspaper articles, or other sources. You can boil down pages of information by drawing this kind of diagram:

Problem

Teenagers want jobs, but many employers prefer to hire older workers.

Solution 1

Lower the minimum wage so older workers who need to support themselves won't want minimum-wage jobs.

Solution 2

The government should subsidize teenage workers by sharing the cost of their wages with employers.

Phrases such as *a problem, a difficulty,* and *a dilemma* are clues to a problem. Phrases such as *a solution, another way of, to solve, to find out,* and *to find the key* are clues to a solution. Words and phrases such as *because, when, as a result, therefore, since,* and *because* are clues to cause and effect.

Causes and Effects

If you throw a rock at a window, what happens? The cause, a thrown rock, will create an effect—a broken window. That effect might also lead to another effect, such as an angry parent. Writers use cause-and-effect patterns to tell why events happened or why things are as they are. One cause can lead to one or more effects. Or several causes can lead to one major effect. Also, an effect can become the cause of something else (the angry parent might be the cause of some discomfort to you).

Comparisons and Contrasts

Writers use this pattern to show how things are alike and how they differ. Example: Margaret Atwood's poems "Snake Woman" and "Buffalo in Compound: Alberta" are *similar* in that the speaker in both poems recalls being a child and seeing animals. The poems are *unlike* in their tone and sensory images.

Sometimes writers compare the unfamiliar with the familiar to help readers make a meaningful comparison. Example:

> Fleas can jump a distance 150 times their own length, **which is like** a person jumping to the top of a 15-storey building. When a flea jumps, its acceleration is **equivalent to** 50 times the speed of a space shuttle after liftoff.

Words and phrases such as *similar, which is like, the equivalent of, in the same way,* and *like* are clues to similarities. Words and phrases such as *unlike, but, in contrast to, however,* and *on the contrary* are clues to differences.

Organizing Ideas from Several Sources

This is especially useful when you're reading factual material for a report or other project.

1. Write down a main idea you have about a topic. Call it A.

    A. When settlers arrived, they needed to build dwellings for shelter.

2. Find information sources that relate to your main idea. Set them side by side, using self-stick removable notes to label them B, C, D, and so on.

Source B	Source C	Source D	Source E
Many settlers hurried to build a soddy before winter. They also tried to plow an area big enough to plant crops in the spring.	Soddies were houses built of blocks cut from the surface of the earth. The thick prairie grasses held these blocks together remarkably well.	Settlers worked hard to build a log cabin before winter. In the spring they planted their first crops among the stumps of the huge trees they had chopped down.	The prairies reminded Ivan and Mary of the Russian steppes they had left behind.

3. Compare A with each source. Write questions and ideas that arise from this.

   A compared with B: Is a soddy a house? It probably wasn't made of wood since prairies were basically treeless.

4. Now compare A with more than one source at once. Write ideas arising from this. Do they answer any of your questions?

   A compared with B and C: A soddy is a sod house.

Let's Practise

1. In your notebook write a paragraph or two to explain what the SQ3R Reading Plan is.

2. Read a passage from a book dealing with a content area such as mathematics, computer science, history, geography, or family studies. During and after your reading, make brief notes on how you are following the SQ3R Reading Plan.

Reading Critically

Focus Your Learning

- Identify main ideas
- Compare similar texts
- Make predictions
- Identify and analyse character and plot development
- Use contextual clues
- Make connections between biographical and historical information and texts
- Identify viewpoints, opinions, bias, false reasoning, and stereotypes
- Distinguish between fact and opinion

When you hear the term *critical reader*, do you picture a person frowning and finding fault with every word? Being critical can mean finding faults, but being a critical reader means something else entirely. It means that you think about what you read. You analyse the content by looking at how it is written and what it is actually saying. You use your knowledge and skill to judge the truth and value of what's in print.

Think While You Read

Reading critically involves several kinds of thinking.

Recognizing: Identify main ideas, facts, opinions, and points of view.

Analysing: Make comparisons, link causes and effects, draw conclusions, and predict outcomes.

Evaluating: Form opinions about how well written, logical, and interesting the work is.

The ways in which you recognize, analyse, and evaluate will vary with the kind of reading you are doing.

Not sure *what* you're supposed to recognize? Read about the different elements of fiction and nonfiction. **See pages 49 and 30.**

Tips for Reading...

An Informational article or book

Ask yourself:

What are the main ideas?

How has the writer organized them?

Does the writer offer support for those main ideas?

What is the writer's point of view and how is it supported?

Is this a useful source of information?

Essay, editorial, letter to the editor, advertisement, or other persuasive writing

Ask yourself:

What is the writer's point of view?

How has the writer presented this viewpoint?

Has the writer used valid reasoning to support this point of view?

Has the writer convinced me?

Short story or novel

Ask yourself:

How are the events in the plot organized?

What are the characters' personality traits?

Is the writer's point of view clear?

Have I gained anything by reading this? Enjoyment? Appreciation? Inspiration?

I started my career as a famous detective...

Recognize Facts and Opinions

What is the difference between these two statements?

> Savitskava was the first woman to walk in space.

> There should be more female astronauts.

The first statement can be proved and universally agreed upon. It is a fact. You can verify it in a book. The second statement is an opinion. It states someone's belief. No one can prove it in a way that everyone will agree on.

Though you may not always recognize them, opinions appear everywhere—ads, editorial columns, conversations, and textbooks. (For an example, check the next sentence.) Learning how to tell the difference between facts and opinions is an important skill for critical readers. If you mistake opinions for facts, you are likely to misjudge or misunderstand situations. You can recognize, analyse, and evaluate opinions by asking yourself certain questions:

- Can this statement be proved and universally agreed upon?
- Is the opinion supported with examples and reasons?
- Might someone disagree with the opinion? Do I?
- Do I need to find out more?

For more on recognizing faulty logic, see page 141.

Opinions tell how people feel about things, how they view or judge them. They often contain words such as these: *should, best, interesting, important, helpful, beautiful.* NASA, in the following paragraph, is the National Aeronautics and Space Administration, the American space agency.

> Some of NASA's most interesting work is the research into voice-operated robots and machines. Recently, designers have tested a voice-controlled wheelchair. Well over one million people in the United States and Canada rely on wheelchairs for mobility; a voice-controlled chair would be a great help to those who also have limited use of their hands.

Here's how one student analysed the NASA information.

> The word interesting means there's an opinion. I guess people could disagree that it's the space agency's most interesting work. Some people might think the space shuttle is more interesting. I'd better keep reading to see if I agree.
>
> The number of people using wheelchairs is a fact. Someone could prove it by looking it up or by actually counting. That "a voice-controlled chair would be a great help" is an opinion. Some people might disagree and think that such a chair would only be a minor help.

Test the Logic

When you find a sentence that expresses an opinion or argues a point, look carefully at the surrounding sentences. Identify the writer's reasons, and check to see if they make sense. The reasons should lead the reader, step by step, to an understanding of why the opinion or argument is valid. Be on the lookout for faulty logic—reasoning that doesn't make sense.

Faulty cause and effect occurs when event A is said to lead to event B, but no proven connection is given. For example:

> Every time I wash the car, it rains.

(Though the writer may believe washing the car brings rain, meteorologists know there are other causes for the rain.)

Either/or fallacy. This kind of reasoning falsely claims that there are only two options when there are actually more. For example:

> Either join this club or be a loner.

Overgeneralization. Statements that reach beyond what the evidence supports are overgeneralizations. They often include words such as *all, never, always, must.* Example:

> *Everyone* loves opera.

Overgeneralization

All is incorrect. Some athletes may think the kind of racket, ball, or glove they use is more important. Swimmers and divers don't even wear shoes for their sports.

All professional athletes know that the shoes they wear are the most important equipment they use.

They know the right shoe makes the difference in scoring that last-minute goal or clearing that final hurdle.

Of course, it's your decision: You can either buy the shoes, or you can get used to losing.

Faulty Cause and Effect

Strength, skill, and timing have more to do with success in sports than the brand of shoe does.

Either/Or Fallacy

There are options besides buying Ace shoes or losing. Many athletes win while wearing other shoes or no shoes.

Check Point of View

Writers' experiences can affect the way they view and write about things. As a critical reader, you'll want to recognize a writer's viewpoint, or bias, and check for how the tone and structure of the writing may have been affected by that viewpoint. The newspaper articles below describe the same soccer match, but the writers had two very different views of the game. What might a third, unbiased reporter write? You could write a report of the same game from an unbiased viewpoint.

The Centreville Chronicle

The soccer championship was stolen from the Centreville Cleats by the Prattville Predators, who enjoyed the home-field advantage in yesterday's match. The Cleats outplayed the Predators during most of the game. Questionable referee calls in the last half gave the game to the Predators, who scored three goals in the last five minutes. Final score: Predators 6, Cleats 5.

The Prattville Press

The Prattville Predators are soccer champions for the third year in a row! The team celebrated its 6–5 come-from-behind victory over the Centreville Cleats, in which it scored three goals in the last five minutes. Everyone made a supreme effort all season, and it paid off.

You can find bias in stories and poems, too. Look at the tone, word choice, setting, and character traits used. For example, in one story a soldier may be described as a brave hero. Another writer, however, might represent a soldier as a mean predator. Descriptions of the battlefield and enemy could also vary greatly.

A stereotype is a fixed idea about a group of people. The idea may be positive or negative. Writers whose minds harbour stereotypes don't take a fresh look each time they meet a person or group. **(For an example of a stereotype, see page 179.)**

Watch for bias and stereotypes in your reading. Don't accept them. They're too simple and unthinking to be true or fair.

Use Historical and Biographical Clues

Suppose you're reading and say to yourself, "I can't believe what this author says. Doesn't she know about the Confederation Bridge linking Prince Edward Island and New Brunswick?" When this kind of thing happens, it's a good idea to check the copyright date. (Usually it's on the second page of a book.)

You may find, for example, that the book was published in 1993. If you look in an up-to-date Canadian almanac or encyclopedia, you'll find the Confederation Bridge didn't open until 1997.

Even if a book isn't quite up to date, it can still be interesting and useful. Just keep in mind *when* the author was writing. If historical questions come up, check with another source such as an almanac, encyclopedia, or textbook.

In much the same way, it's useful to know a bit about the author as a person. For example, did the author of a book about Karen Kain actually meet Karen Kain? If so, his book about her may be more reliable than a book by someone who didn't. Is the author of an Internet article about dieting a medical professional? If so, her article may be more reliable than one by someone with no medical training.

Here's How to

Support a Viewpoint Based on Reading

1. Read about a person or topic that interests you.

2. Write down what you think of this person or topic. For example, after reading the following encyclopedia entry, you might write:
   - I think Tubman was a hero. OR
   - I think Tubman really was a lot like Moses.

Tubman, Harriet (born about 1820–died 1913) African American slavery abolitionist. She escaped enslavement in 1849 and travelled north by means of a secret network of people and "safe houses" known as the Underground Railroad. Tubman often returned to the American South. She risked her life to help other enslaved people escape the same way she had. Many previously enslaved people reached Ontario, where they started communities in and around Windsor, Dresden, Hamilton, and elsewhere. In all, Tubman led some 300 enslaved people to freedom. Her courage and faith earned her the name "the Moses of her people." In fact, "Moses" was a code name for Tubman in the Underground Railroad. It had special significance for the enslaved people, who, while working in the cotton fields, had often sung:
Go down, Moses
Way down in Egypt land
Tell Old Pharaoh
To let my people go.

3. Explain your viewpoint to others, orally or in writing. You need proof to support it. You may find proof right in the selection. For example, to prove Tubman was a hero, you might quote words such as:
   - "She risked her life to help other enslaved people escape."
   - "Tubman led some 300 enslaved people to freedom."

4. Or you may find proof in your own experience. For example, maybe you've seen the museum at Dresden. It includes Underground Railroad history. Maybe you know someone whose ancestor escaped enslavement.

5. You may also find proof in your own knowledge. For example, to prove Tubman was like Moses, you might use your reading knowledge of Moses from history textbooks or sacred writings.

Let's Practise

Look for the following in selections you've read lately or in other reading materials. In your notebook, briefly note examples of at least four of them.

1. Fact

2. Opinion

3. Historical clues

4. Biographical clues

5. Faulty reasoning

6. Bias

7. Stereotyping

For numbers 5, 6, and 7, rewrite to get rid of the faulty reasoning, bias, and stereotyping.

Reading Questions

Say you're filling out an application form to be a clown at the village fair. Or say you're participating in a survey, doing a mathematics assignment, or writing a test. In all these situations and many more, you'll find yourself reading questions. The better you are at reading them, the better you'll be at answering. Here are a few tips.

Reading Short-Answer Questions

Such questions may call for a word or phrase as the answer. Key words to look for in short-answer questions include *who, what, where,* and *when.* Don't be hasty. Read carefully, word by word, to see exactly what information to give.

Sample Question:

Who was the first Canadian astronaut?

Answer:

Marc Garneau.

Sample Question:

What are the colours of the Canadian flag?

Answer:

Red and white.

Some short-answer questions are multiple choice. They give several possible responses, often lettered A, B, C, D. Don't just choose the first response that strikes you as reasonable. Carefully read all responses before choosing.

Sample Question:

In Braille, patterns of raised dots stand for:

A. Oceans and continents

B. Computer terms

C. Letters of the alphabet

D. Numbers

Answer: C.

Watch especially for multiple-choice questions including responses such as "Both B and C" or "All of the above." If you are too hasty, you may choose only the first of two or more correct responses.

Sample Question:

Roberta Bondar was

A. An astronaut

B. Born in Sault Ste. Marie, Ontario

C. The first Canadian woman in space

D. All of the above

Answer: D.

Reading Longer-Answer Questions

Longer-answer questions may call for one sentence or several sentences. If the teacher or other person asking the question expects a paragraph or essay, the question will usually say so.

Key words to look for in longer-answer questions include verbs such as *list, describe, explain,* and *diagram.* **For more on verbs, see page 281.**

❋ **Say you're asked to list.** Usually you are expected to give a series of items.

Sample Question:

List the elements of a short story.

Sample Answer:

The elements of a short story are characters, setting, plot, and theme.

❋ **Say you're asked to describe.** You're often expected to tell how something looks, sounds, feels, smells, tastes, and/or acts.

Sample Question:

Describe the human heart.

Sample Answer:

The human heart is about the size of a fist. Inside are four spaces, or chambers, connected by valves. The heart acts as a pump, pumping blood through its chambers and out through the body.

As the heart pumps, it makes a regular beating sound called a heartbeat.

❋ **Say you're asked to explain.** You may be expected to give reasons, define, and/or tell how something works.

Sample Question:

Explain why people need blood platelets. Explain how platelets work.

Sample Answer:

Blood platelets keep people from losing too much blood when their skin is cut. Platelets are tiny, colourless disks in the blood. They catch on the rough edges of a cut. They make sticky little threads that form a clot to close up the cut.

❋ **Say you're asked to diagram.** You're often expected to make a sketch, drawing, or chart showing what something is or how it works. Usually you are expected to include labels and a caption.

Sample Question:

Draw a diagram showing the colours of a rainbow and their order.

Sample Answer:

red
orange
yellow
green
blue
indigo
violet

Let's Practise

Work with a partner. Write some questions using the models in this section. Answer each other's questions.

Reading Newspaper Articles

Focus Your Learning
- Use comprehension strategies
- Adjust reading/viewing rate
- Check for meaning

Newspapers contain a lot more than just the news. **Feature articles** provide an in-depth investigation of a topic or current event; **editorials**, **letters to the editor**, and **columns** present personal opinions about various issues; **obituaries** and other announcements give important information about the community; **advertisements**, **classified advertisements**, and **job notices** help people do business; and special features such as **comics** and **crossword puzzles** supply an element of fun. News articles, however, are the backbone of a newspaper.

A newspaper article is a factual, objective account of a current event. Its purpose is to give a brief but clear summary of the event, including quotations from eyewitnesses or other key people. Here are some pointers to help you get the most out of the newspaper articles you read.

Scan the Article

You can get a good head start on a newspaper article by checking out these features:

Headline. The headline is a large, bold title that gives a preview of what the article will cover. Headlines are often cleverly written to arouse your interest.

Byline and placeline. Underneath the headline is the byline, which tells who wrote the article, and the placeline, which tells where the news story takes place.

Photographs and captions. Photographs are used to support the message of the story. For example, a photo of a natural disaster can increase the impact of the verbal descriptions. Below the photo you will find a caption that explains the image.

Read the Article

News articles begin with a **lead**—an introductory section that gives the most important information about the story, answering most or all of the W5 + H questions:

Who?   Where?   When?   What?   Why?   How?

After the lead comes the **body** of the newspaper article. It provides details that build on the facts given in the lead.

As you read the article, you may notice that the details toward the end seem less interesting and important than those at the beginning. This is a result of the **inverted pyramid structure** used for newspaper articles. Newspaper editors intentionally put the essential information first.

Check for Objectivity

Newspaper articles should convey facts, not opinions. Use your critical reading skills to evaluate how objective the article is. Here are some questions that can help you detect bias.

❈ Does the article appear to omit important facts or points of view?

❈ Are there loaded words that lead the reader in a certain direction?

Let's Practise

Clip a newspaper article from the front page of a major daily newspaper. Mark where you think the lead ends and the body begins. Identify how the article answers the W5 + H questions. Does the article display the inverted pyramid structure? Do you think the article is objective? Ask a classmate to read the article. Does he or she agree with your conclusions?

Reading Narratives

Focus Your Learning
- Explore texts
- Identify various forms, genres, and texts
- Identify various elements of a narrative
- Analyse interrelationship between story elements
- Identify various techniques and elements of texts
- Produce a book review

Narratives are stories. You've been reading narratives all your life—poring over comic books or following the latest events in the life of your favourite singer, athlete, or film star. Fiction narratives are imaginary stories that are sometimes based on real people and actual situations. Non-fiction narratives tell about true events and real people.

Choose Your Narrative

Narratives come in many forms—short stories, novels, plays, film scripts, magazine articles, and others. Here's a list to choose from.

Adventure stories are action-packed tales in which the characters—either fictional or real—come into conflict with nature or a dangerous enemy.

Biography is the life story of a person other than the author. *Bio* means "life," and *graphy* refers to writing.

Autobiography …
What do you think an autobiography is? *Auto* means "self." It's the story of the writer's own life.

Fantasy deals with the non-existent, the unreal, and the incredible.

Science fiction creates future or other worlds and imaginary characters. Such stories frequently deal with today's issues and problems in futuristic settings.

Mysteries, thrillers, detective stories, and **horror stories** are suspense-filled, sometimes frightening, stories that keep you guessing about what will happen next. The ending may come as a surprise.

Historical fiction takes you back in time, putting you in touch with actual events and people of the past.

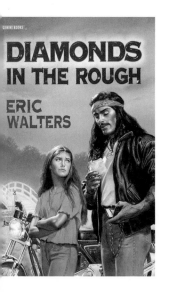

Myths, legends, and **folk tales** have been handed down from past cultures. These are often stories of heroes and gods, and they often explain events or natural phenomena.

Contemporary realistic fiction takes place in the present or recent past. These narratives deal with people—like those you know— and their problems or achievements.

Find the Story Elements

You've chosen your book and settled down in a comfortable spot. You read three pages and … whoa!—it's sort of interesting but you're having trouble figuring out what's going on. A reading strategy might help you. As you read, think about these four basic elements: *setting, character, plot,* and *theme.*

Picture the Setting

You are there. Is it midwinter in the Yukon in 1850? Or is it a sweltering day in downtown Calgary in the year 2040? Watch for details about time and place. Although a story always has a setting, this setting is not always described in detail.

Get to Know the Characters

How do you feel about the *major character* or characters in the story? Often the major character has some kind of problem. Have you gotten to know him or her? What do you think about the *minor characters*? Do they help the major character, cause trouble, or just move the plot along? How do you get to know a character?

★ What does the character look like?

★ What does he or she talk about?

★ What do others say about the character?

★ What emotions does the character show?

★ How does the character act?

★ How believable is the character?

Sometimes it's how he or she changes that keeps you turning the pages. As you read, answer these questions:

★ What choices does the character make?

★ Why does the character make these choices?

★ Does the character stay much the same all the time?

★ Does the character change and develop? If so, how?

Character and Conflict

The main character's problem, or conflict, may play a big part in prompting you to keep turning the pages. Watch for conflicts like these:

❋ Character versus character: A bully is harassing Emiko.

❋ Character versus society: Kevin is outraged that a factory is polluting the river.

❋ Character versus nature: Angie is the lone survivor of a plane crash in the Andes mountains.

❋ Inner conflict: Andrea wants desperately to be on the team. But to join, she has to tell a lie.

Put Yourself into the Plot

When you read a good book, you are often right there with the characters. What's happening? What's the sequence of events? A good story will take you on a roller coaster ride, so hop on …

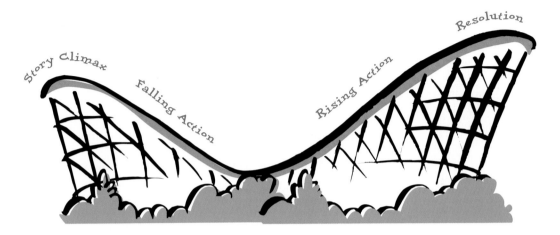

The *rising action* grabs your interest as the main character's problem begins to unfold, and the problem is attacked in various ways.

The *story climax* is the turning point. You hang in suspense waiting to discover if the problem will be resolved.

In the *falling action,* events follow the story climax in quick succession, moving toward resolution.

At the end of the story is the *resolution*, which may—or may not—resolve the problem.

Explore the Theme

O.K. What have you experienced? What's the main idea of the story? Is it to teach a lesson, to entertain, or to inform? What's the author's message to you? Maybe it's "Follow your dream" or "Never give up" or "Animals are smarter than we often realize."

Many modern narratives, like science fiction stories, have a story plot that seems to take you in a circle rather than through a series of events leading to a resolution. Some folk tales and diary stories also loop back to the beginning. As you read, notice if your story plot is circular.

Map a Story

1. **First discover the setting of the story.** Who are the main characters? When and where does the story take place?

2. **Next, recognize the conflict.** What problem do the characters face?

3. **Follow the sequence of events that leads to the resolution.** What situations occur that help to solve the problem?

4. **Then ask how the problem is resolved or *if* it is resolved.** What is the final result? Note that some of the most memorable stories are unresolved, with open endings.

5. **Finally, reflect on the main message of the story.** How did the story make you feel? What's the theme or lesson for you?

This is a Story Map

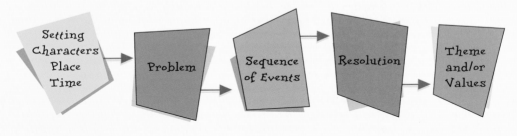

Setting Characters Place Time → Problem → Sequence of Events → Resolution → Theme and/or Values

Relate Story Elements to Each Other

Say a story's characters are skiers. Is the setting more likely to be a ski resort or a sugar cane plantation? Say the theme is "Good triumphs over evil." Is the plot likely to involve much conflict or little? Say the theme is "Life consists mostly of waiting for things to happen." Is the plot likely to be full of twists and surprises, or circular, with the same events recurring several times? As you read, try relating story elements to each other. This can help you grasp a story's structure more quickly and appreciate it more fully.

Interpret and Infer

Authors don't always tell you everything. They carefully pick and choose which details to include and leave the interpreting up to you. That kind of interpreting is called reading between the lines. The conclusions you make are called inferences. Here are some tips on reading between the lines. Ask yourself:

❋ What details are included in the story?

❋ What details have been left out?

❋ Why did the author tell me that?

❋ Why didn't the author tell me about this?

Here's the beginning of a story by Richard Peck called "Priscilla and the Wimps." As you read the dialogue, make some inferences and jot them down. Think about what you learn about the characters and situation without being told.

Points   *Text*

Passes! That sounds like our school—but not having to pay someone for them!

Monk must be smart and also a real bully to have so much clout.

His own gang must be afraid of him if they carry his things around and do his dirty work for him.

---

from "Priscilla and the Wimps"

Listen, there was a time when you couldn't even go to the rest room around this school without a pass. And I'm not talking about those little pink tickets made out by some teacher. I'm talking about a pass that could cost anywhere up to a buck, sold by Monk Klutter.

Not that Mighty Monk ever touched money, not in public. The gang he ran, which ran the school for him, was his collection agency. They were Klutter's Kobras, a name spelled out in nailheads on six well-known black plastic windbreakers.

Monk's threads were more … subtle. A pile-lined suede battle jacket with lizard-skin flaps over tailored Levis and a pair of ostrich-skin boots, brass-toed and suitable for kicking people around. One of his Kobras did nothing all day but walk a half step behind Monk, carrying a fitted bag with Monk's gym shoes, a roll of rest room passes, a cashbox, and a switchblade that Monk gave himself manicures with at lunch over at the Kobras' table.

Explore the Writers' Toolbox

How is a writer like a carpenter? They are both builders. Good story writers use a variety of tools and techniques, called literary devices, to build something that didn't exist before. Think about your favourite stories. They probably use some of the techniques described here.

Point of view is the "voice" of the story. First-person point of view is told by one story character, using *I*. Third-person point of view is told by the narrator, who is outside the story, using *he, she,* or *they.*

Flashback sends you back to an earlier event. The writer may use words or phrases such as *I remember when* or *a few years earlier.*

Figurative language builds comparisons and creates special effects that help you understand characters, places, and ideas. **See simile, metaphor, and personification on page 62.**

Mood is the feeling or atmosphere you get from the story. It may be peaceful, scary, gloomy, funny, weird, or sad.

Symbolism is the use of an object to represent an idea or feeling, such as a grim reaper to represent death or a dove to stand for peace.

Sensory language helps you share sights, sounds, and other sense experiences with the characters.

Foreshadowing is a clue that may create suspense by hinting at things to come.

Characterization is the description of a character's looks, behaviour, motives, emotions, and personality.

Let's Practise

Here's a story that uses many writer's tools. Look for each of the following:

a) Characterization

b) Figurative language
   i. Personification
   ii. Simile

c) Flashback

d) Foreshadowing

e) Mood

f) Point of view

g) Sensory language

h) Symbolism

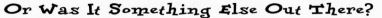

Or Was It Something Else Out There?

I was so tired that I sat back in my chair, just listening to the wind. Suddenly I remembered that August night of long ago.

The dark clouds that night raced across the sky. The wind whined and moaned through the cracks in the cabin. The waves crashed upon the shore. I waited and watched and listened on that stormy night.

Suddenly a flash of light cast the shadow of a raven upon the wall. The air smelled damp and musty, and the rain beat against the window and seeped under the sill. The crying of the wind increased—or was it something else? Something outside?

I leapt to the door and peered outside just as lightning filled the sky and revealed an overturned boat and a man being tossed out to sea. I told myself to keep cool and not to panic, as I rushed out in my motorboat to rescue him. Soon after I reached him, he fell unconscious.

I hauled him to shore. Trying to keep calm, I pumped and pressed him—I kneaded him like a piece of dough until one eye opened, and he gasped for air.

Prepare a Book Review

A book review gives you a chance to become a critic of someone else's writing. It's your personal response to a book, along with information about it and an analysis of its strengths and weaknesses. A review lets you share a cool book with friends or warn them about a time-waster. You could do your book review in one of the following forms.

Short talk or audio recording: Present your responses orally.

Bulletin board display: Use a combination of visuals and written words to present your thoughts about the book.

Poster: Use visuals such as maps and drawings along with words to create a poster about your book.

Book jacket: Find or draw a picture for the front cover, choose lines from your personal response for the back cover, and write your book review on the front and back flaps.

Reading Poetry

Focus Your Learning

- Identify characteristics of poetry
- Explore how language use conveys meaning in popular culture
- Explore and appreciate figurative language and imagery
- Identify and describe characteristics of various forms

What can send a chill creeping down your spine or cause a catch in your throat? What can beat a rhythm in your head? A poem. That's because it taps into your memories and your emotions. You know a poem isn't just words that rhyme. Here is what several poets have said about what poetry is.

> What does it matter what poetry is, after all? If you want a definition of poetry, say: "Poetry is what makes me laugh or cry or yawn, what makes my toenails twinkle, what makes me want to do this or that or nothing," and let it go at that.
>
> —Dylan Thomas

> Poetry is the music of the soul ....
>
> —Voltaire

> I believe that poetry is the heart of the language, the activity through which language is renewed and kept alive.
>
> —Margaret Atwood

Even the poets don't agree on a definition, but probably most would agree it's a unique use of words to communicate something significant or special. **For more on the definition of poetry, see page 117.** Poetry may be a bit tricky to define, but that doesn't mean it's hard to read. Reading poetry does take some practice, though. A reading strategy will help you!

Experiencing a Poem

What makes you remember a poem? Is it the poet's use of sounds, images, and rhythm? Poets choose and arrange their words very carefully. The language of poetry—the images, metaphors, sounds, pauses, and rhythms—creates the meaning of a poem.

Maybe you think all this talk about what a poem means is far less important than the poem itself. If so, the poet Archibald MacLeish agreed with you. He said, "A poem should not mean, but be." The language of poetry *is* the meaning of the poem. The poet John Ciardi believed that readers should concentrate on the *how* of a poem—the way its parts work together—instead of on what a poem means. Look at these two poems about the crescent moon.

The Path on the Sea

The moon this night is like a silver sickle
Mowing a field of stars.
It has spread a golden runner
Over the rippling waves.
With its winking shimmer
This magic carpet lures me
To fly to the moon on it.

—*Inna Muller (age 13)*

Winter Moon

How thin and sharp is the moon tonight!
How thin and sharp and ghostly white
Is the slim curved crook of the moon tonight!

—*Langston Hughes*

Did you notice that Langston Hughes uses cold, cutting words and images, such as *thin* and *sharp, ghostly white,* and *curved crook*? Did you feel the difference in the mood of Inna Muller's poem? The phrases *silver sickle mowing, rippling waves,* and *golden runner* are soft-sounding and call forth rich, pleasant images.

Reading a Poem

Relax and enjoy. Reading a poem involves spending time with it, listening to it. Discover how the poem connects with your feelings. Experience what it means to you. Responding to poetry is not an exercise in finding the hidden meanings.

Begin by reading the poem several times, simply to enjoy it. If the meaning puzzles you, try this process:

1. **First read the poem all the way through.** If you come to a word or phrase you don't understand, just keep going. Let the words have their full effect on you.

2. **Read the poem again.** Concentrate on the parts that seemed unclear. Use context (surrounding words) to unlock the meaning of unfamiliar words, or use a dictionary.

3. **Read the poem a third time, aloud.** As you listen, think about how the sounds in the poem affect you. Think about your reactions to the poem. Ask yourself, "What images do I see? How do I feel? What do I think of?"

4. **Tell what the poem is about.** What is happening in the poem? What does the poet see, think, or feel?

5. **Connect with the poem.** Which feelings, situations, or images remind you of events or emotions in your own life? If none of them do, the poem has given you a new experience.

Discussing a Poem

Reading poetry can be a very personal experience. Even so, pooling your reactions—in a discussion with your classmates—can make the experience of the poem richer for everyone. You will get more out of a poem if you share your thoughts and feelings, using specific examples from the poem to point to what you mean.

Here are some steps to get your group started.

1. **Listen to the poem as it's read aloud.** Ask your teacher, a group member, or someone else familiar with the poem to read it to you. Or listen to it on an audiotape.

2. **Read the poem silently.** Does it remind you of an experience or emotion you've had?

3. **Take turns stating reactions to the poem.** Each group member should answer these questions: "How does the poem make you feel? How does it sound to you? What images does it bring to mind?" You'll get more ideas if everyone speaks without interruption.

4. **Discuss the first round of comments.** After everyone has responded once, answer the question "What related ideas occurred to you as others stated their reactions?"

5. **Open up the discussion.** Try to cover some of these points: Is anything unclear to you? What questions would you want to ask the poet? What's happening in the poem? How do the words and phrases affect you?

6. **Reread the poem aloud.** Try to clear up any confusing points that came up in the discussion. Have a volunteer report on the findings of your group.

The Sounds of Poetry

What makes a poem different from other forms of writing? Do rhythm and rhyme come to mind? Not all poems use both these elements, but most poems have a music of their own. Listen for the music in the poems in this section. How does the arrangement of sounds help to create feeling and meaning?

Find the Rhythm, or Metre

You react to rhythm every day—in the music you hear and the sports you play. In poetry, rhythm is the beat of the lines. Some poems have a predictable rhythm, called *metre*. Here are some tips to figure out the rhythm pattern of a poem.

Here's part of a poem with a strong, regular metre. Try *scanning*, or reading the poem to find the rhythm pattern of stressed and unstressed syllables.

Listen to the beat and mark each syllable. Mark the lighter or unstressed syllables this way: ˘

Mark the heavy or stressed syllables this way: ´

Now listen again to the beat of the lines: duh-DAH, duh-DAH, duh-DAH, duh-DAH.

After marking the beat, look for the pattern. Usually the rhythm pattern repeats.

The sun / that brief / Decem/ber day
Rose cheer/less ov/er hills / of / gray,
And, dark/ly cir/cled, gave / at noon
A sad/der light / than wan/ing moon.

—*John Greenleaf Whittier*

Locate the Rhyme

You've been listening to rhymes for years! Rhyme is the repetition of the same sound in different words. Poets use rhyme for the same reason they use rhythm—to help organize the poem and to suggest meaning and emotion.

The most common type of rhyme in poetry is called *end rhyme*, which occurs—you guessed it!—at the end of lines, like *day* and *gray* in the poem above. *Internal rhyme* occurs within a single line. Example:

See the *mean gleam* in his eye and *deep crease* in his *cheek*.

Of course, some poems have no rhyme at all! Often poets repeat a rhyme scheme or metre pattern within a four- or five-line stanza. A *stanza* is another word for verse. It's a group of lines standing together. Check out the rhyme scheme in the following stanzas.

Dust of Snow

The way a crow	a
Shook down on me	b
The dust of snow	a
From a hemlock tree	b

Has given my heart	
A change of mood	
And saved some part	
Of a day I had rued.	

—*Robert Frost*

Each line is marked according to the sound at the end. Mark the first line with an *a*. If you find another line-ending sound that rhymes with the first line ending, mark that with an *a* also. Then mark the next line-ending sound with a *b*, and so on.

Mark the rhyme pattern of the second stanza. Watch for a pattern as you mark the stanza. Each new line-ending sound should be marked with a new letter.

Look for Repeated Words

Why do parents repeat the same comments? Why do *you* repeat the same comments? Is it to make sure the listener gets the point? Look at the repetition in the poem on the next page.

Poetry

What is Poetry? Who knows?
Not a rose, but the scent of the rose;
Not the sky, but the light in the sky;
Not the fly, but the gleam of the fly;
Not the sea, but the sound of the sea;
Not myself, but what makes me
See, hear, and feel something that prose
Cannot: and what it is, who knows?

—*Eleanor Farjeon*

Why does Eleanor Farjeon repeat words and phrases in her poem?
What effect does the repetition have?

Note the Line Breaks

Line breaks help set the pace and rhythm of a poem. They tell you
where to pause and where to take a breath. Try reading "Poetry" to
see where you pause. Poets arrange their poems carefully. Try to
follow the signals given by line breaks, rhythm, and rhyme.

Listen for Alliteration

In the poem below, listen for the *l* sound in *like* and *licorice*, and
the repetition of the *t* sound in *twisting*, *traffic*, and *taste*. Can you
taste the rain? The taste image travels all the way through the
poem, strengthened by *alliteration*, which is repetition of the same
consonant at the beginning of words.

rush hour in the rain

wet streets
shiny black like licorice
twisting through the city
traffic tastes its way home

—*Tiffany Stone*

Alliteration is not always the repetition of a beginning consonant
sound. Sometimes the sound is hidden within the words. For
example, listen for the repetition of similar consonants in the
words *sad*, *uncertain*, *bustle*, and *symbol*.

The Language of Poetry

Imagery is language that creates pictures and sensory impressions. Often you remember a poem because its images appeal to your sight, sound, touch, taste, or smell.

Can you see the giant, rolling sea-dog in this poem? Hear the clashing of teeth and jaws? Touch the greasy paws?

from The Sea

The sea is a hungry dog,
Giant and gray.
He rolls on the beach all day.
With his clashing teeth and shaggy jaws
Hour upon hour he gnaws
The rumbling, tumbling stones,
And, "Bones, bones, bones!"
The giant sea-dog moans,
Licking his greasy paws.

—*James Reeves*

Simile

The sea is like a hungry dog.

Metaphor

The sea is a hungry dog.

Figurative language uses images that cannot be taken literally. If your dad says, "Your room looks like a cyclone hit it!" what do you think of? You will have a personal reaction—but it won't be fear that a big storm has ruined your room! Figurative language suggests similarities in things that are not usually compared. A comparison using the word *like* or *as* is called a *simile*. In a *metaphor* the comparison is made more directly, without either of those words, as in "The sea is a hungry dog ..."

In *personification* an animal, object, or concept is given human characteristics, as in this poem, "Eclipse."

Eclipse

I looked the sun straight in the eye.
He put on dark glasses.

—*F. R. Scott*

The Forms of Poetry

Poetry has been growing and changing since ancient times, and there are many different poetic forms. All over the world, people of all ages have enjoyed singing, chanting, reciting, writing, and listening to poetry. The roots of modern poetry go back to prehistoric songs, chants, and prayers.

Do you ever wonder how poets decide which poetic forms to use? Sometimes they create new forms to fit what they want to say. But poets may also choose a particular poetic form for the fun and challenge of fitting words, sounds, and meaning into its structure. You will find examples of some common poetic forms below. See if you can figure out how the structure contributes to the meaning of the poem.

Haiku

Haiku, a three-line poem that captures a moment in nature, originated in Japan. Its seventeen syllables are arranged in three lines in a five-seven-five syllable pattern. Look for haiku collections, such as *The Haiku Anthology*, edited by Cor Van Den Heuvel.

Haiku

In the bent birch tree
wind ruffles the fur and quills
of a porcupine.

—*Bruce Meyer*

Free Verse

Free verse is a common form of modern poetry that does not follow a set metrical (or rhythmical) pattern. It may include rhyme. Free verse can be found in most modern poetry collections.

Elephants

aren't any more important
than insects,
but I'm on the side
of elephants,
unless one of them tries
to crawl up my leg.

—*John Newlove*

Sonnet

A sonnet is a fourteen-line poem that usually follows a set rhyme scheme and metrical pattern. Look for collections of works by the famous sonnet writers—William Shakespeare, John Keats, Elizabeth Barrett Browning, and Edna St. Vincent Millay.

If I should learn, in some quite casual way,
That you were gone, not to return again—
Read from the back-page of a paper, say,
Held by a neighbor in a subway train,
How at the corner of this avenue
And such a street (so are the papers filled)
A hurrying man, who happened to be you,
At noon today had happened to be killed,
I should not cry aloud—I could not cry
Aloud, or wring my hands in such a place—
I should but watch the station lights rush by
With a more careful interest on my face;
Or raise my eyes and read with greater care
Where to store furs and how to treat the hair.

—Edna St. Vincent Millay

Ballad

A ballad is a short narrative poem told in songlike form. Many ballads have been passed down as folk songs that tell love stories or tales about heroes or historical events. Look in collections of folk ballads for well-known ballads such as "Frankie and Johnny" or "The Cremation of Sam McGee." To learn what happens to Annabel Lee in the following poem, find the entire poem in a volume of the works of Edgar Allan Poe.

Annabel Lee

It was many and many a year ago,
In a kingdom by the sea
That a maiden there lived whom you may know
By the name of ANNABEL LEE;
And this maiden she lived with no other thought
Than to love and be loved by me …

—Edgar Allan Poe

Let's Practise

1. Look through a book of poetry or another suitable source. Find one example of each of the following types of poems.
   - Haiku
   - Free verse
   - Sonnet
   - Ballad

2. In the poems you have chosen, identify at least three examples of the following poet's tools.
   - Rhythm
   - Rhyme
   - Line breaks
   - Alliteration
   - Simile
   - Metaphor
   - Personification

3. In your group, or with the class, discuss which examples are the most effective and why.

4. If you wanted to write up the exploits of a school volleyball team in a humorous way, which type of poem would you use? Explain your choice.

5. Brainstorm words in the English language that don't rhyme with anything. As a class, discuss ways that poets who want to use rhyme deal with this problem.

6. Choose one of the forms of poetry that you have studied in this section. Write a poem in this form.

Measure Your Growth

Write the numbers 1 through 12 in your notebook. Beside each, rate yourself according to the following scale:

A Excellent

B Good

C Fair

D Needs a lot of work

1. Before I read, I set a purpose for my reading and predict what the material might be about.

2. I choose my reading speed to suit my situation and reading material.

3. I note design, layout, and other aspects that help me understand what I read.

4. I express my responses to reading through methods such as discussion circles and a reading log.

5. I choose and use a reading plan that works for me.

6. I recognize customs, or conventions, that writers use to get meaning across. I use these conventions to preview information and to help me understand it.

7. I can get useful information from what I read.

8. In some situations I read from several sources, summarizing and using ideas from all of them.

9. I read critically, watching for faulty reasoning, bias, and stereotyping.

10. I can read questions, determine what the questioner is asking, and answer appropriately.

11. I recognize story elements and characteristics, using them to help me understand and appreciate narratives.

12. I recognize poetic language and forms, using them to help me understand and appreciate poetry.

CHAPTER *two*

Writing

CONTENTS

Journals and Writing Folders

Focus Your Learning
- Create original text in journal
- Use various forms of note making

When you face a blank paper or empty computer screen, do you wonder how you will ever fill it with finished work? Don't let writing frighten you! It's a process of discovery that's different for everyone.

The best writing often comes from moments such as getting a story idea from a song lyric or finding a great word you want to use later in your writing. How can you keep track of your discoveries so they're there when you want to write? Many writers use journals.

Key Features of Journals

The word *journal* comes from the French word *jour*, which means *day*. A journal is anything you write in daily or regularly. It is a record kept for your personal use. It may be disjointed. One entry does not necessarily follow from another. This is O.K. Also, you may choose whether or not to share your ideas.

A writer's response journal is a book in which you write about your experiences, ideas, and feelings. You can use it to help you think about what you already know, wonder about what you don't know, or express opinions.

A diary is usually used for briefly noting personal feelings and day-by-day events.

"I wore my red jacket today, and everyone liked it."

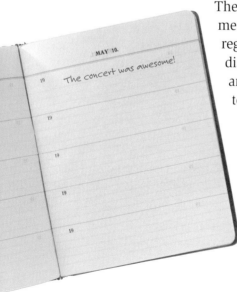

MAY 10.

The concert was awesome!

Here's How to

Keep a Writer's Response Journal

1. **Choose your tools:** lined paper in a notebook or loose-leaf binder, a computer, index cards, or a small pocket-size notebook.

2. **Try to write regularly, though it need not be daily.**

3. **Try writing about interesting people.** A student wrote the following journal entry to develop a character for a short story.

   Becky transferred to our school in the middle of the year. She had travelled the world, and could speak four languages.

4. **Try writing about embarrassing experiences.** These can be a big help in writing a personal narrative or humorous story.

   I didn't want to look too eager, so I rocked back in my chair as if I had to think about his offer. The next thing I knew, I, my chair, and my lunch were on the floor.

5. **Try describing funny or interesting sights.** Use this opportunity to develop descriptive writing skills.

   Matthew, the little boy next door, brought us a zucchini from his garden. It was as green as his shirt and nearly half his size.

6. **Include quotations, poems, newspaper clippings, photos, and sketches, and make notes around them.**

7. **Write about your feelings.**

Organize with a Writing Folder

A writing folder is a place where you store ideas for easy reference and keep your writing in one place so you can see your progress as a writer. You might use a folder with several pockets, a loose-leaf notebook with dividers, or a directory of computer files.

"Reading, though, is the way to learn to write. Someone interested in writing should just read .... Writers can show you directions."

— Carol Shields

Here's How to

Set Up a Writing Folder

1. **Create a section for writers' helps,** such as a revising checklist, proofreader's marks, transition words, interesting words, hard words, and your most frequent errors. **See pages 95 and 303.**

2. **Create a section for writing ideas**, from cartoons, quotations, maps, ads, photographs, postcards.

3. **Create a section for works in progress.**

4. **Create a section for published works.** Save pieces that you might use as models for writing in a particular genre and pieces you might want to discuss with a classmate or teacher. Date each work.

Let's Practise

If you haven't already done so, start either a writer's response journal or a writing folder.

The Predrafting Process

Much of the writing process occurs before you start putting words together. It may involve any or all of the following, in any order.

1. **Search for Ideas:** Ideas for writing are all around you—in this room, out the window, in your family, on the news. When you're stuck for an idea, try thinking of one in each of those categories. Drawing and doodling can also trigger ideas.

2. **Freewrite:** When you freewrite, the goal is to produce ideas, not polish them. Write quickly and freely with a pencil or at a computer. Don't worry about complete sentences and don't stop to evaluate your ideas. Freewriting at the computer can be even more productive if you write without seeing the words. Darken the screen while you write. Then turn up the brightness and read what you've written. You may be surprised by your own creativity.

> Trail bikes — zoom along trail — fly over ditches ...

3. **Brainstorm:** You can brainstorm by yourself or with several others. When you brainstorm, choose a topic and list every related idea that occurs to you—even those that seem a little wild. A word or phrase will do for each idea.

4. **Use a Web or Clustering:** Start by writing an idea, a word, or phrase, and drawing a ring around it. Surround this idea with related ideas and draw a line connecting each new idea to the original one. Then branch out to ideas suggested by the new ones.

5. **Match Objects and Emotions:** Think about a general topic such as shopping malls, baseball diamonds, or provincial parks. What specific objects come to mind? List them. Beside your objects, list emotions—any emotions. Then try making matchups. What writing ideas do your matchups give you?

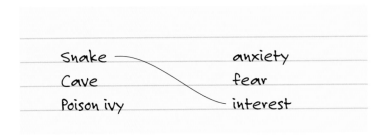

6. **Try Looping:** This can help you find a new way to look at your idea. Follow these steps:

❊ Freewrite several sentences about your idea. Underline the most interesting word or phrase.

❊ Freewrite about the underlined word or phrase. Again, underline the most interesting word or phrase, and freewrite again.

❊ Repeat this process as many times as you want.

❊ Reread all your sentences. Linking the underlined words and phrases may give you a new angle.

> Provincial parks are special places. Many people love to visit them.
>
> People go to parks to camp out and hike, to see the wildlife, and to enjoy the peace and quiet of the wilderness.
>
> Unfortunately, too many people go, and noise and crowds are a problem.
>
> New angle: We could lose the peace and the quiet that make provincial parks such special places.

7. **Narrow Your Subject:** Run a big topic such as space exploration or endangered species through an imaginary funnel. Choose the aspect, the one species, the one personality you most want to write about.

8. **Fill in Missing Information:** Research by collecting information from interviews, books, magazines, videos, CD-ROMs, the Internet, and other sources. **To learn about doing research, see chapter 6.**

Make Key Writing Decisions

Once you have an idea that inspires you, make some plans. Answering the following questions will help you chart a course through the rest of your writing process.

Form: What kind of writing best fits the subject? An e-mail or letter that will describe, inform, or persuade? A story that relates an adventure or a mystery? A poem that focusses on narrative, description, or humour?

Purpose: Why are you writing? To explain, persuade, or describe? To express feelings? To condemn or support?

Tone: How do you feel about your subject? Think of tone in writing as similar to tone of voice when you speak. The tone you take usually reflects your feelings.

Audience: For whom are you writing? Visualize your audience as you plan.

Plan: Informal or Outline

Gather all your clusters, drawings, lists, and any notes you've made. Keep them close at hand and look at them often. Before you write, you need to select your main points and the details that support each idea. You also need to try different arrangements of both ideas and details.

Bright Ideas

for Planning Your Writing

Here are two ways to plan. You may be able to develop another way to plan, one that works especially well for you.

Informal Plan

Put your ideas on index cards and rearrange them until you have a workable order. Informal planning works well for poems, short stories, and other creative writing.

Formal Plan

Write main ideas and supporting details on separate index cards. Organize the cards and then use them to create an outline showing each main idea with the details that support it. Formal planning usually works best for research reports, persuasive letters, essays, and other factual writing.

Here's How to

Make an Outline

1. Write a title for your essay, article, report, or other piece of writing.

2. List your main topics or parts. Leave several lines of space after each heading.

3. Under your main topics or parts, list subtopics or subdivisions. Indent them.

4. A writing outline is not carved in stone. You don't have to follow it exactly. If better ideas come to you as you write, go for them!

For more on making a working outline, see page 114.

Let's Practise

1. Choose four or more ideas from the preceding section. Use them to predraft a story, poem, book review, or other piece of writing.

2. Identify an issue that concerns you, such as racism or the environment. Write a paragraph for your principal, outlining your thoughts on the issue. Then redraft the paragraph for Grade Five students. Notice how the change in audience may require changes in the way you express your ideas.

Graphic Organizers

In many cases, the formal outline described above will provide the best way of structuring your ideas. There are several **graphic organizers** that can also help you put your thoughts in order. A graphic organizer is a tool that shows the relationships between ideas in a visual way. Each one is suited to a specific purpose.

Main Ideas and Supporting Details

The organizer below is just another way of presenting the formal outline you have already learned. This two-column chart allows you to see the way the writing will unfold, and provides room to list details in point form.

Main Idea	Supporting Details
Columbus did not "discover" America	● The Vikings made the sea voyage between Europe and North America hundreds of years before Columbus. ● Aboriginal peoples have lived in the Americas for thousands of years.
Aboriginal peoples developed sophisticated cultures and civilizations	● The Incas had a vast trading and communications network. ● Mayans constructed elaborate temples and created beautiful works of art. ● Huron peoples practised agriculture and built fortified settlements.

Time Line

A time line shows the order in which events occurred. It can also indicate the pace of change.

Electricity in Canada

1877	1883	1888	1906	1920
first use of electricity for lighting		first generation of hydro-electric power	generation of hydro from Niagara Falls	97% of Canada's electricity generated by hydro-electric power
	electric street lighting in Toronto and Montreal			

Venn Diagram

A Venn diagram shows the features shared by two or more things. Place the shared features in the space where the circles overlap.

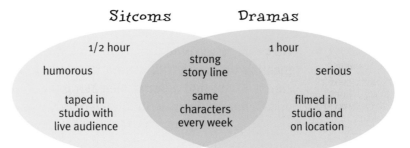

Sitcoms   Dramas

1/2 hour   1 hour
humorous   strong   serious
                 story line
taped in   same   filmed in
studio with   characters   studio and
live audience   every week   on location

Comparison and Contrast

A comparison and contrast chart is another way of exploring the similarities and differences between two or more things.

Competitive Skating   Cross-Country Running

Similarities

- requires serious training
- leg strength and endurance important

Differences

- controlled indoor environment (rink)
- success subjectively evaluated by judges

- natural outdoor environment
- success measured objectively at finish line

Tree Diagram

A tree diagram sorts things into categories.

Transportation

Air
- jet
- airplane
- helicopter
- balloon

Land
- automobile
- bicycle
- train
- snowmobile

Water
- ship
- sailboat
- hovercraft
- jetski

The Drafting Process

Now you're ready to write your first draft. As you put words together on paper, follow your plan. But don't be afraid to change course if you find a better idea along the way. Since you'll want to make changes later, write on every other line (double space if you are using a computer) and leave wide margins. Don't stop to correct spelling, grammar, and punctuation; you can do that later.

Focus Your Learning
- Create original text in a variety of forms
- Use various forms of note making
- Choose style and pace

Start with a Strong Lead

The best leads start with a dramatic moment, a description of a scene, a surprising statement, or lively dialogue. They grab readers and encourage them to read on. One good strategy for finding a lead is to freewrite as many possible leads as you can and then pick the best one. Another option is to write your lead last.

Article or essay, serious tone
Provincial parks face a growing danger—if we are not careful, we may love them to death.

Personal narrative, informal tone
My parents and I had spent an entire month packing for the canoe trip, and we still weren't ready.

Short story, suspenseful tone
"Leave that bear cub alone! There's a mother bear around here somewhere!"

Poem, lyric tone
Cranes rise from misty marshes.

Show—Don't Tell

The best writing allows a reader to see or experience a subject through the use of vivid words and specific details.

Telling

My upstairs neighbour is noisy.

Showing

The thumping bass of my neighbour's CD player made the windows rattle and the vases dance across my coffee table.

Develop a Writing Voice

Nobody in the world is just like you. When you write short stories, essays, or other works, look for ways to express your unique personality and voice.

1. Think about what you enjoy reading. Your reading preferences are clues to your unique personality and voice. Try writing the kinds of details and explanations you yourself enjoy reading.

2. Tape-record a conversation between yourself and someone you like. Then listen to the tape. Look for ways to include your own words in your writing.

3. Suppose you're writing and you sense an inner voice saying, "Write it like this." Try listening to your inner voice. When you do, you may find yourself doing your best writing ever.

Consider Connotation and Tone

Use a thesaurus to find exact words. **(See page 321 for help with using a thesaurus.)** However, stick to synonyms that have the right connotation; that is, words that make the right suggestion. *Relax* and *loaf* are synonyms, but they have opposite connotations. *Relax* has a positive connotation, while *loaf, loiter,* and *vegetate* have negative connotations.

When choosing from among synonyms, also keep tone in mind. Suppose you are writing in a sophisticated and elegant tone. You might write *promenade* rather than *street, shoppes* rather than *stores,* and *adolescent* rather than *teenager.*

Be Gender-Inclusive

Canadian society is working toward equal treatment for males and females. As a writer you can help by using gender-inclusive language. This means language that includes both females and males.

Instead of ...	use gender-inclusive language such as ...
mankind	people, human beings
chairman	chairperson, chair
man-made	synthetic
Each student can make up his own mind.	Students can make up their own minds.
mailman	letter carrier
stewardess	flight attendant
fireman	firefighter

Be Unbiased

Canadian society is working toward equal treatment for all peoples and groups. As a writer you can help by using unbiased language.

Instead of ...	prefer unbiased language such as ...
old person	senior citizen
disabled	physically challenged
blind	visually challenged
Eskimo	Inuk for one; Inuit for more than one
General names for groups of people	• Name the First Nation to which the person belongs. For example, Haida, Blackfoot, Mohawk, or Wahta First Nation. If you don't know specifics, you could use the term Aboriginal. • Use a name that indicates the country from which the person comes. For example, Ugandan, Swedish, Somali, Israeli, Jamaican.

Finish with a Good Ending

Your conclusion can be as important as your lead. It's the last thing your readers see and may be what they remember best. A good ending can summarize what you've been saying, add a final bit of information, or even pack a surprise.

Article or essay, formal tone
Too many people and too much noise can make the forest feel like a busy city street.

Personal narrative, informal tone
As we dragged the canoe back on shore, I knew I'd never been tireder—or dirtier!

Short story, suspenseful tone
"We'll tell you all about our adventure," said Ed. "Just bear with us!"

Poem, lyric tone
Hoarse bird-voices crying free.

Think of a Good Title

Like the aroma of a delicious meal, a good title gives the reader a hint of what the piece is about. It arouses curiosity and interest, but doesn't tell all. Some writers think of a good title first. Others wait until they've finished a piece.

Article or essay
Provincial Parks: An Endangered Species

Personal narrative
Misadventures in the Wilderness

Short story
Bear with Me, Please!

Poem
Winter Flight

Let's Practise

1. Choose a piece of writing you've done recently or sometime in the past. Think of a good title for it.

2. Choose an article from a magazine or newspaper that you've recently read. Think of a better title for it than the one it has.

Constructing Paragraphs

Whether you write a letter, a story, an essay, or a research report, paragraphs are your building blocks. A paragraph is a group of sentences that develops a main idea. The beginning of a paragraph signals that a new idea will be introduced, a new voice will speak, or the main idea of the previous paragraph will be expanded.

Parts of a Paragraph

In nonfiction writing, good paragraphs have three main parts: a main idea expressed in a topic sentence or implied directly, one or more supporting sentences, and a closing sentence that lets readers know you've completed your thought.

Main Idea: This can be clearly expressed in a topic sentence, which can appear anywhere in the paragraph. A main idea can also be implied, or suggested, though not spelled out in one sentence.

> Walking is probably the best all-around exercise for you, whether you're age nine or ninety!

Supporting Sentences: These explain the main idea of a paragraph. They develop the idea with logically related details, facts, reasons, and examples.

> It can strengthen your heart and lungs without overworking them. It can give your whole body a good workout without straining any part of it. Better still, expensive equipment and flashy outfits aren't required. You need a comfortable pair of shoes or sneakers and your everyday clothes. You don't have to find a special stadium, court, or track. No matter where you live, it should be possible to find a safe place to walk. At the end of a good walk, you'll find yourself refreshed and cheery, rather than exhausted and dripping with sweat.

Closing Sentence: A good closing reinforces the main idea, adds something new, and leaves the reader with a manageable chunk of information to think about.

> Walking has all of these advantages and, best of all, it's fun.

Features of a Paragraph

Besides the three basic parts, a good paragraph has other important features: organization, unity, and coherence. Organization allows for an orderly development of the main idea. Unity means all the sentences are focussed on the main idea. Coherence provides smooth connections between the sentences, like links forming a chain.

Order

The information in your paragraph can be organized to follow a variety of "orders." With these orders you can argue a specific point, narrate a sequence of events, or describe a particular place.

1. Logical order.

Organizing a paragraph in logical order means arranging its details and information in a way that makes sense. Logical order can help you position your ideas so they are clear and easy to follow.

Most important to least important
I had run the race of my life. The crowd cheered.

Least important to most important
The crowd cheered. I had run the race of my life.

General to specific
It was a beautiful day, but I felt sad that summer was almost over.

Specific to general
I felt sad that summer was almost over, but it was a beautiful day!

Most familiar to least familiar
I glanced at my dog. Then I faced the snarling bear.

Least familiar to most familiar
I faced the snarling bear. Then I glanced at my dog.

Simplest to most complex
That single drop of rain grew into a mighty storm.

Most complex to simplest
That mighty storm began with a single drop of rain.

2. Time order.

This ensures that events in a story or personal narrative unfold in the proper sequence.

Time Expressions

within minutes	now	then
before	later	as time passed
eventually	immediately	soon
previously		

From the moment I left the starting block, I tried to keep my mind on just one lap at a time. **First** I pulled my thoughts away from the poor start I'd made. **Then** I focussed on the goal ahead. **Before** I knew it, I had reached the finish line and everybody was cheering.

3. Spatial order.

This method focusses on where things stand physically in space. Spatial order can help you describe your settings and characters so that your readers will imagine them vividly.

Spatial Expressions

across	down	between
beyond	over	next to
distant	nearby	adjacent

The ballpark was quiet and empty. I pushed my cap **back** on my head and looked **down** at Daisy, my dog. She was walking **between** me and Kate as we crossed **centre** field and moved **toward** home plate. The game was over. We had lost, but there would be other games.

Paragraph Unity

Your paragraph has unity when every sentence focusses on the main idea. All the pieces fit together.

Unifying Expressions

in addition to	furthermore	in the same way
all together	also	but

Weak unity

Some people, such as Wayne Gretzky, are natural athletes. My sister is a great runner. One day last month, I tripped over the curb and broke my arm.

Better unity

Some people, such as Wayne Gretzky, are natural athletes. **In a similar way**, my sister has always been a great runner. I **also** dream of having natural grace and agility, **but** since the day I tripped over the curb and broke my arm, I have had my doubts.

Paragraph Coherence

Even if every sentence is hard at work developing the main idea of your paragraph, your writing may still be difficult to follow. Make your sentences flow together and build on one another. This will help your paragraph make sense.

Transitional Expressions

first, next, then, finally, but, even though, because, however, therefore, for example, meanwhile

Weak coherence

This spring I decided to try the low hurdles. I didn't know how I'd do. I hoped I wouldn't fall flat on my face. I got into the starting block. I took off. I knocked down the first hurdle. Sailing over the second and third hurdles, I had room to spare. The fourth hurdle came up. I felt as if I'd learned to fly.

Better coherence

This spring I decided to try the low hurdles. I didn't know how I'd do it, but I hoped I wouldn't fall flat on my face. First I got into the starting block. Next I heard the coach blow the whistle. Then I took off. Even though I knocked down the first hurdle, I sailed over the second and third hurdles with room to spare. By the fourth hurdle, I felt as if I'd learned to fly.

Types of Paragraphs

There are different types of paragraphs for different kinds of writing. Your choice of paragraph depends on your purpose in writing. Sometimes different types of paragraphs may need to be combined. For example, an explanatory paragraph may include description or persuasion.

Descriptive Paragraph

This kind of paragraph describes a person, place, or thing as vividly as possible. It helps the reader see, hear, and sense things that will bring the subject to life.

> I arrive here in the valley of Williams Creek on a sunny day cooled by clouds that hang over the Cariboo Mountains. A breeze rustles down the creek, shimmering the cottonwoods, quaking the aspens. The town is bustling, for this day marks the end of a depressing wet period. The warm air has dried the street so I can walk the roadway rather than the boardwalk that fronts the buildings.

From *Discover Barkerville: A Gold Rush Adventure* by Richard Thomas Wright

Bright Ideas

for Writing Descriptive Paragraphs

1. Create an overall impression of the person, place, or thing you are describing.

2. You can use sensory details of sight, sound, taste, smell, colour, and touch as well as details of time, space, and motion.

3. Similes and metaphors can make your description more interesting. **For an explanation of these writing tools, see page 62.**

Narrative Paragraphs

A narrative paragraph tells a story or relates an event. You can use this type of paragraph not only in a formal narrative, but also in any form of writing whenever you want to tell a story.

> Also, he told me about the ... carpenter who had been standing in line all day to get his name down on the prospective list of employees. When he had given the employment clerk all the

required information about himself, he said, "Now you had better put my two-year-old son on your list, too." The clerk said, "Why should I do that?" The ... chap replied, "Because by the time he gets up to your desk, he'll be old enough to work."

From *"Come 'Ere Till I Tells Ya"* by Al Clouston

Bright Ideas

for Writing Narrative Paragraphs

1. Establish the point of view from which you are writing: first person, second person, or third person.

2. Set the scene or the tone with your opening sentence.

3. Organize the events of your paragraph in time order.

Explanatory Paragraphs

Explanatory paragraphs explain a circumstance, event, or experience. They answer some or all of these questions: *who, what, when, why, where,* and *how.* You can use description, comparison and contrast, or cause-and-effect relationships to make your explanation clear.

> The world of media has taken to the Internet by storm. Today, you can find tens of thousands of magazines, newspapers, journals, and other publications online, each of which is providing regularly updated information. Hundreds of radio stations broadcast their signals live through the Internet, providing a global reach that has previously been restricted to shortwave stations. Television stations have established web sites in order to reach their viewers.

From *Canadian Internet New User's Handbook* by Jim Carroll and Rick Broadhead

Bright Ideas

for Writing Explanatory Paragraphs

1. Clearly state the topic that needs explanation.

2. Support your topic sentence with detailed information.

3. If necessary, research your topic to make your explanation accurate and complete.

Instructive Paragraphs

An instructive paragraph gives detailed, step-by-step instructions.

> Take a piece of paper and outline all seven continents. Then cut out each continent separately and lay all the pieces on a table, positioning them to resemble the earth's surface. Now push the continents together and try to fit them into one big land mass .... it's easy to imagine that they once were part of the same continent— which, in fact, they were. It's all a matter of plate tectonics.

From "Travelling Turf" by Neal Shusterman

Bright Ideas

for Writing Instructive Paragraphs

1. State your main idea clearly.

2. You can organize your instructions step by step in logical order.

3. Be sure to warn the reader of possible difficulties in the procedure you're describing.

4. Remember to use explanation, description, comparison and contrast, or cause-and-effect relationships whenever they may be helpful.

Summary Paragraphs

This kind of paragraph summarizes, in one or more stand-alone sentences, the information or events from a longer piece of writing. You can use it as the closing paragraph of an essay or report, or by itself as a brief review.

> Today Lydia lives quietly in the Pyrenees Mountains near her close-knit family. Memories of her Arctic ordeal stay fresh. It was there she learned of human courage and resilience and the fragile preciousness of life. Her determination to survive stands as an inspiration to others—just as Jean-Jacques was to her.
>
> From "Terror Above the Arctic Circle" by Sheldon Kelly

Bright Ideas

for Writing Summary Paragraphs

1. Briefly restate the main points or events that have been outlined.

2. You can summarize conclusions that may be drawn from these points.

Edit Your Paragraphs

Studying the questions about the following paragraph and how it was edited will help you learn to improve your own paragraphs.

Draft

Some people want to be part of a team and aren't good at team play. Why don't you try out for track and field? If you're a good runner, there are lots of events to choose from. Javelin and discus throwers develop strong arms. Sprinters develop strong legs. Find out what you're good at. I'm sure there's a track and field event that you could enter and have fun at.

Questions and Comments

Topic sentence—This draft has a weak beginning. Combining the first two sentences into a strong topic sentence will express the main idea more effectively.

Organization—The paragraph moves from the topic of running, to throwing, and back again. Stick to one organizational plan, such as running fast and then throwing.

Closing sentence—This could be more effective if it had a stronger link to the sentences before it.

Supporting details—Try comparing and contrasting events for athletes who like to run with events for athletes with strong arms. Use more detail about running events. What about the high jump or other jumping events? Give as many examples as you can to make your argument complete.

Coherence—This paragraph is choppy and unclear in spots because the sentences do not build on one another. Make each sentence flow smoothly to the next one by using effective transitions.

Revised paragraph

If you want to be part of a team, yet enjoy competing on your own, consider trying out for track and field. If you have strong legs, the running events will develop your speed and endurance. The high jump and the long jump (and—for the especially co-ordinated— the jazzy hop, skip, and jump) will take you into the air. Try the javelin or discus if upper-body strength is your specialty. With so many events to choose from, I'll bet there's a track or field event that's just right for you.

Let's Practise

Choose at least three types of paragraphs discussed in the preceding section. Write them, using what you've learned.

The Revision Process

Focus Your Learning
- Use the steps in the writing process
- Appraise your own and others' work
- Revise to improve

If you can, put a little space between yourself and your draft. Tuck it away for a few days and work on something else. When you look at your draft again, imagine you're seeing it for the first time.

As you reread and revise any draft of your writing, remember you can always return to the predrafting and drafting stages!

You might make minor adjustments in content, or you might want to create an entirely new draft.

Big Changes

Changing a main idea

Changing the form or tone

Changing the purpose or audience

Major reordering or **adding** of information

Small Changes

Substituting words

Rewriting lead or ending

Adding or **deleting** information

Reordering details or paragraphs

The new work that results from these changes will be a second draft or perhaps a new piece of writing. You could keep your drafts in your writing folder.

Use a Revising Checklist

A handy tool to keep in your writing folder is a revising checklist like the following one. Include questions aimed at your own specific writing problems.

☑ Are my purpose and main idea clear?

☐ Do my language and content suit the audience?

☐ Have I kept the same tone throughout?

☐ Have I considered connotation in my choice of words?

☐ Are the title and lead interesting? Is the ending strong? Does the writing lead readers from one detail to the next?

☐ Is every idea supported with details?

☐ Are the ideas in a logical order?

☐ Does each sentence fit?

☐ Is there unnecessary repetition?

☐ Have I used my own unique "voice" in my writing?

☐ Have I used gender-inclusive and unbiased language?

Revision Conferences

A conference with a classmate or your teacher can be a great help when you're revising. You have a chance to see your writing through another person's eyes. In peer conferences, you get to look at another student's writing process as you discuss that person's draft. In teacher conferences, you benefit from your teacher's knowledge and writing experience.

After the conference, look over the suggestions. You may find contradictions. Only you can decide which changes will improve your writing.

Let's Practise

Choose a piece of writing you've done recently or sometime in the past. Revise it using ideas from the preceding section.

The Editing and Proofreading Processes

Focus Your Learning
- Check spelling
- Check capitalization
- Check punctuation
- Check grammar
- Check usage
- Revise and edit
- Appraise your own and others' work

When you wrote and revised your draft, you paid most attention to content. Now is the time to focus on making your writing smoother. Let it communicate your ideas as successfully as possible. You can correct any errors in grammar, punctuation, word choice, and spelling. **For tips on identifying and fixing problems at the word and sentence level, see pages 266–342.**

Since you must focus on so many aspects of your writing when you edit and proofread, it helps to work with a peer editor. It also helps to have a system.

Here's How to

Look for Errors

1. **Check for problems in grammar and usage.** Decide how to make each improvement and carry it out.

2. **Check your capitalization and punctuation.** A computer grammar checker can help with this.

3. **Look for weak nouns and verbs.** If you find any, use a thesaurus—either a reference book or a software program—to help you come up with better ones. **For more on using a thesaurus, see page 321.**

4. **Look for spelling errors.** A computer spell checker can be useful. Keep in mind, however, that it isn't foolproof. It may not have every word, and does not recognize when you have used a word incorrectly.

5. **Proofread all your changes.**

"The current has you!" yelled Lisa, who

hadnt taken her eyes off me. She ~~tells~~ told

me exacly what to do.

My sisters were watching from the

shore. and I could feel my face turning

red. That day I learned about the

danger of being too confident and I

discoverd the power of the sea.

Let's Practise

Make a "watch list" of your most frequent errors. Include the following:

1. your most frequent grammar and usage errors

2. capitalization and punctuation errors you tend to make

3. the words you most often misspell

Keep the list in your writing folder.

The Publishing and Reflecting Processes

Focus Your Learning
- Choose form to meet purpose and audience
- Appraise own and others' work
- Reflect on personal growth

You're finally satisfied with your writing. Now that you've invested so much time, effort, and creativity, your work deserves some form of presentation. Here are some publishing ideas you might try:

Make an audio tape of your work. Send it to a local radio station or share it with your class.

Record your work on videotape. Show the video to friends or family.

Perform your work as a play.

Submit your finished work to a contest, magazine, or newspaper.

Illustrate your work with drawings or photos. Then display it or present it to a family member or friend.

Read your work aloud to friends, family, or another class.

Your previous work can be your best teacher, but only if you save it. Make an extra copy or printout of each finished work. Put it in your writing folder along with your drafts.

Here's How to

Reflect on Your Writing

1. **Ask yourself questions such as these to help you think about the work you just completed and published:**

   What do I like best about this piece?

   What could be improved?

   Which stage of writing went most smoothly?

   Which ideas might I develop into new writing?

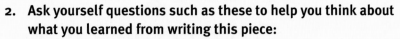

2. **Ask yourself questions such as these to help you think about what you learned from writing this piece:**

Did I find a new way to generate ideas?

Did I make a new discovery about myself or an experience?

Did writing this piece help me to better understand a type of literature?

Did I experiment with a new form of writing?

Let's Practise

1. Choose a piece of writing you particularly like. Decide on an effective way to present it. Before you decide, consider the following:

   a) What form bests suits this piece of writing—oral, written, or some other?

   b) Who is the intended audience?

2. Prepare and present your piece of writing.

3. Ask for feedback on your work. Decide what suggestions will help you next time. Enter these ideas in your writing journal.

Using a Computer to Write

Focus Your Learning
- Create original text in journal
- Use various forms of note making

The computer is a powerful tool that can help you at each stage of the writing process. Here are some suggestions.

1. During the **predrafting** process you can put a computer to work in two important ways. First, most computers give you access to encyclopedias and other resources stored electronically on CD-ROMs. You can use these resources when you are searching for ideas or conducting research. If the computer is connected to the Internet, you can explore a whole world of information. **To learn more about doing research, see page 254.**

   Second, you can use a computer to help you create an outline. Most word processing software has a special outline feature that makes it easy to set up headings and subheadings. When your outline is complete, you can develop your ideas in paragraph form right on the computer.

2. People with relatively good keyboarding skills find that the computer helps them with the **drafting** process. They find keying less tiring than handwriting. It is also much easier and neater to make corrections on screen. Others prefer to create a first draft using pen and paper. They don't key in their work until they are ready to revise.

3. Computers can simplify the **revision** process immensely. With pen and paper, the mess of scratching out sentences and moving paragraphs around can be discouraging. Word processing software makes it easy to cut material from one place and paste it to another. It is easy to experiment with different words and sentence structures because there is never any erasing to do.

   One disadvantage of using a computer is the small viewing area the screen provides. It is hard to flip from one part of the writing to another, and you may not be able to get a sense of your work as a whole. You may therefore want to print sample copies of your writing as you revise.

4. Computers are just as useful when you are **editing and proofreading**. Almost all word processing software includes a spell checker that can help you identify misspelled words. (But remember, a spell checker will not tell you when you have used a word incorrectly. For example, it won't warn you that you typed *cast* instead of *cats*.) A grammar checker can help you find grammar and usage errors, and might even suggest corrections.

5. When it is time for **publishing** your writing, use the computer to finalize the formatting. You can add graphics, use special fonts and colours for headings, and adjust the type size to make your work easy to read and pleasing to the eye.

Here's How to

Use the Computer Effectively

1. **If you are doing an assignment, find out what format your teacher expects.** Have you included a cover page? Have you used the right spacing?

2. **Save your documents frequently, and always make a backup copy.**

3. **Use the search feature to help you catch errors you tend to repeat.** For example, if you confuse *accept* and *except*, search for both spellings and correct any errors you find.

4. **Before you share your work, print out a hard copy and proofread it carefully.** Ask a peer to proofread as well.

Let's Practise

Input a first draft of some of your writing into a computer. Use some or all of the following features as you bring your draft to completion:

cut and paste   spell checker   thesaurus (electronic)

search   undo   fonts   print preview

Writing Letters, Faxes, and E-mail

Letters, faxes, and e-mail have similar purposes and contents. Faxes (facsimile transmissions) and e-mail (electronic mail) are quicker than regular mail and don't need envelopes or stamps.

Since you send letters, faxes, and e-mail in different ways, you use a different format for each. For all three, the body provides the main content.

Friendly Letter Format

Medicine Hat, AB
November 3, 2005

Dear Grandpa,

Body of message

Love,
Rocco

Envelope for Friendly Letter

Rocco Apostolic
39 Grassmere Rd.
Medicine Hat, AB   T1A 7Y2

Mr. Franco Bucci
177 Ralston Court
Toronto, ON   M2R 2S7

Business Letter Format

Ashley Miller
7 Aberdeen Ave.
Elbow, SK   S0H 1J0
November 3, 2005

Mr. Andrew Steenstra
Public Relations Officer
Sandvik Inc.
34 Supra Drive
Vancouver, BC   V6E 3T2

Dear Sir :

— Body of message —

Sincerely,

Ashley Miller

Envelope for Business Letter

Ashley Miller
7 Aberdeen Ave.
Elbow, SK   S0H 1J0

Mr. Andrew Steenstra
Public Relations Officer
Sandvik Inc.
34 Supra Drive
Vancouver, BC   V6E 3T2

Fax Format

January 17, 2009

Fax to: Ms. Karla Klassen, Click Cameras Inc.,

Fax (306) 749-2395

From: Candace Winslow, Fax (306) 255-3856

2 pages including this

— Body of message —

Sincerely,

Candace Winslow

Let's Practise

1. E-mail is like having a conversation. **A sample e-mail format appears in the Reading chapter on page 19.** Using the template, write an e-mail to a friend or relative.

2. How does e-mail differ from formal letters?

Writing to Persuade

In a persuasive message, you set forth your opinion about an issue or problem as convincingly as you can. You want people to understand your view. Then you want them to agree with you. You may even want them to take some kind of action.

To start, you need to ask yourself two big questions:

❋ What problem is most important to me right now?

❋ Who can help me fix it?

Major issues such as pollution, war, poverty, and injustice are too big for one person to solve. Try focussing on a small piece of a big issue. Or choose a smaller issue that bothers you in a big way.

> Dear Editor,
> My friends and I are angry because all of our ramps in the skateboard park were thrown in the river.

Build and Organize Your Arguments

Once you have chosen an issue to write about, jot down every reason you can think of that supports your opinion and any action you plan to suggest. Your opinions will need to be supported by facts.

1. **Research.** It's not enough to say, "Our town needs a food bank" or "We need a bike path." You'll need to convince your readers by providing answers to the questions in their minds. List questions people might ask about your issue. Research up-to-date answers in sources such as computer web sites, the library, the yellow pages, almanacs, newspaper and magazine articles, TV and radio news programs. **For help with researching, see Chapter 6.**

2. **Consider your target audience.** Write to people who can take that action you want.

   Issue
   Students want to plan the next class field trip.

   Your opinion
   Students should make the choice of destination.

   Purpose and audience
   • To persuade the teacher that students can make a good choice.
   • School administrators.

3. **Write differently for different readers.** Adapt your writing to the readers you have in mind.

Bright Ideas

for Writing Persuasively

1. Get to the point right away.

    On May 18 I plan to take part in the Walk for Bread to raise funds for our new food bank. I hope you will sponsor me.

2. Include personal experiences and feelings.

    Picture me in the Walk for Bread on May 18: I'm on kilometre 15. My legs feel like lead. My feet are killing me. But I won't give up! I owe my best effort to the food bank—and to you, my sponsor. You will sponsor me, won't you?

3. Use appropriate language.

    Formal language

    Dear Mr. Li,

    Would you please consider sponsoring me in the Walk for Bread on May 18? I would appreciate your support.

    Yours truly,
    Benjamin Kornblum

    Informal language

    Hey Guys,

    What about sponsoring me in a walkathon next week? I'll take any and all donations.

    See ya,
    Benjie

Here's How to

Draft Your Persuasive Message

1. **State your purpose, opinion, or request.**

   Dear Channel 6:

   Recently you moved my favourite program, *Tales from Outer Space*, from 4:30 p.m. to 1:30 a.m. Please reconsider. Your viewers will be asleep at that hour!

2. **Follow your plan for ordering your arguments or reasons: one reason or category in each paragraph.** To help readers follow your ideas easily, use introductory words and phrases such as: *first of all, furthermore, next, another thing that, finally.*

   First of all, this is my favourite program and .... Furthermore, I am unable to tape the show because ....

3. **Restate your purpose. Ask for support.**

   Students at our junior high miss this show! Won't you please return it to its old time?

Let's Practise

1. With a group, brainstorm to create a list of issues.

2. Decide which issue you care about the most. Write on that issue.

3. Consider the action you would like taken.

4. Write a persuasive letter about the issue.

5. Use the revising tips on page 92 to help you make improvements.

Writing Personal Narratives

Focus Your Learning

- Use prewriting strategies
- Use an organizational pattern
- Use various forms of note making
- Revise and edit to improve
- Retell from different points of view

A personal narrative is a true story that you write about yourself. You tell the story in the first person, using the word *I*. A personal narrative is written to share experiences, thoughts, and feelings with others. This makes it different from private writing you do in a diary or journal.

"The fascinating thing about writing is that it's a way of transforming the things you've experienced; it's like being able to live twice."

— Jacques Godbout

Here's How to

Plan Your Personal Narrative

1. Select the experience you want to write about, using your predrafting notes.

2. Outline events in the order in which they happened.

3. List words describing how you felt during the experience.

4. Name other people who were involved.

5. Identify where and when the events took place.

6. Review your notes and decide whether you have all the information you need. If not, do research.

Let's Practise

1. Write a personal narrative of an experience which you shared with at least one other person, preferably of a different age or gender. Rewrite the narrative from what you think that person's point of view might be. What perspectives and details might change?

2. Read a personal narrative such as Anne Frank's "The Diary of a Young Girl" or Budge Wilson's "Thirteen Never Changes."

3. After writing a personal narrative, use the following questions to help you make revisions:

   ❋ How can I improve the lead?

   ❋ Can I make the ending more effective?

   ❋ How can I improve connections between ideas?

   ❋ Do the characters act and speak convincingly?

   ❋ Is the tone right for the story? Is it consistent?

See page 92 for help with revising your narrative.

Writing Short Stories

Do you ever tell a friend about something that just happened? You might tell a story to make sense of an event or just to make your friend laugh. When you write a short story, you can do the same things. You can also create a partly or entirely imaginary world and see what happens.

Key Features of Short Stories

A short story is a brief narrative written in an artistic way. It usually presents a conflict having a definite beginning, middle, and end. A short story may be partly true or completely invented. Unlike a mere incident, a short story has a theme. It leaves the reader with one main idea. Besides a theme, other elements of a short story include setting, characters, and plot.

Search for and Explore Ideas

Stories can grow out of small moments that have personal meaning. Your experiences don't have to be earth-shaking to make interesting stories.

Search for ideas using the methods discussed earlier in this chapter. Try choosing one of the types of stories described in the chapter on Reading, page 48. The kind of story you like to read may be the best kind for you to write.

To help you judge how workable each story idea is, answer the following questions. **(See page 49 to review these elements.)**

Character: Who is at the centre of the action? Do I know anyone like this character?

Plot: What starts the action rolling? What happens in the story? What might the characters do as a result?

Theme: What is my theme or main idea? Do I want to show something about courage or hope or friendship or life?

Setting: When and where will the action happen? Is the setting important? Do I know enough about the time and place?

Do you want to keep your readers turning the pages? A good way to do this is by building your story around a problem or conflict.

Beginning: Set up the problem or conflict.

Middle: Show how the main character struggles to solve the problem and how she or he changes as a result.

End: Resolve the problem, happily or not.

If you want to tell the story from a character's point of view, the narrator will be limited to what that character knows. A *limited narrator* tells the story in the first person (using *I*).

> **Limited first person**
> I knew I had to focus on the race, but I kept wondering why Nadia was angry.
>
> A limited narrator may also tell the story in the third person (using he, she, they).
>
> **Limited third person**
> Ahmed knew he had to focus on the race, but he kept wondering why Nadia was angry.

If you want to describe the thoughts and feelings of all the characters, make the narrator all-knowing or *omniscient*. An *omniscient narrator* always tells a story in the third person and is not a character in the story.

> **Omniscient**
> Ahmed's taunting had made Nadia furious, but she wasn't going to think about that now. The starting signal went off. Nadia took off like a shot, but Ahmed fell behind, distracted by Nadia's anger.

Draft Your Story

Now is the time to get your story down on paper. One way to start is to create a rough draft. Write as quickly as possible. Don't think too much about any particular scene or conversation, and don't try to shape perfect sentences. If this approach doesn't work for you, try beginning with the scene you picture most vividly. Then write the rest of the story, forward and backward, from that special scene.

Use Dialogue

Story characters should sound like real people, but their conversations should usually come to the point more quickly. Use dialogue to show what your characters are like, but make sure it also moves the story along.

Weak

"I saw you in the mall," Romalda's mother argued.
"But I was at school," she responded.
Her mother insisted, "I don't believe you!"

Stronger

Her mother gave Romalda an accusing look. "I saw you at the mall," she said.
"But I was at school," Romalda replied coolly, staring her mother down.

Improve Your Story

Revising is part of creating a story. Answering the following questions will help you decide what to do.

❁ Is the plot believable?

❁ Would the characters behave as they do if they were real people?

❁ Have you included everything the reader needs to know?

Let's Practise

Write a short story. Use an idea from the Representing chapter to publish it.

Writing Essays

Key Features of Essays

An essay is a short nonfiction discussion of a topic. It is usually composed of several paragraphs. Most essays have an introduction, body (main part), and conclusion. There are many kinds of essays, including opinion essays, explanatory essays, narrative essays, humorous essays, and descriptive essays.

Planning a Descriptive Essay

When you write a descriptive essay, you use your senses, memory, and imagination to re-create a real-life experience. You try to write so vividly that readers will feel as if they are standing in *your* shoes and seeing with *your* eyes.

What should you describe in your essay? You can choose

★ a person, such as your uncle

★ a place, such as a noisy elevator

★ a thing, such as a strange pet

Here's How to

Build an Essay

Use Ginger's Pizzeria as a sample subject. The *goal* is to enter an essay contest. The *purpose* is to convince people Ginger's is a great place to eat. The intended *audience* is local kids and adults.

1. **Introduce your essay with a catchy first paragraph that does two jobs:** It gets the reader interested in your subject. It lets the reader know what point you will be making. The last sentence of the first paragraph is a good place to do this.

I think of Ginger's Pizzeria as my second home. It's Ginger's attitude that gives me that feeling—the pizzeria is both a successful business and a great place to visit.

2. **Compose the body of the essay with paragraphs that tell about the subject. Most descriptive details go here.**

   First sentence of first body paragraph
   Walk in, and Ginger will give you a friendly wave.

   First sentence of second body paragraph
   Sit down, and sniff the rich aromas.

   First sentence of third body paragraph
   By the time you leave, the warm room seems to be a place you've always known.

3. **End the essay with a paragraph that reminds readers of the point you made and leaves them with a closing thought.**

   Ginger's Pizzeria has succeeded where others have failed because Ginger treats her customers like family.

Let's Practise

1. Once you've written the first draft of your essay, have a peer editor read the draft and make suggestions. Use these to help you make revisions.

2. In your revised draft, choose the best descriptive words you can—but don't overdo it.

   Cut redundant words: Avoid words that mean almost the same thing.
   He laughed **loudly** and **uproariously**.

   Too many adjectives can blur your picture: Eliminate the ones that aren't as important.
   Her mop of **long, shiny, wild, unevenly cut, flaming red** hair was tightly confined in a **new jade green** hair net.

Writing Research Reports

When you write a research report, you're presenting information and your own ideas about a subject. You get to play detective as you gather information, organize it, think about it, evaluate it, and add your own thoughts. In presenting your report, you inform your readers by showing what you've learned.

Focus Your Learning
- Use various forms of note making
- Use prewriting strategies
- Use the steps in the writing process
- Organize

Key Features of Research Reports

A research report is a factual report based on information from one or more sources. Many research reports consist of several written paragraphs. A good research report begins with an attention-getting introduction, presents factual information in a logical order in the body, and ends with a strong conclusion. Many research reports include visual materials such as charts and graphs.

In research reports, any quoted material is set off with quotation marks, and its source is acknowledged. Most research reports include a bibliography of sources. People write research reports for many purposes, including school assignments, work reports, and web site information.

Select and Explore a Subject

If you're free to choose the subject of your research report, think about something you *need* to know or *want* to find out. If your teacher assigns a general category (such as ancient civilizations, vision, animal defences), choose a subject that

❋ interests you

❋ has enough available information—more than a single book or article

If possible, check to see what the Internet can tell you about your subject. **Check the chapter on researching for other useful sources. See page 238.**

Make a Working Outline

You have a pile of pages or a directory of computer files with information that answers your questions. Use this information to make a *working outline,* a list that shows how your facts and ideas are related. Organize your pages or files by grouping together all the answers to each of your questions:

❋ If you're working on pages, you could colour-code your notes with crayons or markers. All notes about biting could be marked in blue. All notes about mosquito control could be marked in red.

❋ If you're working on a computer, try sorting your notes with the *Cut, Copy,* and *Paste* functions. (Since software varies, you may find they have slightly different names.)

Once you have your groupings, use them to make your outline. Keep renumbering them or moving them around until you have an order that makes sense.

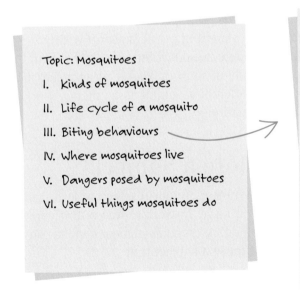

Topic: Mosquitoes

I. Kinds of mosquitoes

II. Life cycle of a mosquito

III. Biting behaviours

IV. Where mosquitoes live

V. Dangers posed by mosquitoes

VI. Useful things mosquitoes do

III. Biting behaviours
  A. Only females bite
    1. Need blood to reproduce
  B. Biting process
    1. How mosquitoes bite
      a. Six mouth parts pierce skin
      b. Damage small blood vessels
      c. Two pumps in head suck up blood
    2. Effect on victim
      a. Saliva causes itching and swelling

Each *main topic* (after a Roman numeral—I, II, III) can be turned into a paragraph or section of the report.

Subtopics (after capital letters) can be divided into *subsections* (after Arabic numerals—1, 2, 3) and *details* (after small letters). These show what information will be included.

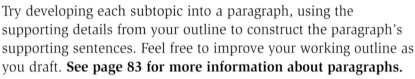

Draft Your Research Report

Now that you've collected and outlined your information, it's time to begin your rough draft. Use a standard organization similar to that of a business letter or essay. This will make it easier to write clearly. The basics include three parts:

1. The *introduction* is usually a single paragraph. Tell your readers what the report is about and use a strong lead to get them interested.

2. The *body* of the report is made of several paragraphs, each built around one main idea. Follow the order of your outline.

3. The *conclusion* is a paragraph that sums up the main points. Try to leave your reader saying, "This really is a fascinating subject."

Try developing each subtopic into a paragraph, using the supporting details from your outline to construct the paragraph's supporting sentences. Feel free to improve your working outline as you draft. **See page 83 for more information about paragraphs.**

As you write, note places where a drawing, graph, map, or diagram could help you explain an idea. Make sketches that you'll later turn into finished pieces of art. **For information on preparing visuals, see pages 214–221 in the Representing chapter.**

Check Your Report for Accuracy

After drafting and revising your report, double-check the accuracy of your facts as you prepare the final version. Go back to your notes or sources to make sure you've copied all dates, numbers, names, and terms accurately.

As you edit your prose, remember to check the visuals too!

❊ Are all labels and captions clear and accurate?

❊ Are the drawings neat, not smudged or crooked?

Add a bibliography of your sources. **For information on how to write a bibliography, see page 263.**

Evaluate Information

Take a final look at your report. Does your information have the following qualities?

Relevance: The information should be "to the point" and relevant to the subject, purpose, and audience of your research paper. Does your information answer the kind of questions that you need to answer? Was it written for the same kind of purpose and audience as you have for your research paper?

Currency: Often, you will need to have the most up-to-date information available, especially in fields such as science and technology. For books, read the copyright page to see when it was published. For magazines and newspapers, check the dates of the issues. For web pages, look for the date the article was written or the page updated.

Accuracy: Your information must be accurate. A good way to check accuracy is to compare two reliable sources. If they don't agree, keep searching until you get sources that agree.

Reliability: You will want to know if the source of your information can be trusted. What is the writer's (or speaker's) background in the subject area? Is this person considered to be an expert? Is the web site sponsored by a reputable institution or group? Does the writer of the web page provide a name and e-mail address?

Objectivity: You will need to know if the information has any bias. If it is arguing for a point of view (a newspaper editorial or a political speech) or appealing to your emotions (an advertisement), then you know that it will be biased. Is the material made up of facts or of opinions? Does it offer factual evidence to back up any claims?

Let's Practise

Write a research report on a subject that interests you. How can you research your subject? How will writing your report help you learn about it? How will it help others learn about it?

Writing Poetry

Writing a poem is finding just the right words to capture a moment, an idea, a feeling, an observation.

Key Features of Poems

A poem is an arrangement of words in lines. Some poems use rhyme and rhythm. Others do not. Many poems use strong, beautiful language. A poem often surprises readers, leading them to see something in a new way.

Predraft: Capture a Poem Idea

Your world is full of ideas for poems. You can find ideas hidden in objects as different as a fine painting and a garbage bin. You can write about a tiny moment or a huge event, a close friend or a stranger you passed on the street.

Ideas of Poetry

My cat
Computer games
Grandpa

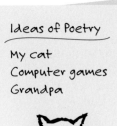

How do you recognize a good idea for a poem? Start with your list of ideas. Which one evokes a powerful feeling? Why do you feel that way? Which subject brings a vivid picture to your mind?

Think about your subject. Quickly list words and phrases to describe it. Does your subject have a particular size, shape, mass, or colour? How does it affect your senses? Can you smell, touch, taste, or hear it? Can you compare what you see or feel to something else?

You have spent some time living with your idea—finding details to express it and discovering more about how it affects you. Now it's time to think about the poem you will write.

How do you feel about your subject? That feeling often sets the tone of your poem. List the first emotions that come to your mind. Or talk aloud about your subject and listen for your tone of voice. The words on your list may also suggest the tone you're after.

Draft Your Poem

Just let the words and ideas flow freely in the first draft of your poem. You may wish to follow these four steps:

1. **Freewrite your poem.** Describe your subject in words, short phrases, or sentences. Unless you have a definite sense of words breaking themselves into lines, write your poem in your natural voice—just the way you would tell it to a friend.

2. **Condense.** Take out uninteresting or unnecessary words. You can leave out articles, verbs, adjectives, prepositions— whatever leaves your poem strong without being confusing.

3. **Find the line breaks.** Read your draft aloud. Where do the natural breaks come—the ones made as you speak, or the ones made by your changing thoughts? Rewrite your poem. Use these natural breaks to shape your poem into lines.

4. **Choose a matching form**. You can write your poem in a traditional form, with a rhythm and rhyme pattern. Or you can write it in free verse, without a set pattern of rhythm or rhyme. If your poem is short and describes nature, look at an example of a haiku. If your poem tells a story, look at a ballad. **For information on poetic forms, see page 63.**

How do the words and phrases in the following free verse make the shark come to life?

The Shark

He seemed to know the harbour,
So leisurely he swam;
His fin,
Like a piece of sheet-iron,
Three-cornered,
And with knife-edge,
Stirred not a bubble
As it moved
With its base-line on the water.

His body was tubular
And tapered
And smoke-blue,
And as he passed the wharf
He turned,
And snapped at a flat-fish
That was dead and floating.

And I saw the flash of a white throat,
And a double row of white teeth,
And eyes of metallic grey,
Hard and narrow and slit.

Then out of the harbour,
With that three-cornered fin
Shearing without a bubble the water
Lithely,
Leisurely,
He swam—
That strange fish,
Tubular, tapered, smoke-blue,
Part vulture, part wolf,
Part neither—for his blood was cold.

— *E. J. Pratt*

Use Literary Devices

Try using some literary devices to liven up your poem. **For more information on literary devices, see pages 59–62.**

Many poets use *onomatopoeia*. Onomatopoeia refers to words like *gurgle*, or *slap*, or *murmur*, in which the sound suggests the meaning.

Let's Practise

Use the following questions to help you revise a poem you are writing:

❋ What's the main image or idea I want my poem to communicate? Does the poem accomplish this?

❋ Would my point be clearer if there were fewer words or phrases? Which ones can I cut?

❋ Is each word the best possible word?

❋ Does the poem end with force, surprise, or a message? How might I improve the ending?

Measure Your Growth

Write the numbers 1 through 20 in your notebook. Beside each, rate yourself according to the following scale:

A Excellent

B Good

C Fair

D Needs a lot of work

1. I regularly record experiences, ideas, and feelings in a writer's response journal or writing folder.

2. I use a writer's response journal or writing folder to help organize my writing.

3. I understand and use the predrafting process.

4. When I draft pieces of writing, I try to write in my own unique "voice."

5. I consider connotation and tone.

6. I use gender-inclusive and unbiased language.

7. I understand paragraph parts and features, applying this knowledge when I construct paragraphs.

8. I can identify and write different types of paragraphs.

9. I understand and use the revision process.

10. I edit and proofread my writing.

11. I use various methods of sharing my writing with others.

12. I reflect on what I have written.

13. I can identify and use the specific formats of friendly letters, business letters, faxes, and e-mail.

14. I write differently for different readers.

15. I can choose an event from my life and write a personal narrative based on it.

16. I can write a short story, using short story elements: theme, characters, setting, and plot.

17. I can write an essay, stating my viewpoint clearly and backing it up with supporting facts, opinions, and details.

18. I can do research and write a research report.

19. I effectively use the elements of essays and research reports: introduction, body, and conclusion.

20. I can capture poem ideas and write poetry that communicates ideas and feelings in ways others appreciate.

CHAPTER *three*

Speaking and Listening

CONTENTS

Conversation

Conversation is an informal exchange of spoken words between people. Two people, or sometimes more, share ideas or feelings or information, usually in a casual way. This takes place in informal situations where you can express yourself naturally.

Do you express yourself differently depending on the person you're talking to? Most of us do. But even if you know a person well, what you mean to say may not be what he or she hears you say. Take heart! There are ways to speak and listen better.

Focus Your Learning
- Recognize and use the conventions of formal and informal speech
- Listen

Speak and Listen Appropriately

Good speakers	Good listeners
♣ speak in a style and vocabulary their listeners will understand.	👁 are respectful, polite, and interested. Their behaviour helps the speaker feel more confident.
♣ talk clearly, not too quickly, and loudly enough for their listeners.	👁 pay attention. If they can't hear, they let the speaker know.
♣ use language that expresses how they feel. They use slang that's familiar to the listener, but only in informal situations.	👁 listen closely before drawing conclusions.

Discussion

Discussion is an exchange of ideas or viewpoints between many people.

In a discussion you share ideas with others, think out loud, speak clearly and thoughtfully. You listen carefully, considering other viewpoints, stay open to new ideas and ways of looking at things, and treat one another with respect.

Discussion involves making sure everyone gets a chance to talk, helping one another to learn, solving problems and making decisions together.

Focus Your Learning

- Use appropriate verbal and nonverbal feedback
- Seek and respond to diverse opinions and ideas
- Use inclusive language and actions
- Contribute to group harmony
- Explore, compare, listen, and respond to other ideas and opinions
- Assume a variety of roles in group work
- Analyse factors of a successful/ unsuccessful discussion

Do's and Don'ts of Discussion

	Hot	Not
To recognize others' ideas and invite them to speak	★ Smile and nod. ★ Say, "I agree!" ★ Say, "That's a good point!" ★ Look encouraging.	✎ Clap wildly and cry, "Yes, YES!" ✎ Say, "Let me interrupt to say that I agree with you completely, Sarah and ... (blah, blah, blah)."
To disagree with a group member	★ Look puzzled. ★ Say, "But have you thought about ... ?" ★ Say, "I have another suggestion."	✎ Roll your eyes and sigh. ✎ Shake your head violently. ✎ Mutter, "What a silly thing to say!" ✎ Shout, "You don't know what you're talking about!"
To present points of view	★ Listen to what others are saying, and think of ways you can add to what someone else has said. ★ Say, "That's a good point, Gerardo, because...." Or say, "That's true, but on the other hand...." ★ Jot down some notes on the discussion. Read one aloud and comment on it.	✎ Mutter, "Well, I guess no one here cares what I think!" ✎ Slump in your chair and refuse to make eye contact with anyone. ✎ Wait for someone else to ask you what you have to say. ✎ Try to get the group's attention by stretching, clearing your throat, and tapping the table.

Hot	**Not**
To keep one member from monopolizing the discussion	★ Hold up your hand and say, "I have something to add when you're finished, Kim." ★ Say, "Interesting point, Kim. Can we discuss that? Mashid, what do you think?"	💣 Clear your throat loudly. 💣 Stare angrily and hope the person takes the hint. 💣 Exclaim, "Kim! Would you please give someone else a chance!"
To make sure you and your group understand something	★ Check to see if anyone looks confused or puzzled. ★ Ask, "Are we all clear on this?" ★ Say, "Excuse me, Kyoka, do you mean that … ?"	💣 Sit back and hope everything will become clear later. 💣 Cry, "What on earth are you talking about, Kyoka? You've got everyone confused!"
To deal with group members who interrupt you while you're speaking	★ Make sure you aren't monopolizing the discussion. ★ In a pleasant voice, say, "Could you give me another second, Sam? I'm almost done."	💣 Get angry. 💣 Hiss, "Thanks, Sam. I'll finish my thought when you're done."
To keep group members from being rude	★ Be a good example. ★ Keep your tone light but firm to avoid bad feeling. ★ Direct a rude person toward the issue. Ask, "Do you have something to add to the discussion, Josh?"	💣 Let someone get away with rudeness. 💣 Shout, "What makes you think you're so great?" 💣 Cry, "Hey! You want name-calling? Here's a name for you!"
To reach group agreement	★ Say, "Let's keep talking this out. I don't think everyone agrees." ★ Say, "I think we need to get more information before we can agree." ★ Ask, "Has everyone had a say?" ★ Say, "We're ready. Let's vote."	💣 Move around restlessly. 💣 Announce, "I say we go with Sergei's proposal. And that's that!" 💣 Demand, "We've got two minutes to agree—starting now."

Respect Differences in Opinions

Express your own opinions, but do this in a way that is sensitive to the feelings of people from other backgrounds. Not everyone will agree with you; their backgrounds or views of life may be so different that you could never convince them. And when they are speaking, be willing to listen to them with an open mind.

Keep in mind different cultural backgrounds too. If you mention a holiday some class members don't celebrate, briefly explain what it's about. If you want to use a word or phrase that some students might not be familiar with, explain it.

Kinds of Groups

Different kinds of discussion groups have different goals, and group members may have different roles and responsibilities.

Group Investigation

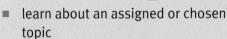

3–5 Members

Goals and Uses

- do a research project
- learn about an assigned or chosen topic
- share responsibility for learning

Roles and Responsibilities

- The team has a topic to investigate or a project to complete.
- The team divides the topic into subtopics to investigate or divides the project into tasks to accomplish.
- The members share what they learn or accomplish.

The roles of leader, clarifier, recorder, and reporter may be assigned. **See the Group Roles section on page 129.**

Pairs

2 Members

Goals and Uses

- brainstorm or exchange ideas on a topic
- learn or study together
- tutor each other
- hold a peer conference

Roles and Responsibilities

- Take turns speaking and listening.
- Alternate acting as teacher and as learner. One or both might be the recorder.
- Go through the material together or separately, then quiz each other.
- In a peer conference, one asks to hear the other's thoughts about the topic or asks for help learning or understanding it.

Literary Circles

3–8 Members

Goals and Uses

- examine critically a piece of literature
- share personal responses to a reading
- compare critical responses to a literary element, such as plot or characters

Roles and Responsibilities

Each member reads the same piece of literature. Or each reads a different piece—on a similar topic, or in the same genre, or by the same author. The roles of leader, clarifier, recorder, and reporter may be assigned. **See the Group Roles section on page 129.**

Jigsaw

3–5 Members

Goals and Uses

- discuss the material in a textbook chapter
- learn about an assigned topic
- share responsibility for learning

Roles and Responsibilities

- The class chooses a project and divides it into topics. It forms groups, assigning one topic to each group.
- Each team member studies a subtopic of its group's topic.
- Team members then teach each other what they have learned.
- From each team, representatives go to other teams and find out what they have learned.
- The representatives return and teach this to their own teams.

Whole Class

All Class Members

Goals and Uses

- learn together
- think critically, analyse
- problem-solve
- make decisions
- carry out a project or other task

Roles and Responsibilities

The teacher is often the leader. In some cases a student or group of students may lead the discussion. All class members are encouraged to participate. The roles of leader, clarifier, recorder, and reporter may be assigned. **See the Group Roles section on page 129.**

For more on presenting to a small group and the whole class, see page 138.

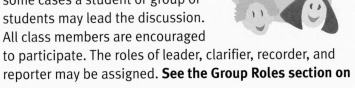

Group Roles

Leader   Keeps discussion on topic.

"Good point. What does that teach us about the rain forest?"

Clarifier   Makes sure everyone understands what a speaker has said.

"Alice, do you have a question about how trees produce oxygen?"

Recaller   From time to time, summarizes what has been learned or discussed before the group decides to record something.

"We've learned there are important medicinal plants that grow in the rain forest."

Recorder   Writes down the main subjects of discussion.

"Why the rain forest is important: medicinal plants, ... oxygen ...."

Reporter   Shares the group's findings with others.

"In addition, our group learned that the oxygen produced by the rain forest... "

Here's How to

Discuss a Class Project

You can follow these steps in any order. The order will vary depending on how the discussion and the project are going.

- **Follow up on each other's ideas.** Suppose Karin suggests asking a scientist to speak at the class science fair. Julio may know a chemist to ask.

- **Work together to advance your thinking.** For example, some students may not know what a chemist is. The class might look up the word in a few dictionaries and develop a definition.

- ☀ **Suggest alternatives.** For example, suppose Julio's chemist friend can't come. Class members could suggest other speakers to invite.

- ☀ **Listen to a variety of points of view.** For example, Kelly may think posters work best in advertising a science fair. Ryan may think brochures are better. Perhaps the class will decide to use both, or something else entirely.

- ☀ **Assign tasks.** Have various class members take on specific parts of the project. For example, Kelly, Ryan, and Nando might make posters and brochures. Austin, Maria, Elio, and Hayley might set up the science displays.

- ☀ **Share resources.** Arrange among yourselves how you will share art supplies, computer time, fax machine, photocopier, and books.

Let's Practise

Hold a class or group discussion using what you have learned in the preceding sections. You could discuss a question such as:

- ❇ Why is computer technology changing so rapidly?
- ❇ Why is it important to learn math?
- ❇ If we could have any kind of school we wanted, what would it be like?

If you prefer, you could have a class discussion to plan a project such as a trip to a historical site or a bake sale to raise money for gym equipment.

For tips on speaking to the whole class or a small group, see page 138.

Inform and Persuade

You want to tell someone how to get to a theatre, or you want the class to vote for you. You have to give a report or take part in a debate. How do you do it? You use a form of oral communication, one that gives information or persuades the listeners to do a particular thing or agree with a particular viewpoint.

Oral Directions

If you're writing directions, it's easy to check how accurate your information is. But when you're giving or getting oral directions, that can be harder to do. The following tips can help.

When you're giving oral directions:

Give it some thought. What are you explaining to someone? Directions to a particular location? Instructions for programming a VCR? Whatever it is, think it through. Imagine the whole process as a series of steps.

I'd like to talk about my great trip to Spain.

I wonder when he went? What did he see? What is it like to go to another country?

Explain each step, in order, clearly and simply. Pause after each step to make sure your listener is following you.

Give it a second chance. Encourage your listener to repeat what you have said.

Consider your listener's needs. Consider how much your listener already knows and what ideas and language he or she is likely to understand.

When you're getting oral directions:

Get the picture. As you hear the directions, try to picture yourself performing each step of the process.

Listen for clue words. These tell you when one step ends and another begins. Some common clue words are: first, next, after, before, while, then, and last.

Get it straight. How many steps do you have to complete? Do you have them all? Are they in the proper order? Go through the complete process in your mind. You can repeat what you were told, using gestures if this helps.

Check it. Make sure you have all the information you need. Don't be afraid to ask questions if something is unclear to you.

Interviews

People can be wonderful sources of information. But conducting a good interview requires careful planning. Suppose your research topic is recycling, and you want to interview Dr. Uzita Genn, the supervisor at a local recycling plant. What do you do?

Before the Interview

Know something about your topic. You won't be able to fully understand Dr. Genn if you know nothing about recycling. Do a little research.

Decide what you want to find out. What kind of information do you want? How much? When you first contact Dr. Genn, introduce yourself. Then give her a general idea of what you want to know and how long the interview will take.

Make an appointment. Explain your project and invite Dr. Genn to talk with you. Ask when and where she'd like to meet. Write down the time and location. If you plan to use a tape recorder, ask Dr. Genn's permission.

Write a list of questions you want to ask. Make them clear and simple.

Questions to Ask

1. Begin with a few direct questions about basic factual information. Answers to such questions are often short.

   Sample Direct Question:

   "Dr. Genn, what is your job title?"

   Sample Answer:

   "I'm the acting supervisor for the Crowfoot and Kelsey County Recycling Plant."

2. Ask more detailed factual questions. These could be connected to the person's area of expertise or the specific event that led you to ask for the interview.

   "What area of recycling do you work with?"

3. After asking direct questions, move to open-ended ones. These are questions that draw out the interviewee's experiences and opinions.

"Why did you decide to work in recycling?"
"What materials do you think are most important to recycle?"

4. Avoid questions that can be answered with just "yes" or "no." Rather than asking, "Do you like your job?" ask, "What do you like about your job?"

5. Don't ask leading questions. These are questions that tell the interviewee what answer you expect. Which of the following examples is more likely to draw out an interviewee's real opinion?

"Do you agree that recycling is necessary for our planet to survive?" or "Why is your work important? What will happen to our planet if we don't recycle?"

During the Interview

Get off to a good start. Introduce yourself again. Remind Dr. Genn of the purpose of your interview.

Be responsive. Look and act interested. Make eye contact. Ask questions clearly and politely.

Take careful notes. If you aren't taping the interview, write down every word of those statements you might want to quote. For everything else, write down only the most important points, words, and phrases. If you are taping, your hands are free to write down new questions that the speaker's responses may raise in your mind.

Be polite, but follow up. In answering a question, suppose Dr. Genn mentions a topic worth pursuing. Don't interrupt her; just jot a note to yourself to go back to it.

Get it right. If you don't understand something Dr. Genn says, ask her to explain. Check your notes to make sure everything is clear. If you want to quote Dr. Genn, ask her permission and check the wording of quotations.

After the Interview

End it right. Thank Dr. Genn for her time. Ask if she would like a copy of the interview.

Take some time. As soon as possible, organize your notes. Transcribe your tape—that is, make a word-for-word copy. If you're unsure of something, ask Dr. Genn before including it.

Write up the interview. You can write up the interview using only what was said, including your questions and Dr. Genn's answers. Or you can make a summary of the interview, using some paraphrases of Dr. Genn's words and some direct quotations.

A paraphrase is a summary of a direct quotation.

Sample Direct Quotation

Sample Paraphrase

"I'm concerned," Dr. Genn said, "that we are using up our non-renewable resources."

Dr. Genn is concerned that her country is using up its non-renewable resources.

Publish your work! Send a copy of the interview, with a persuasive letter, to the editor of your school or local newspaper. Explain why you think readers will enjoy it.

It's Your Turn

Perhaps you are the one being interviewed. A radio host may be interviewing you about your CD collection. A neighbour may be interviewing you about a summer job working in her garden. You may be attending a basketball club meeting at which you're expected to answer questions. Many situations in life call for responding to oral questions. Here are some suggestions for effective responses.

Elicit Effective Reponses

1. Listen carefully so you know exactly what the questioner wants to know. Clue words include who, what, where, when, why, and how.

   "What place did the team finish in last season?"
   "Where did you work last summer?"

2. Don't interrupt while the questioner is speaking.

3. Look at the questioner and make eye contact while responding. (Sometimes this may not be possible or suitable; for example, when speaking on the telephone.)

4. When you respond, speak loudly and clearly enough to be heard.

5. Make your responses complete but brief. Be alert to what types of responses the questions call for. Don't include a lot of details that have nothing to do with the question. They waste the questioner's time, and may confuse him or her. For example, if you are asked, "How did you raise the money to pay for your skis?," which of the following answers is clearer?

   ✳ "Last summer I delivered advertising flyers on Stanley Street."

   ✳ "Last summer—the summer my sister went to New Brunswick and my uncle had his tonsils out—I delivered advertising flyers to the Taylors, Lees, Wilsons, Obratovs, and others on our street, Stanley Street."

6. Give more details if the questioner asks for them.

   "I've lived on Stanley Street for four years."

Oral Presentations

Oral presentations are part of every student's life and part of many working people's lives, too. An oral presentation is a verbal description of any kind of project or activity done by an individual or a group, in which one person presents the results. It could be a report on a research project or a group discussion, or it could be an individual talk or an information session. It might include displays, models, charts, or other visual aids; or it might rely on words and gestures.

Need help giving a talk? Is it an informal talk about your own experiences? Is it a speech that expresses your viewpoint on an issue—a viewpoint you want others to share? **For tips on storytelling, see page 158. For more about giving a speech, turn to page 147.**

Mateo asked his friend Isha to help him practise giving his oral report. He prepared a checklist of things to do and remember. Isha agreed to make up a checklist of things the audience might watch and listen for during Mateo's presentation. Here are their checklists.

Checklist for My Oral Report

Ahead of time

☐ Make notes of main points to cover.

☐ Organize notes. Print large so I can read fast and not lose my place.

☐ Mark places to show pictures and charts.

☐ Write interesting, dramatic opening.

☐ Do a trial run to check time (I have only 15 minutes).

☐ Practise using slide projector. Do slides look OK?

☐ Get organized. Is projector set up? Are slides & notes in order?

While speaking

☐ Relax! This can be fun!

☐ Don't slouch!

☐ Keep hands below shoulders so they won't be distracting.

☐ Glance at notes only now and then.

☐ Don't read everything. Speak spontaneously part of the time.

☐ Sweep eyes over audience. Then look up at people often.

☐ Speak up. Can everyone hear me?

☐ Speak slowly! (Listen to voice—am I racing?)

☐ Sound interested.

☐ At the end, give people time to ask questions.

Feedback for Your Oral Report

Opening

Got audience's attention?

Yes   No

Presentation

Was clear and easy to follow?

Yes   No

Covered topic well?

Yes   No

Made information interesting?

Yes   No

Delivery

Good appearance?

Yes   No

Voice clear and natural?

Yes   No

Speed good?

Yes   No

Sounded interested/interesting?

Yes   No

Looked at audience often?

Yes   No

Sample Comment:

Mateo, you started out talking a little fast. When you slowed down, it was easier for me to take in all the information you were giving. But you really made me feel like I was there in the Rockies. Thanks for the trip!

Your friend,

Isha

Class and Group Presentations Differ

Presenting to the Class	Presenting to a Group
Subject	
When you are making a presentation to the entire class, you are likely to be giving a report or making a speech. Examples: "Anne Frank's Life in Hiding" or "What My Group Discovered about Dinosaurs."	When you are speaking to a small group, you might be giving your ideas on how to solve a problem that the group has been asked to discuss, such as "What to Do if You Meet a Bear While Hiking" or "Find Five Ways to Determine the Height of the CN Tower."

Presenting *to the* Class	Presenting *to a* Group
Delivery	
Presenting to a class is more formal, like a speech. You are the only one speaking until you invite questions at the end of your presentation.	Presenting to a group is more informal, closer to a conversation or discussion.
Prepare the presentation ahead of time. Speak from notes but look up and ad lib from time to time.	Think about what you want to say before your presentation. You can use notes but they are not always necessary.
It may be best to stand during the presentation so the class can see you better. Speak loudly enough that those at the back of the room can hear you.	Since there are fewer people in a small group, you can remain seated if you prefer. Speak in normal conversational style, but clearly.
It's harder to hold the attention of the class than that of a small group. Use some gestures. From time to time during the presentation, look at different people, trying to make everyone feel involved.	It's easier to hold a group's attention. You can see everyone at a glance. You will probably naturally make eye contact with all group members, one at a time.
If you photocopy an outline, list of videos, or other handout, you will need to make enough copies so each class member receives one. If you show pictures or other visuals, they should be big enough so even those at the back can easily see them.	You will not need as many copies of your handout. You can show pictures or other visuals of any size, and you can easily pass them around to every member of the group.

Presenting to the Class	Presenting to a Group
Interaction	
Questions should be left until the end of your presentation. Ask members to raise their hands before speaking.	Because there are fewer people, questions and answers can be more informal. You can invite group members to ask questions at any point in your presentation. Eye contact or body language may be enough to tell you when a person wishes to ask a question.
You present information or ideas, and class members listen to you.	You can ask for reactions during the presentation. Or invite group members to add their ideas to yours at certain points in the presentation, so that your own ideas are expanded. At this point you may become a discussion leader as well as a presenter.

Here's How to

Listen for Main Ideas

Maybe you're listening to a presentation given in class, a 4H meeting, a dog obedience session, or a soccer coach's strategy presentation. Many situations in life call for listening attentively. This means listening carefully in order to pick up main ideas and remember what you heard.

1. Pay attention to any opening remarks. They often give clues to main points that will follow.

2. Set a purpose for listening. This will help you identify main ideas, or key points. For example, your purpose is to score a goal from your position. You'll be listening to identify which strategies you can apply best.

3. Consider taking notes. You might have in mind a few questions you'd like answered. As you hear answers, jot them down. These answers are likely to be main ideas. Also briefly note any other key points you identify.

4. Practise tuning out background sounds such as coughing, foot-shuffling, or cars driving by, so that they don't distract you.

5. Look at the speaker often. Speakers tend to signal main ideas by leaning forward, waving their hands around, or using other body language.

6. Listen for tone, pitch, and emotion in the speaker's voice. Speakers often use these to signal key points.

7. Listen for words and phrases such as "here's the strategy for … ," "first," "second," "next," and "in conclusion." They help you follow the speaker from one main idea to another.

Is It Logical?

It's hard to contradict an argument that you build logically. Logical ideas are like steps leading to a conclusion that really makes sense. But faulty logic is like a staircase with some of the steps missing. What sounds logical at first may not be convincing when you really think about it. Knowing what to avoid and what to listen for can help you make your case or help you avoid being fooled. Here are some common examples of faulty logic.

Irrelevance: "And that reminds me ..."

Sometimes, instead of giving reasons to support a main idea, a speaker wanders into another idea. For example:

> Marta says, "Our community centre needs more funding. The sports equipment is old and in poor shape. We only have one basketball. I saw some basketballs at Speedy's. Speedy's has the best prices in town."

Irrelevance gets off track. Speedy's prices have nothing to do with why the community centre needs more funding. Make sure your reasons lead back to the main point—not away from it.

Incomplete Comparison: "It's better!"

Better than what? Better than whose? Incomplete comparisons say less than they pretend or mean to say. Advertisers often use them to make you think their product is best. Here's another example:

> Kay says, "In the old days, students learned more than they do today. Teachers made kids work hard. When they graduated, they knew how to read and write. So those students definitely learned more."

Half a comparison isn't a comparison. Kay begins to compare how much students used to learn with how much they learn today. But she never describes how much students learn today. The incomplete comparison makes her conclusion illogical.

Wrong Conclusion: "The sky is falling!"

In a popular tale, Chicken Little gets hit on the head with an acorn and concludes that the sky is falling. Here's another example of an illogical conclusion:

> Joe says, "Medical experiments have brought us cures for certain types of cancer. Animal-rights activists are against hurting animals in medical experiments. So animal-rights activists are against finding a cure for cancer."

Wrong conclusions don't add up. Joe begins by stating two separate facts that have nothing to do with each other. The two facts don't lead logically to any conclusion. So Joe's conclusion is wrong.

Are You Listening Critically?

Can you tell whether the speaker is knowledgeable about the subject? Has the biologist done her research? Does the actor understand his lines? Can you separate the speaker's facts, which can be proved, from the speaker's opinions, which can't? Listening critically doesn't mean trying to find fault with everything someone says. It means evaluating what you hear before deciding what you think of it.

Persuasion…or Propaganda?

"Everybody who's cool is wearing designer jeans, so you should too." Sound familiar? You've heard manipulative reasoning such as this in speeches, ads, and conversations. It uses generalizations, false information, or other devices to persuade you to do or believe something without asking why. Sometimes it's called propaganda. Critical thinking can help you spot it.

There are many persuasive techniques. Some are designed to benefit others, and some are designed to manipulate people. When you want to be persuasive, you might try some of the following techniques.

Persuasive Techniques

Bandwagon:

Hockey is this town's most popular sport. So join us in supporting our hockey team!

Inviting people to jump on the bandwagon often works because most people like to do what other people around them are doing.

Testimonial:

Razell Dazell is doing her part. "All the money from my last concert went toward saving the rain forests," she says. Shouldn't you help, too?

Quoting people is fine, if you have their permission. If you don't, describe what they've said or done.

Repetition:

Do you want safer schools? Vote for Pete.
Do you want safer streets? Vote for Pete.
Do you want safer lives? Vote for Pete.

Repetition helps people remember. But that means Pete had better be able to provide all that safety!

> Do you want safer schools?
> Vote for Pete.
> Do you want safer streets? Vote for Pete.
> Do you want safer lives? Vote for Pete.

Emotional words:

Can we support a company that dumps poisonous, deadly chemicals into our waters? Their cold indifference to our health is appalling.

Emotional language can be a good means of reaching people, so long as it isn't overdone.

Recognize Bias

Are you aware that telephone marketing companies may target certain telephone numbers because of the kinds of houses they know are in those neighbourhoods? This is an example of prejudice, or prejudgment. A prejudice is a judgment based on opinions formed previously, before an actual situation arises. Often such opinions are not based on facts.

Say you enter a public speaking contest. You feel your speech is excellent, but the top prizes go to students from a school that has placed first for the past ten years. This may be an example of bias. A bias is a leaning of the mind in a certain direction. Often it makes a person favour one group too much. **For more on bias, see page 80.**

How can you recognize prejudice and bias in oral presentations? Here are some tips.

★ Notice when presenters are stating facts and when they're stating opinions.

Sample fact:

"Canada is one of the wealthiest countries in the world."

Sample opinion:

"I think all Canadians are wealthy."

★ Watch for words such as "I think," "in my judgment," and "as far as I know." Presenters often use them to signal opinions.

★ Sometimes presenters do not use such words. They simply state opinions as if they were facts. Examples:

"People who live in small towns are friendlier than people who live in big cities."

"Young people care about the environment."

Watch out when you hear opinions stated as if they were facts. They may signal a prejudice or bias.

Watch for connotation. Connotation is what a word suggests besides its simple meaning. For example, young has a positive connotation. Immature has a negative one. Adventuresome and daring have positive connotations. Dare-devil and foolhardy have negative connotations. **For more on connotation, see page 79.** Words with negative connotations may signal prejudice or bias.

Debates

In a debate, two individuals or teams present opposite sides of an issue before an audience or judges. The debate topic is called a proposition. It's a single idea that can have strong arguments for it (an affirmative side) and strong arguments against it (a negative side).

Learn the Art of Debate

1. **Talk.** Meet with team members to discuss arguments both for and against the proposition. Zero in on the main issues. Collect evidence for your side.

2. **Gather evidence.** Look for facts that support your team's argument. Refer to books and magazines, call agencies and organizations, and talk to professionals. As you collect evidence for their case, note evidence the other side might use.

3. **Plan.** Meet with your team to share the information you've collected. Put it together into a case for your side. Back up each main point with evidence—maybe a few strong facts, the results of a study, or a quotation from an expert. Discuss the arguments the other team is likely to make and how to refute them. Check your own arguments for any weak or faulty reasoning.

4. **Practise.** Choose two people to present the team's viewpoint. Help them make notes of the team's arguments and backup evidence. Listen and make helpful suggestions as the presenters practise.

5. **Present.** Each speaker has a chance to present arguments from that speaker's team and to refute or argue against points from the opposing team.

6. **Rethink.** Team members can huddle to consider the other side's arguments. They can discuss flaws in the other side's reasoning and plan new ways to show that their own case is stronger.

7. **Rebut.** Each team has time to explain the weaknesses of the other side's arguments. Speakers remind the judges and audience of why their own team's case is stronger. Team members listen without interrupting.

8. **Judges' decision.** The judges decide which team has won the debate by presenting its position more persuasively.

Panel Discussions

A panel discussion is an organized discussion among several people, less formal than a debate but more formal than most discussions.

Panel members are both speech makers and informal debaters. Panels usually consist of three or four people who explain their ideas on a certain subject. This is the speech-making part. After all their positions have been presented, panelists are invited to join in a general discussion, responding to one another's comments. This discussion may become an informal debate. Panelists take turns restating their points of view or responding to someone else. A chairperson keeps order and makes sure everyone who wishes to speak has an opportunity to do so.

Speeches

You deliver a speech alone, in front of an audience. It's about your thoughts, your opinions, or your experiences, and it's in your own words. Maybe that's why speeches are so challenging—and nerve-wracking—but also why making them can bring you enormous satisfaction.

Check out the Details

Who will the audience be? Your peers? adults? a mix? Who they are may affect what you say and how you say it. **For tips on presenting to groups and the whole class (or other larger audiences) see page 138.**

Where will you speak? Outdoors? in an auditorium? Will you have a microphone? If so, learn how to use it.

How big will the audience be? Smaller audiences pay closer attention. It's harder to keep a large group interested.

How long will you have to speak? You don't want to run out of time—or end too soon and be left with nothing to say.

Plan the Speech Itself

Decide on a topic and a goal. Your speech could inform your audience about something you know ("My Cambodian Heritage").

It could persuade them to agree with you ("Why I Should Be Prime Minister"). Or it could entertain them with your experiences ("The Thrill of Windsurfing").

Make notes. They're handy for an informal speech. On separate index cards, write a sentence to introduce each important point. Below it, jot down details. Write out any jokes, quotations, or statistics you plan to use. If you use these cards when you make your speech, they are called *cue cards.* They "cue" your next point.

Or, write the whole speech. If it has to be formal, or if you're worried about the time limit or afraid you'll leave something out, this way is best. Print or type, so the speech is easy to read. Number the pages and put them in order, unstapled.

Polish your delivery. Practice is the only way.

My speech is on why I hate giving speeches.

Use Visual Aids

Visual aids get an audience's attention and help get your point across. Use a chalkboard, posters, charts or diagrams, slides, or a video. Use puppets, an overhead projector, photographs, maps, or relevant objects such as a T-shirt and a lobster trap. Be creative.

Visual aids can help remind you of main ideas in your speech. They'll also help your audience understand your speech.

Plan a Few Gestures

A few gestures will help the audience pay attention and understand your ideas. For example, as you list items, you could count them out on your raised fingers: "first," "second," "third," and so on. To indicate a wide area, you might sweep your hand in a semicircle in front of you. You could point at the floor with dramatic words such as, "It could happen right here."

A little walking around can also be effective. For example, when making an important point, you could step forward. When moving from one main idea of your speech to the next, you could take a step or two to the side.

Watch yourself in a full-length mirror to make sure your gestures look natural. If, during your speech, you don't remember all your planned gestures, don't worry. As you speak, you may come up with others that work just as well.

Blown away

Impressive Speech Techniques

Speech Part	Techniques to Try	For Instance ...
Introduction: First, get their attention. Then tell them what you're going to tell them about.	Open with a quotation by a famous person.	"Blue Jays player Carlos Delgado once said ...."
	Start with a dramatic example or statistic.	"Do you know how many people died last year in car accidents?"
	Tell an anecdote (a short personal story).	"Two weeks ago, for the very first time, I talked to a homeless person."
Body: Tell them what you want to tell them.	**Repetition:** Repetition emphasizes an idea and helps people remember. But be careful: enough is enough.	"They asked us for money. But no one gave. They asked us for help. But no one came."
	Rhetorical questions: Set up the body as a series of questions that you ask and answer.	"How can such a plan work? Let me explain .... What would it cost? The figures may surprise you ...."
	Emotional words: Use words that people react to strongly, but don't overdo it. Avoid stereotyping. **For more on stereotyping, see page 179.**	"Our public road system is in crisis. Our city streets are choked with cars ...."
	Humour: Jokes can backfire. Ask yourself the questions at the right. If you can answer yes, the joke should work.	Will the joke fit my topic? Will my audience get it—and like it? Is it short and easy to deliver? Is it fresh or probably new to my audience?
Conclusion: Remind them of what you've told them. Then end dramatically!	End with a quotation, a dramatic example or statistic, or an anecdote.	"Yesterday, I was reminded of how common this experience is. A woman at the bus stop turned to me and said ...."
	End by going back to the beginning of your speech and briefly adding a point.	"I began my speech by looking with hope toward our future. I end it by asking you to join me in ...."
	End with an emotional plea.	"And that's why we can't survive without your help!"

Tackle Nervousness

Do you feel nervous when all eyes are upon you? At such times it may help to remember that your audience is on your side to begin with: they want to enjoy what you have to share. If remembering that doesn't help, then try this: what you're feeling is normal! Even the greatest speakers and performers have had sweaty palms. They've just learned some tricks to relax and gain confidence.

Exercise your fear away.

Go off alone. Run in place or jump up and down to let off steam.

Take deep breaths and exhale slowly. Do slow stretches at the same time.

Figure out which part of you feels tense, and tighten it. Then relax it. Do this several times.

Swing your arms — together, one at a time, together.

Practise, practise, practise! The more you practise, the better you do, and the better you do, the bolder you feel. Try talking in front of a mirror to see how you look and move, and talking into a tape recorder to hear how you sound. Ask some friends to be your practice audience. This might feel awkward at first, but it'll help you get used to having listeners. Practise in the place where you'll be speaking, if possible. See how loudly you have to speak to be heard.

Make Eye Contact

Making eye contact with your listeners can help you feel less nervous. As you look over the audience, pick a person who looks especially kind and interested. Make eye contact with your chosen person. Pretend you are talking to this person alone, not to the whole room. After a few minutes, switch to another interested person. Pretend you are talking to this person alone.

As you gain confidence in making speeches, switch your gaze from person to person more often during a speech. Eye contact helps you overcome stage fright; it also helps your audience feel involved.

Give Feedback to a Speaker

Speakers are only human. They like to know how you're reacting to what they're saying. As you listen, don't look down at your notes or the floor all the time. When you agree with something a speaker says, give him or her an encouraging look. Clap if appropriate. When you're puzzled, you could give the speaker a puzzled look. It might prompt him or her to explain so that everyone understands better. When you're amused by something the speaker says, smile or laugh.

If you're bored, it doesn't hurt to show it, perhaps by politely glancing at your watch or shifting in your chair. This may prompt the speaker to show a visual, speak in a livelier way, or otherwise improve the presentation. But remember, speakers are human. Don't show boredom in a way that hurts the speaker's feelings. Next time the speaker may be you.

Let's Practise

Choose one of the following: oral directions, interview, oral report, debate, panel discussion, speech. Using what you have learned, prepare and present it to the class.

As you practise, remember the following:

★ Think positively about how well you do and how well your audience responds.

★ Visualize yourself doing everything the way you planned.

★ Practise making eye contact with your audience.

★ Exercise your fear away before you perform. This can be done by deep breathing or by moving your arms and body.

★ If you make a mistake, don't worry—improvise.

Speaking and Listening in Performance

Focus Your Learning
- Read aloud showing understanding of text and awareness of audience
- Rehearse and use feedback from rehearsals to make modifications
- Enhance presentation by varying volume, tempo, rhythm, pitch, and pauses

The curtain goes up. The spotlight comes on and finds an inventive person working magic with the spoken word. Perhaps this person is reading a nature essay to a writing club, performing a rap, mesmerizing a group with a story, ad libbing in radio comedy, reciting a soliloquy in a school play. Who is it? It's YOU, using your voice in performance!

Read Aloud by Yourself

The best part of reading aloud is that you get to bring a piece of writing to life for others. Often you can hear them respond—laughing at humour, gasping at suspense, even crying at something sad. And reading aloud is a skill. You can make money at it—as a disc jockey, a TV or radio news anchor or sports commentator, a reader of literature for audio books, a narrator of documentaries, a voice in TV or radio ads, or even as the voice of a character in an animated film.

1. **Select a written piece you think your audience would like to hear.** It shouldn't be very long or complicated. It should keep you interested from beginning to end.

2. **Use your understanding of the writing.** What's the general mood of the piece—humorous? tense? sad? Decide what you want your audience to understand about it from your reading.

3. **Practise.** On a photocopy of your piece, mark pauses as well as passages you want to read in a certain way. In a dictionary, check the pronunciation and meaning of any words you aren't sure of. Then read the piece aloud a few times. Try different ways to express the mood. Use your voice comically as you read something funny. Use it dramatically as you read a passage that's full of suspense. Read some passages more slowly or quickly, more loudly or softly than others.

4. **Captivate your audience.** Make eye contact with them. Read clearly and with feeling. Don't rush: The audience is probably hearing this piece for the first time. Take time to use the techniques you have practised! Pause at special points to give your listeners a chance to react.

These students are discussing plans for an oral reading.

Read Aloud with Others

Have you ever joined with a partner or group performing a rap or a choral reading of a poem? If so, you already know that a choral presentation can be as much fun to perform as it is exciting to hear. When you put together a choral reading, you're like a composer arranging music for a show. The poem is the music. Your voices are the instruments.

Pick a poem you'll all enjoy working with. It could include strong rhythms, repeated lines, dramatic passages, rhymes, and places where switching from one voice to another would add to the effect.

Experiment with Sounds

Try these ways to "play" with volume, tempo, rhythm, pitch, and pauses.

Adjust the *volume.* Should words or passages be louder? softer? Change your volume, gradually or abruptly.

Play with the *tempo.* Some lines work best when they're read rapidly or slowly.

Bring out the *rhythm.* The poem already has rhythm; your voices can use *stress*, or emphasis, to help others feel it. You may also want to give extra stress to certain words because they're important to the meaning of the poem.

Change *pitch*. Try using high voices for humorous or playful parts and low voices for serious, sad, or scary parts.

Use *pauses* and *stops.* These are good places to switch voices. Remember, a poet may expect readers to pause in the middle, and not at the end, of a line.

Arrange your voices. Decide whether you want each line to be spoken solo (by one voice), as a duet (by two voices), or in unison (all together). (You will probably find that speaking in unison is hard to do for very long.) In most choral readings, two or more voices or sets of voices take turns speaking lines. In another pattern, one voice after another joins in, until all voices are reading together. You may want to use a combination of patterns. Experiment.

Scoring System

/   a pause

//   a full stop

~   no pause

>   softer

<   louder

/   accent word or syllable

Score the reading. A composer scores music with special marks and words to show how the instruments should play each musical phrase. In the same way, you can use special marks to score your choral reading piece.

Indicate who says each line. Use your names, or call yourselves Voice 1, Voice 2, Voice 3, and so on.

Make copies of the score. Give a copy to everyone in the group.

A Choral Reading Score

Here is a poem by Langston Hughes, marked for a choral reading using three voices. You can also read the poem alone or experiment with using a different number of voices. Sample scoring marks have been added.

Voice 1

Dream Dust
by Langston Hughes

Voice 1   Gather out of star-dust /

Voice 2   > Earth-dust, /

Voice 3   > Cloud-dust, /

Voice 2   > Storm-dust, /

Voice 3   And splinters of hail, /

Voice 1   One handful of dream-dust ~

Not for sale. //

For dramatic flair, add gestures and movement to your choral reading. You might try stepping forward a bit when it's your turn to speak.

Rap It Up!

What we know as rap is a kind of "talk singing." Like some poetry, rap uses rhyme, repetition, and other patterns that play with word meanings and sounds. Here is an excerpt from the rap "Our Time Has Now Come" by Soul II Soul. It has been scored for choral reading to show how it was recorded.

Voice 1

Take my time to create this rhyme

Words of inspiration drew me time after time

I was flowin'

Goin' on and on

Inducin' motivation, knowin' made me strong

So clear in my mind with intentions and thoughts

Like the ones that brought us here

Here to this place

So now you gotta gain

Your own time and space

By movin' in the right direction

Aided by a selection of actions

Enrich your positivity

There's no time for negativity

It's prosperin', developin'

And we're envelopin'

And I'm here

Showin' you all something

Flowin'

Goin' on and on

Our time has now come

Our time has now come

Refrain

Our time has come
to be together and live as one
Forever livin' free, happily
Our time has come, yeah

All Voices   [Sing refrain twice]

156   ResourceLines 7/8

Storytelling

Thousands of years ago—before TV, even before books—people gathered to hear their storytellers. They listened to learn—about their ancestors, about nature, about themselves. And they listened just for the fun of hearing a well-told tale. Today, from Saskatoon to San Salvador, for the same good reasons, people are still telling and listening to stories. Are you about to try the ancient craft of storytelling? Of course, there's no one "right" way to tell a story. But here are some tips.

Find a Tale to Tell

The first thing is personal: You, the storyteller, must really *like* the story. Beyond that, the story should have these elements:

A good plot: A good opening will draw in the audience. Story events shouldn't be too complicated or be in a confusing order. The ending should be interesting, too.

A good length: A relatively short story is easier for you to learn and less likely to bore your audience.

Howard Contin, an *Anishnabe* elder from the Henvey First Nation, tells stories to counsel young people.

Interesting language: The story might have vivid descriptions, humorous or very realistic dialogue, or a dialect. The language might build a magical mood or an atmosphere of suspense. Where do you find such a tale? Go to libraries and bookstores. Skim picture books, folk tale collections, and story anthologies in the fiction sections. Ask relatives and neighbours to tell you their favourite tales (ask if you can tape them). Or look through your own writings. After all, storytellers don't tell only other people's stories.

Tips for Storytelling

Learn the Tale. There are two basic ways. When you just *get the gist* of a story, your goal is to learn its plot, characters, and general language so you can bring them to life in your own way, with your own words. When you *memorize* a story, your goal is to use the author's or previous storyteller's exact words. Pick the way that works best for you.

"I don't *memorize* my stories," says Spalding Gray, a professional who specializes in monologues. "In fact, I'm not a good memorizer. Instead, I see images …. I know that I'm never going to go blank as long as I know the topic and focus on it, because I'm describing an inner film running through my mind as I go through the story."

Make the Story Your Own. Maybe you think it sounds most natural to tell this story in a conversational tone. Or to have the villain tell it, in a hoarse whisper. You may decide to leave out an unimportant story event. Or to shorten the ending. Maybe you want to add more dialogue. If the language is old-fashioned or too hard for your audience, you can substitute other language or define the hard words. As the storyteller, you can do anything you (and your audience) like!

Move with It. Some storytellers like using hand gestures. Others avoid any movements that might distract the listeners from what they're "seeing" in their imaginations. Experts know that a single dramatic movement at the story's climax (maybe you LEAP forward) can electrify an audience like nothing else. There's no rule about how much you should move. Just concentrate on feeling the emotion and mood you're telling about. The rest will probably come naturally.

Keep Your Listeners with You. You know when your listeners are "with" you—when they're laughing, or wiping their eyes, or hanging on every word. You also know when they're restless, or whispering, or dozing off. If you're losing them, try moving more quickly through that part of the story—by leaving some of it out, not by speeding up. Or pause. Add a gesture or a sound effect.

Doc McConnell, a storyteller, explains how he keeps his listeners with him:

> "To enhance the stories I tell, I often stop for a moment ... to give a twinkle of the eye, a slight smile, an expression of disbelief that helps reinforce and make powerful the statements I've just made. And during those pauses, I'm thinking ahead, to my next words, and my listeners are given time ... to build the mental images of the story."

How Does It Sound? You can tell the whole tale in your own voice or in the voice of a character who is the narrator. Use a different voice and manner for each character.

Use sounds to create mood and express emotion. Howl like a wolf. Moan like the wind. Sigh. Make the door creak.

For more ideas on using your voice, see page 162.

Let's Practise

In the library or on the Internet, find a story you would like to retell. Practise it, then tell it to a friend and ask for suggestions about how to improve your presentation.

Bright Ideas

for Improvising

To *improvise* means to invent, recite, or do something spontaneously, without planning it. Storytellers—as well as actors, dancers, and other performers—sometimes like to improvise. To practise, try some of these exercises.

❋ **Talk to music.** Put on a tape or CD of instrumental music (without voices). Close your eyes and move your body to the music. Then begin saying things that come to mind as you're moving, until you're talking non-stop. (The words don't have to make sense. Just keep talking!) Try many kinds of music, including classical, jazz, and music from unfamiliar cultures.

❋ **Become a machine.** Be a can opener (solo), an alarm clock (duet), or a chain saw (group). Express yourself with sounds and motions.

❋ **Ad lib a dialogue.** With a partner, invent the conversation between two people in a particular situation—a salesperson and a customer, two strangers stuck in an elevator, an art critic interviewing a rock star, two residents of a nursing home, a parent and a teenager having a talk. Don't discuss beforehand what the people would say (and no scripts allowed!).

❋ **Do an impression or a parody.** Your imitation could be a serious or a humorous one. Pretend to be a famous or a familiar person. Stand in front of the mirror and talk for five minutes straight, as though you're that person. (Don't pause. Don't be shy.)

❋ **Tape your improvisations.** Record some short narratives, monologues, or dialogues that you think up as you go along, using different characters' voices. (You could pretend they're telephone answering messages.) Then listen to the tape. What works? What doesn't?

Radio Play

Good radio shows depend on actors who can use their voices well, narrators who explain what can't be seen, vivid sound effects, and mood-making music. To create a radio play, you don't need scenery, props, or costumes. You need only one or two tape recorders, and dramatic voices.

Sound effects: The train's whistle, the ringing phone, the echoing footsteps, the crack of thunder: you can take them from sound-effects recordings at a library or (for more fun) make your own. Unless you want to make the sound effects as you're taping the play itself, use a second tape recorder. For a sound-effects tape, record sounds in the order in which you'll use them. Designate a "sound person" to play parts of the tape as each effect is called for in the script.

Music: Does the play have dramatic episodes? sad or frightening ones? Find some background music that will add to the mood. You can have class musicians play it, live. Or make another tape, combining your musical selections in order, and have the "sound person" play each selection on cue.

Get used to the tape recorder and microphone. How close must you be to get good sound? If you have only one mike, put it where all the actors can easily reach it. Or designate a "mike mover," someone to quickly take it to each actor.

Act with Your Voice

Use volume, rate, pitch, rhythm, pauses, and projection.

When you're portraying a character, give him or her a special way of speaking. Does she sound as though she's racing to finish each sentence? Does he nervously say "uh" before every phrase, then clear his throat? There are many vocal techniques you can use to convey your character's personality and emotions.

Use This	To Express Character	To Express Emotion or Purpose
volume	Shy people often speak softly. Confident characters may have booming voices.	Angry people may yell or stress their words in a lowered voice. People giving orders may talk loudly. Those who are scared, menacing, or telling a secret may whisper.
rate	Thoughtful individuals may talk slowly. An energetic or aggressive person may speak quickly.	People speak quickly when excited or in a hurry, slowly when tired or trying hard to be understood.
pitch	Adult male voices tend to be lowest. Older people usually speak lower than young people.	Angry or excited people often speak at a higher pitch. Frightened, sad, or quiet people usually speak in low tones.
rhythm	A character from a particular region or country may speak with a distinctive rhythm.	Someone feeling unsure may speak in a halting, stop-and-start pattern. A happy person may speak in a bouncy, laughing manner.
pauses	Pauses can be very effective. They can show that a character is thinking, or hesitating, or in shock.	They can also be used to draw attention to an important point or to ... create ... suspense.

Use This	To Express Character	To Express Emotion or Purpose
projection		Project your voice as if you're speaking to someone in the back row.
pronunciation		Pronounce words clearly. If they can't hear, many audience members will try to read your lips.

Readers' Theatre

This is a dramatic reading, with a minimum of fuss. The readers typically sit or stand together, facing an audience. Each reader reads from a script or text but often looks up to make eye contact with the audience. Readers do not move or gesture. They rely on their voices for expressiveness. Readers may wear regular clothes, or they may dress alike in something simple—such as dark sweat shirts and jeans. They may also use a few character props, such as hats or eyeglasses. No scenery is necessary, though a simple curtain or backdrop may be used to create a mood or set a scene.

Stage Play

As an actor in a stage play, you have numerous tools for communicating with an audience. Like the storyteller, you have your voice, facial expressions, posture, and hand gestures to help you express a character's personality, thoughts, and feelings. But you will rely more than the storyteller on dramatic body language and movement. You can use make-up and costumes to tell even more. And you can take advantage of stage props and lighting.

Learn Your Lines

Read the lines *aloud,* over and over, until you can say them with your eyes closed. If you have a big part, memorize your lines one scene or one act at a time.

Visualize what your character will be doing as you speak each line.

Practise your lines "in character," with all the expression and gestures you plan to use on stage. Remember, you aren't just memorizing words; you're memorizing how your character speaks, feels, and behaves.

Don't learn only your own lines and cues. Instead, read the entire play several times. Get a sense of what the other characters do and say in each scene.

Attend *every* **rehearsal**, because just hearing the lines again and again will help "set" them in your mind.

Bright Ideas

for Speaking on the Stage

✳ **Pay careful attention** to how real people talk, and (when they aren't around) mimic them.

✳ **See some actors at work,** if possible, in rehearsals and plays in your area. Notice how they use and project their voices.

✳ **Listen to accents.** But use a foreign or regional accent only when you *know* you can do it well *and* it's right for the character. An accent that sounds fake can spoil an otherwise good performance.

✳ **Watch a good film actor** in several roles. How does he or she use voice (and body language) to become each character?

✳ **Do improvising exercises,** alone and with friends. **See page 160 for improvising ideas.**

Use Feedback from Rehearsals

After a rehearsal it's a good idea to talk about what happened. The people involved can make suggestions for improving their performance. Examples:

> "I think some people said their lines too quietly. Let's speak up a bit."

> "Sorry I forgot my lines in the tree house scene. I'll practise them at home."

> "Could we change the blue light to a white one? Blue seems too cold for that scene."

You could also ask outside people to watch a rehearsal and give suggestions for improvement. Some students' parents or grandparents may be happy to help in this way. Or maybe a few students from another class could watch and comment during a spare period.

Remember the Others

Play to the front. This means keeping your face partially turned toward the audience, even when you're talking to another character who is beside you. It looks and sounds better.

Don't upstage another actor. When it's another actor's turn to talk, don't distract everyone with actions or ad libbing that will draw attention to you.

Watch your timing. Delivering your lines late or early can throw off the other actors. But if you really listen, your timing will take care of itself. Bad timing usually occurs when someone's attention has wandered.

Use Images and Sounds

In a stage play, the audience sees lots of images. These include stage sets, lighting, costumes, make-up, props (chairs, bows and arrows, umbrellas, and so on), and—most important—actors. At the same time, the audience hears sounds. The most important sounds are the actors' voices. But you can also use other sounds along with images to help create effects.

Try sound effects to back up your images. You could use prerecorded ones or make your own. For example, if the image the audience sees is an actor walking through snow, back it up by crunching a box of cornstarch backstage. (This sounds amazingly like the crunch of boots on snow.) If you use lighting to create an image of fire, back it up by crumpling paper backstage. You may need to record your sound effects and amplify them so the audience can easily hear them.

Also, use music at some points. For example, every time a certain actor comes on stage, you could use a certain threatening, happy, or silly tune. Use something that fits that actor's appearance and character. You could use recorded music, or students could play it live on violins, guitars, or other instruments. **For more on sound effects and music, see page 161.**

Role Play

When you role-play, you step into the shoes of a character. You try to see the world through the character's eyes. The thoughts, feelings, attitudes, and values you express in your role play should fit the character. Sometimes you will role-play a situation that you have read about in a story or poem. But other times you will role-play the characters in new situations. Then, you really have to think your way into the role and react to new situations as though you were the character.

Try to assume the voice and characteristics of the character. Costumes can help. Use body language that will help you develop the scene.

Let's Practise

1. **a)** Choose one of the following: oral reading by yourself, choral reading, radio play, readers' theatre, stage play, role play. Using what you have learned, prepare and present your performance. Depending on which kind of performance you choose, you could work by yourself, with a group, or with the whole class.

   b) Develop a script showing what you plan. It will help you to organize.

Measure Your Growth

Focus Your Learning

- Reflect on personal growth to set goals
- Evaluate personal contribution

How are you doing as a speaker and listener? Write the numbers 1 through 12 in your notebook. Beside each, rate yourself according to the following scale:

A Excellent

B Good

C Fair

D Needs a lot of work

1. I speak in a way my listeners understand.

2. I follow the do's and don'ts of discussion.

3. I can give oral directions.

4. I can listen attentively to oral directions and follow them.

5. I can plan and conduct an interview.

6. I respond effectively to oral questions.

7. I can plan and give an oral report or speech.

8. I can listen attentively to identify main ideas.

9. When listening I can identify faulty logic, propaganda, opinions, prejudice, and bias.

10. I can read aloud effectively, by myself and with others.

11. I can tell a story in a way that interests my listeners.

12. I can make effective use of volume, rate, pitch, rhythm, and other performance elements.

Measure Your Class's Growth

What has your class learned about speaking, listening, and working together? Write the numbers 1 through 8 in your notebook. Beside each, rate your class (or group) according to the following scale:

A Excellent

B Good

C Fair

D Needs a lot of work

1. When we discuss things, most people take part and feel involved.

2. We can take roles and carry out responsibilities in various kinds of discussion groups.

3. We can use discussion to get things done; for example, a class project or oral presentation.

4. When class members give oral presentations, the class listens attentively.

5. Class members give helpful feedback to oral presenters.

6. We respect differences in each other's cultures, languages, and opinions.

7. We can inform and persuade through oral presentations such as debates and panel discussions.

8. We can plan and present oral performances such as choral readings, readers' theatre, and stage plays.

CHAPTER *four*

Viewing

CONTENTS

The Viewing Process

Focus Your Learning

- Examine dramatization techniques that communicate meaning
- Explore how visuals convey meaning
- Explore how imagery conveys meaning

As a Canadian, you receive much of your information through visual images. Photographs and paintings are visual images, of course, but so are television sitcoms and news broadcasts; movies; advertisements; and even the logos on your shoes, jackets, and T-shirts. This chapter will help you think more carefully and critically about these images.

You are used to the distinction between "hearing" and "listening." You know that in order to listen, you have to pay close attention to what you hear. The same principle applies to viewing. You may have seen a television advertisement so many times that you can repeat every detail. But have you looked beneath the surface of the ad to try to understand the meaning and significance of the message? Have you viewed the image as a media "text" to be read, analysed, and evaluated?

Visual Literacy

In order to become an active rather than a passive viewer, you will need some viewing skills. In this chapter you will learn, first, how to identify the features of a visual image text. What do you look for when you study a visual image? How do you identify its most important features?

You will also learn how to use strategies to understand the message in the visual. What are the hidden messages? What questions might help you understand these messages? How do visual images influence the way you see the world?

Many of the principles and strategies described in the Reading and Listening chapters of this book also apply to the viewing process. As with reading, your success in reading visual texts will improve as you learn to pay close attention to what you view and to apply the appropriate strategies at each stage of the viewing process.

1. Pre-viewing

Sometimes you just want to browse through images. Other times you need to study them more closely. It depends on your purpose. First, skim and scan (preview) the visual text. Then, ask yourself questions and make predictions as you view. Use your prior knowledge about, and experience with, similar texts to help you with your questions and predictions. And remember that the person who created the image had a purpose in mind.

2. During viewing

As you view, keep asking questions based on your experience of the particular visual image. Of what does this advertisement remind you? Why does it show that particular character taking that action? What does it mean? Does it make sense to you? As you experience any visual, try to predict. What is this television sitcom all about? What is the plot? Is the ending likely to be a surprise?

Use a viewing response journal to keep track of your questions and responses. You can also use graphic organizers (for example, web diagrams or timelines) to help organize your thoughts.

3. Post-viewing

After viewing, take some time to think and write about what you have viewed. Ask yourself questions about your experience; for example: What did you feel as you viewed the visual? Of what did it remind you? What did you think about the characters and their actions? What caught your attention in the image? What do you think the intended meaning was? Was there anything that you would like to get further information on? Do you agree with the values portrayed?

You can also share your responses with others. Compare responses and explore reasons why others reacted differently. You may get some of your questions answered. You may even want to go back and revise your first evaluation.

Be a critical reader of visual images. Ask questions about them. For example: What was the artist's purpose in creating this visual image? What was his or her point of view? Who was the intended audience? How does this visual compare to similar visuals? What visual techniques did the artist use to achieve the desired effect? What values does the visual image embody?

Mass Media and Popular Culture

Focus Your Learning
- Explain how sound and imagery work together
- Examine composition techniques that communicate meaning
- Explore how visuals convey meaning in popular culture

Many of the visual images you see are produced by mass media. Mass media include radio, television, films, books, newspapers, magazines, recordings, and popular web sites on the World Wide Web. Popular culture is the culture that you have in common with other Canadians and North Americans. Popular culture includes not only shopping malls and popular sitcoms on television, but also the values, ideals, and beliefs held by the majority of people in the society.

The following key concepts will help you view the mass media more carefully.

1. All media texts are constructions.

All media productions are carefully planned and "constructed" to create an intended effect on their audience. A documentary on polar bears may look completely natural, but many people have worked together to build just that effect. Directors, producers, technicians from many specialties, and film editors chose the story-line, decided which pictures would be taken and where to place the camera, wrote the script for the narrator, and selected the footage and the sound effects.

2. Media texts have their own codes through which they communicate.

Each medium has its own language. You already have years of experience interpreting these codes. You know how to use the codes for viewing a comic strip, for example. You know that the four panels of a comic strip tell a story that happens through time and that uses plot and characters, conflict, a setting, and theme. You also know that the same characters (with the same characteristics) usually continue in the strip from day to day.

You know that, if the character's words are written in a balloon connected to the character by a tail, then they are spoken words. If the artist uses a series of small circles instead of a tail, then the character is thinking and not speaking.

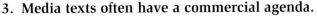

3. Media texts often have a commercial agenda.

Many of the media images you view are created for commercial purposes. In other words, the creators and/or sponsors are trying to sell you something. The purpose of most television programs is to sell the products of the advertisers. Without the commercials, there would be no commercial television. If a television show has fewer than six million viewers in North America, the show may be cancelled because it is not a commercial success.

4. Audiences make the meaning of a media text.

As a viewer of media images, you bring yourself to whatever you are viewing. You make your own meaning depending on who you are: your age and gender, your needs and anxieties, your economic, family, and cultural background. Many media texts are aimed at a target audience. A television show may be aimed at very young children. A big-budget movie may be aimed at a wide audience of all ages and cultural backgrounds.

5. Media texts express values.

You may not have stopped to think about a message or its values, but you may have absorbed the message all the same. As a critical viewer of media images, you need to look carefully at the values underneath the surface of media texts.

Let's Practise

Working in a small group, select six representations from different media: for example, one television sitcom, one currently popular movie, one painting, one comic strip, one advertising image, and one poster. Use the following questions to start your discussions about these visual media texts.

1. What is my personal response to each of these visual texts? What effect do they have on me? How do they make me feel? How do they accomplish this effect?

2. Who is their intended audience?

3. How do they represent a culture (popular or otherwise)?

4. How were they put together? What techniques do they use?

Visuals: Bird's Eye View

Focus Your Learning
- Identify a variety of print media
- Express interpretations of fine art
- Identify multimedia sources
- Identify characteristics of different types of media
- Evaluate effectiveness and limitations of various forms

Have you looked at a painting, magazine, or video today? These are all visual presentations. They appeal to your sense of sight. Visual presentations differ from those that appeal to other senses. Radio and tape recordings, for example, appeal to your sense of hearing. They are audio, not visual, presentations.

Fine Art and Print Media

The following charts give a bird's eye view of the two main categories of visual presentations.

Fine Art

Fine art is an imaginative expression of artists' ideas about meaning, beauty, and harmony, using a variety of means, or *media,* such as sculpture, painting, music, writing. Fine art is not necessarily created to make money—or to complete a school assignment.

Example	Features
Sculptures	three-dimensional (3-D) works of art done in metals (such as bronze), marble, soapstone, wood, papier-mâché, or other materials
Paintings	pictures done with paints (often oil paints or acrylic paints) on canvas or other materials, like wood
Water colours	pictures done in water colours; often more delicate-looking than oil paintings
Drawings	pictures done in ink, charcoal, pencil, etc.
Collages	works of art created by gluing a variety of materials and objects to a flat surface

Strong Points. Fine art is a kind of universal language, one that can be understood and appreciated by people of all languages and cultures. It often represents a society's finest, newest, or most meaningful ideas.

Weak Points. People sometimes find works of art baffling. Some groups of people do not have access to art galleries.

For more on fine art, see pages 182–184.

Can you think of other examples of fine art? What are their features? What are their strong and weak points?

Print Media

Media are different means or avenues of communicating with large numbers of people. They are sometimes called *mass media* because they reach "masses" of people. Print media are created by pressing ink or similar material onto paper or another surface.

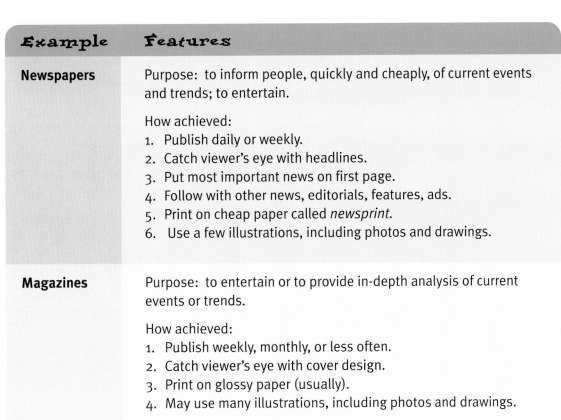

Example	Features
Newspapers	Purpose: to inform people, quickly and cheaply, of current events and trends; to entertain. How achieved: 1. Publish daily or weekly. 2. Catch viewer's eye with headlines. 3. Put most important news on first page. 4. Follow with other news, editorials, features, ads. 5. Print on cheap paper called *newsprint*. 6. Use a few illustrations, including photos and drawings.
Magazines	Purpose: to entertain or to provide in-depth analysis of current events or trends. How achieved: 1. Publish weekly, monthly, or less often. 2. Catch viewer's eye with cover design. 3. Print on glossy paper (usually). 4. May use many illustrations, including photos and drawings.

Example	Features
Instruction booklets	Purpose: to teach people a specific skill, like using an interactive CD-ROM. How achieved: 1. Use explanatory paragraphs and lists of steps. 2. Include diagrams and drawings to help teach. 3. Give cross-references to other parts of booklet. 4. May have footnotes to give extra help on specific points. 5. May include troubleshooting section (to help the reader identify causes of trouble in equipment operation). 6. Provide addresses and numbers of experts to consult.
Schedules	Purpose: to inform people of times for events such as bus departures. How achieved: 1. Use few words, since people are often in a hurry. 2. Use tables, charts, and diagrams.

Strong Points. Print media are easy for people to carry and hold in their hands. People do not need expensive or complicated technologies to use them.

Weak Points. Print media can go out of date quickly. Materials are costly to the environment—especially trees and rivers.

For more on print media, see pages 224–227 and pages 234–235. What other examples of print media can you list? What are their purposes, and how do they achieve them?

CD-ROMs, Web Sites, and More

What about CD-ROMs and computer web sites? They're media, too. Where do they fit? CD-ROMs and web sites fit into a category called *multimedia*.

Multimedia appeal to more than one of the five senses. Many appeal to both sight and hearing. Computerized multimedia often mix together video, photographs, animated (moving) diagrams, written words, music, and sound effects.

Example	Features
CD-ROMs	Purpose: to educate; to provide in-depth information; to entertain; to serve as references. How achieved: 1. Provide extensive, in-depth, lasting information. 2. Lead people to more specific information as they make selections by clicking on highlighted text (*hypertext*). 3. May include animation—for example, flashing words, moving diagrams, 3-D charts. 4. Include drawings, photos, and short videos. 5. Use spoken words, sound effects, and music. How found: borrow from libraries; buy in computer stores or bookstores; order by mail.
Web sites	Purpose: to share current, up-to-date information and opinions; to entertain; to persuade people to act; to sell goods and services; to give access to a network of other web sites. How achieved: 1. Provide access to current information in broad subject categories. 2. Lead people to more specific information as they make selections by clicking on highlighted text (*hypertext*). 3. May include animation—for example, flashing words, moving diagrams, 3-D charts. 4. May include drawings, photos, and short videos. 5. May use spoken words, sound effects, and music. How found: by computer, through an on-line service (more user-friendly); or directly, through an Internet service provider.
Films (movies), TV, and videos	Purpose: to entertain; to inform; to get emotional responses from viewers. How achieved: 1. Feature famous actors, if possible. 2. Use a good script and effective camera work. 3. Include adventure, humour, action, and suspense. 4. Use effective dialogue, sound effects, and music.

Example	Features
Animated cartoons	Purpose: mainly to entertain; also to inform and get emotional responses from viewers. How achieved: 1. Often use recognizable characters—for example, Pocahontas or Homer Simpson. 2. Use effective drawings and motions. 3. Include adventure, humour, action, and suspense. 4. Include effective dialogue, sound effects, and music.

For more on web sites and CD-ROMs, see pages 254–255. For more on films, TV, videos, and animated cartoons, see pages 192–199.

Strong Points. Many multimedia presentations entertain as well as inform. Some—including CD-ROMs, web sites, and video games— are *interactive*. That is, they encourage people to use them in highly personal ways. Example: An educational CD-ROM may encourage students to use its content to create their own multimedia presentations.

Multimedia encourage a variety of learning styles. They are easier to update than print media, especially books. They also take up less space than print media, and are friendlier to the environment because they don't use paper.

Weak Points. Multimedia require more expensive, complex technologies to use than books and magazines. They may take more time to use than such print media as newspapers. Using them requires special skills that some people don't have. Some people find a computer screen hard on their eyes, and a computer keyboard and mouse hard on their hands and wrists.

Which of these strong points do you agree with most? Which of the weak points do you agree with most? Do you disagree with any points? Which ones? Why? Can you suggest any other strengths and weaknesses of multimedia?

Multimedia Stereotypes and Violence

A stereotype is a fixed idea about a group of people. Examples:

❊ Tall people make good basketball players.

❊ Thin people are bad cooks.

❊ People from other countries are different from us.

A stereotype may be positive or negative. In either case it isn't fair or true. People who have stereotyped ideas don't take a fair, fresh look each time they meet a person or group. They mentally drop a new person they meet into the "good basketball player," "bad cook," or "different" box they've created.

"Different" can come to mean "unwanted." And this can lead to violence, if the person or group seems to get in someone's way. Violence may be defined as rough or harmful physical force against property or individuals. Examples: throwing garbage on someone's lawn, vandalizing a car, pushing or hitting someone, throwing someone downstairs.

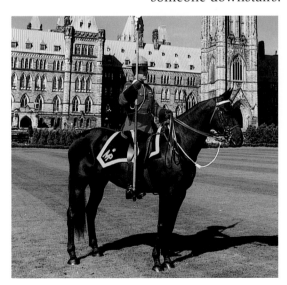

If multimedia producers have stereotyped ideas about people, these ideas can creep into the TV shows, movies, music videos, computer web sites, video games, and other works they create. Analyse and evaluate the following examples. Which ones show stereotypes? Which show violence? Do any examples show a combination of both?

This picture is actually a stereotype. Today, male and female Mounties wear a different uniform and rarely ride horseback—except for special occasions such as their Musical Ride.

* A movie in which a boy rescues a girl, who is shown as having no idea how to help or defend herself.

* A TV show in which a teenage boy spray-paints graffiti on the wall of a public building.

* A music video in which people are tied to railway tracks.

* A video game in which all people from a certain group are portrayed in a negative way.

* A computer web site in which all people from a certain group are shown as having no sense of humour.

* An animated cartoon in which a rabbit is pushed over a cliff.

Here's How to

Deal with Stereotypes and Violence in Multimedia

1. Realize that some multimedia producers may not understand the people and groups they're portraying. You, however, can think and choose for yourself. You don't have to let their stereotyped ideas influence you.

2. Analyse and evaluate the multimedia productions you view or are thinking of viewing. Do they seem to include stereotypes or violence?

3. Realize that multimedia producers usually want to make productions that people will buy and view. If you and enough others stop buying and viewing stereotyped and violent productions, fewer will be made.

4. Look for multimedia productions that present people and groups in positive ways, and that uphold values such as kindness, truth, freedom, and justice.

5. Consider writing to multimedia producers and objecting to their stereotyped or violent productions. Also, consider writing to multimedia producers who are doing a good job. Show your appreciation for productions that present people and groups in a fair and favourable light, and that uphold positive values.

Let's Practise

1. Choose one of the following categories of media. Write a paragraph telling why you like it. Or write a paragraph telling how you learn through this kind of media.
   - Fine art
   - Print media
   - Multimedia

2. For this exercise, you can work alone, with a group, or with the whole class.

   a) List TV shows, music videos, web sites, and other multimedia productions that you think are free of stereotypes and violence. Make notes on the positive values they seem to present. (If necessary, research by viewing some multimedia productions.)

   b) List multimedia productions that include stereotypes and violence. Make notes on the kinds of stereotypes and violence they present.

   c) Use your notes as the basis for a bulletin board display on multimedia productions you do and don't recommend to other viewers. Or, if you prefer, use your notes as the basis for an article in your school newspaper.

Fine Art

Why do some works of art make you smile and others make you feel sad? Why are you sometimes not sure if you even *like* a work of art? Becoming familiar with the basic elements of art will help you understand the "cause" or "reason for" your feelings when you're viewing art.

Elements of Art

Any work of art begins with one or more of these four elements: line, shape, form, and colour. Together they can create powerful emotional effects.

Line

Any image begins with a line.

Straight lines suggest order, direction, and motion.

Jagged lines, like lightning bolts, can suggest power, disruption, or chaos.

Curved lines may suggest motion, like waves, or softness, like a smile.

Form

The illusion of three-dimensional forms having height, width, and depth can be created on a flat sheet of paper. Size can create a sense of depth, called perspective. Objects or people that are far away look smaller than those that are nearby.

When one object overlaps another, the object shown in full view seems to be in front of the other object.

Shape

When a line turns, it creates a shape. Shapes are flat, with only two dimensions: height and width.

When shapes are balanced, they create a feeling of harmony.

When shapes are not symmetrical, they create a feeling of tension.

Colour

Colour can communicate shape, perspective, and emotion. It can convey the true appearance of an object. Many dark colours together can create feelings such as mystery or sadness.

Shading a colour can create an illusion of curves.

Art: Reasons for Responses

When you look at a work of art, ask yourself, "What's happening in this work?" Once you've identified the subject matter and how the artist felt about it, you can probably figure out why you have the emotional response that you do. Following are some ways your interest may be sparked.

- **People are interesting.** That's why people are often the subjects of songs, works of art, and conversations. When you look at a work of art, look at the people in it. What are they doing? How are they relating to each other? to their surroundings? If the people look sad, they may make you feel the same way.

- **Beauty draws us in.** Everybody likes a beautiful picture. If a work of art presents a beautiful subject or scene in a new way, you'll probably appreciate it.

- **The unusual sparks curiosity.** Unusual subject matter presents a mystery that makes us pause, take a second look, and try to figure it out.

- **Some subjects guarantee certain responses.** Most people react the same way to certain subjects. For example, images of mothers and babies or happy homes create warm feelings. On the other hand, images of danger, death, and severe weather create apprehensive feelings.

Memalilaqua, Knight Inlet   Emily Carr, 1912

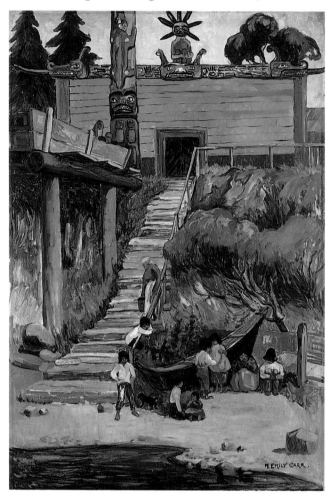

Answer these questions about Emily Carr's painting:

1. What is shown in this picture?
2. What people do you see in the picture?
3. What "story" does this painting suggest?
4. What feelings does this painting arouse in you? Why?

5. How did the artist use straight lines? What do they suggest to you about her attitude toward her subject?
6. How did the artist use colour? What does this suggest to you about her attitude toward her subject?

Art Critique

A written opinion of a work of art is called a critique. The word *critique* comes from a Greek word meaning "to criticize." In English we often use the word *critic* in a negative way. But a critique looks at the positive as well as the negative aspects of a work of art.

Art isn't like spelling or math. There are no right or wrong answers when you give your opinion about art. Yet some people consider some works of art to be better than others. That's where criticism comes in.

Sample Student Critique

At first I didn't like "Patriarche" very much. It sort of weirded me out. The colours are intense, and the guy is shaped like a refrigerator. It reminded me of one of those costumes in a monster video.

Then I looked again. The guy's head is really big, and he's wearing a crown. Actually, the crown doesn't exactly look like a crown, but somehow you just know it's a crown. So that made him seem like a king. The crown and the king's outfit are covered with little figures of people. Maybe the artist is saying something like we're all made up of the people who are part of our lives. Now the sculpture seems friendly—maybe even happy.

Patriarche

Mickaël Bethe-Selassié
papier-mâché sculpture, 205 cm high, 1991

Compare Drawings

Look closely at the two drawings on these facing pages. How do you think the artists' personalities come through in their drawings? What is the feeling you get from Käthe Kollwitz's thick charcoal lines? Why do you think Henri Matisse made his drawing so simple?

Comparing drawings can help you better understand each one. When you look at two drawings together, observe the kinds of materials, colours, and techniques each artist used.

For example, when you look at Matisse's work, consider the lack of detail. No line is wasted.

What do you think Matisse had in mind when he drew this figure? Do you think this was a completed drawing, or a sketch for another work?

What would be the effect of this drawing if it were sketched with a felt-tip pen? If it were shaded?

Look at Kollwitz's drawing. What effect did Kollwitz create by drawing just the subject's head and arm?

Artists decide how much of a subject to show in order to focus our attention on what they feel is important.

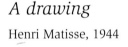

A drawing

Henri Matisse, 1944

Self-Portrait   Käthe Kollwitz, 1933

Rosenwald Collection, 1993 National Gallery of Art, Washington, D.C.

Compare Lines

Compare the lines in the drawings on these two pages. Notice how Kollwitz used charcoal to create her drawing. How would you describe the lines in her drawing? Thick? Dark? Smudgy? What would be the effect if Kollwitz had used a fine-point pen? Notice the kind of lines Matisse used. What kind of lines would make each drawing look more forceful? gentler?

Let's Practise

Answer these questions about the two drawings on this page.

1. What does each drawing make you feel? Why?

2. What was each artist trying to express?

3. How well did each artist's message come across?

4. What materials did each artist use? In each case, how did the artist's choice of materials affect the drawing?

Colours and Emotions

Have you ever been green with envy or red with anger? Colour is often linked in our minds with emotions. That's one reason colour in a work of art can bring out a viewer's emotions. Shades of blue can be calming and soothing. Yellows and reds are often exciting.

Combining colours and using certain colours next to each other can create almost any effect the artist wants. Some colours are comfortable together, and others clash or contrast sharply. Think about the colours you pick to wear together or to decorate your room. What effect are you creating?

Primary Colours. There are only three primary colours: red, blue, and yellow. From those three colours you can mix any other colour.

Secondary Colours. The secondary colours are orange, green, and violet. Each one is made by mixing two of the primary colours. Orange is made by mixing red and yellow.

Complementary Colours. The colour wheel shows both primary and secondary colours. Any two colours that sit directly opposite each other on the colour wheel are a complementary pair. The colours in these pairs strongly contrast with each other. When they are used together, each makes the other seem more brilliant.

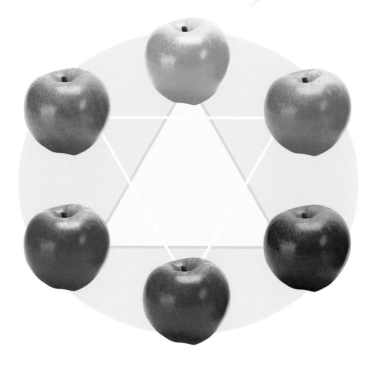

Respond to Paintings

Paintings capture feelings, memories, and thoughts, and communicate them to an audience. In the painting below, Marc Chagall used strong colours; large, basic shapes; and playful, curving lines to express childhood memories of his village. What did he convey by making his painting unrealistic rather than showing the village as it really looked?

How do you respond to a painting? Do you respond to it in the same way you'd react to a poem? If you do, you probably begin by just examining your emotional reaction to it. Then, you give the painting a second look to see what it reminds you of and what it could mean. A third look might focus on the painter's artistry. **Need help focussing your responses? Check out responding to reading, page 17.**

I and the Village
Marc Chagall, 1911

Oil on canvas, 6' 3 5/8" × 59 5/8" (192.1 × 151.4 cm). The Museum of Modern Art, New York. Mrs. Simon Guggenheim Fund. Photograph ©1999 The Museum of Modern Art, New York.

Your first reaction to the painting by Chagall was probably an emotional one. The painting "Spring Salmon" is very different, and your reactions to it are likely to be different as well.

When you look at a painting for the first time, you can sometimes tell when it was done, by whom, or maybe even why. These clues help you understand what the artist tried to express. The artist intended the "Spring Salmon" painting to represent his family, who for generations have fished for salmon. The faces represent past generations. The eggs represent the generations still to come.

Spring Salmon   Roy Henry Vickers, 1979

© Roy Henry Vickers, 1979.

Look at Collage

Painting and drawing create images on flat surfaces. Collage is often made by gluing various materials and objects to a firm, flat surface. Artists use magazine clippings, swatches of fabric, photographs, sports programs, buttons, pressed flowers, and even garbage!

Look at the collage on the next page and take note of the materials the artist has used. This collage was created by Francisco Rios, a university art student. His assignment was to tell a story in a collage. Look carefully at the objects in the collage. What do the photographs show? What words did Rios include? What is your response to the whole collage? The incident Rios described in this collage involved a ballgame and an angry dog named Fletcher.

Fletcher   collage, Francisco Rios, 1992

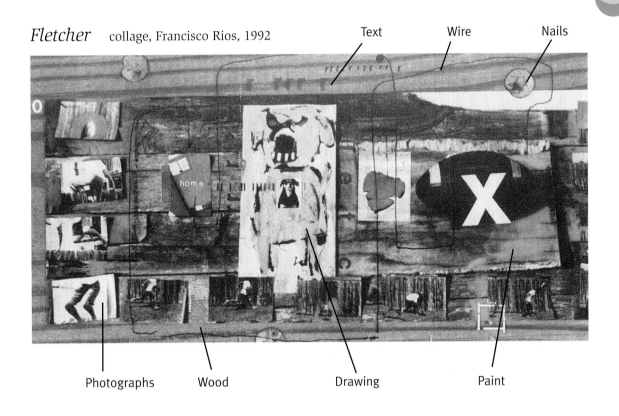

Text   Wire   Nails

Photographs   Wood   Drawing   Paint

Let's Practise

Look at a piece of fine art. It might be a painting, sculpture, drawing, collage, weaving, tapestry, or some other form of art. If you cannot view the actual art, look at a picture of it. Answer the following questions.

1. How does this work of art make me feel?

2. Does this piece of art remind me of something? an idea? a feeling? an experience?

3. Are there objects in this work of art? If so, what are they?

4. Why are they there and what do they say?

5. What story does the picture suggest?

6. Do I like it?

Film, TV, and Videos

Focus Your Learning

- View film, TV, animation, and video
- Explain how sound and image work together to create effects
- Discuss usefulness of different types of media
- Discuss characteristics of different types of media
- Express preferences for different types of media

What's in a name? The other names for film—*motion pictures* and *movies*—point out the basic difference between film and photographs. A photograph is a *still* (unmoving) picture. A film uses many still photographs to show things in motion. The photographs are in small rectangular *frames* on a long strip of film wound onto a reel. When the reel is rolled, the film moves quickly in front of a light and the images, projected onto a screen, make one big picture that moves … a movie!

These days it's hard to imagine our world without the *big screen* and the *small screen.* But actually they haven't been around long.

Pictures That Move: A History

Filmmaking began in the late 1870s in California when a young British photographer, Eadweard Muybridge, wanted to capture on film the motion of a running horse. He placed a series of cameras at equal distances along a racetrack. Then he attached a separate string to the lens shutter of each camera and stretched the string across the track. As the horse ran by, it tripped the strings, making the cameras take pictures only instants apart. Muybridge's experiment paved the way for modern filmmaking. The following time line traces this and other highlights in the history of film, TV, and videos.

1877–1878 Eadweard Muybridge creates the first moving pictures.

1904 The first movie theatres, called *nickelodeons,* are built. Entrance fee: five cents.

1909–1927 The silent film era brings stars such as Canadian Mary Pickford to audiences everywhere.

1927 The film *The Jazz Singer* is the first "talkie"—a film with sound.

1928 The Walt Disney Company produces an early Mickey Mouse cartoon film.

1939 The first regularly scheduled telecasts in the United States take place on the NBC network.

1953 The first colour TVs appear on the market.

1962 For the first time, a TV program is broadcast across an ocean. It is watched in the United States, Great Britain, and France.

1965 The world's first commercial communications satellite is launched, making worldwide TV broadcasting possible.

1970s Video cassette recorders (VCRs) arrive on the market, allowing TV viewers to watch films in their own homes and to record their favourite TV shows.

1980s Two cable networks—MuchMusic in Canada and MTV (Music Television) in the United States—are first to entertain viewers with music videos.

2000 and beyond High-definition TV, virtual reality, and interactive video may be the wave of the future.

Viewing Habits

There are many kinds of films, TV programs, and videos. The following Venn diagram lists some. In spite of the many kinds, most share one goal: to entertain you. Some may also hope to inform you or persuade you of something—or to do all three.

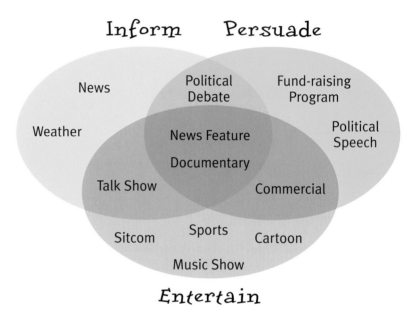

Inform   Persuade

News

Political Debate

Fund-raising Program

Weather

News Feature

Political Speech

Documentary

Talk Show

Commercial

Sitcom   Sports   Cartoon

Music Show

Entertain

Let's Practise

What Do You Watch?

1. List your three favourite films, videos, or television shows. For each, write a short explanation of why it has a strong effect on you.

2. Most TV programs, films, and videos are designed to draw an emotional response from viewers. Write down the three things you have recently seen on TV, film, or video that affected you most. Did they make you feel inspired, amused, sad, or afraid? Consider all genres including news, music videos, and cartoons, as well as religious programs and dramatic ones. Then write whether you'd watch this film, program, or video again.

3. Pick one film, video, or television show whose ending you would change if you could. Write a persuasive letter to the director suggesting the new ending. Explain how you think the new ending would be an improvement.

4. Analyse your viewing patterns. Do you watch mostly sitcoms (situation comedies) or crime dramas? Do you prefer to have film, TV, and videos take you to places you might never go, such as the rim of a smouldering volcano or backstage at a rock concert? Film, TV, and video producers know that viewers have different interests, and they provide a wide variety of productions.

Animators and Technology

One of the oldest kinds of film is the cartoon, which is a form of animation. The word *animate* means "to give life to." Like all moving pictures, an animated film or video is made up of single frames, or images, on a reel of film or videotape. On film there are 24 frames per second; on videotape there are 30. Since film is finer grained than videotape, it produces sharper images. Though animation and live-action filming are similar in some ways, they differ in important ways.

How do animators make characters and objects move? One way is to make drawings of each character's or object's actions. One action requires many drawings, each slightly different from the one before. For example, the animator would draw the monster with its head in the swamp, its head slightly above the swamp, its head slightly higher, and so on and on and on. All these separate drawings are filmed, one after the other, in a way that gives the impression of motion.

Since the 1980s computers have made animation quicker and easier. Animators can scan their drawings into a computer, which preserves and colours them according to the animators' instructions. Animators can also use computer software to produce multiple characters. If the animator needs hundreds of actors for a crowd scene, for example, the animator creates only a few characters. Based on these, the computer creates more—with specified variations such as different colours of clothes and different ways of moving their arms.

Many animators create their characters right on a computer screen. Using the computer, they draw key frames of a character's movements; for example, the monster with its head in the swamp and the monster with its head in a tree.

The computer does much of the *in-betweening* (drawings between the beginning and end of the movement). The animation, instead of being filmed, is recorded by the computer's processor onto a disk. Later the information on the disk can be transferred onto videotape or film.

Today animation is used for more than making cartoons.

🐄 Makers of video games use animation to make figures and objects move.

🐄 Film and video makers use it for special effects such as a volcano blowing or a figure running from a burning factory.

🐄 Business people use it for presentations. Example: They might make a moving diagram showing how an oil refinery works—or how quickly the company is reaching its sales goals.

🐄 TV advertisers use it to transform, or *morph*, objects and figures. Example: They may morph an automobile into a tiger to show how fast and strong their cars are.

🐄 Doctors use it to learn how someone's body is working— without having to do investigative surgery.

NOVEMBER 5-14, 1998

THE COLISEUM, NATIONAL TRADE CENTRE

TORONTO ONTARIO, CANADA

THE ROYAL AGRICULTURAL WINTER FAIR

Royal Agricultural Winter Fair, November, Exhibition Place, Toronto.

This illustration is similar to a famous painting by Grant Wood titled *American Gothic*. Why might advertisers want familiar people and images in their ads? **For more on advertising, see page 234.**

Watching Television

In 1953 only about ten percent of the Canadian population had a television at home. Today, ninety-eight percent of Canadian households have at least one TV, and about thirty-three percent have three or more. In fact, the average Canadian views about twenty-three hours of television every week. That's fifty days of solid TV-watching every year!

As you know, television provides a wide variety of entertainment and informational programming. The chart below shows the most common kinds of shows.

Show	Characteristics
Soaps	A kind of drama shown in the afternoon. Plots focus on complex interpersonal relationships, and story lines extend for several episodes—sometimes for years.
Sitcoms (situation comedies)	1 half-hour-long episode per week; with the same characters and similar plot lines used every episode. A laugh track (taped laughter) is used to emphasize the humour.
Talk shows	1 hour-long show per day, with a host interviewing different guests. Some talk shows specialize in celebrity guests; others focus on the personal lives of ordinary people.
News	Shown daily. Some feature prominent national and international news, while others deal with local and provincial stories. One or more anchors read the news, and other hosts specialize in weather, sports, and entertainment stories.
Sports	Sports broadcasts last 2 or more hours and air mainly on weekends. Hosts and colour commentators describe the sports event as it occurs and provide background information.
Information shows	Some information shows appear weekly and focus on a particular area, such as cooking or history. Documentaries are special shows that provide an in-depth look at a particular subject.

Show	Characteristics
Movies	The television version of a movie differs from the original version because commercials have been added. Movies are often censored, with potentially offensive language and scenes removed.

Television and Advertising

The main purpose of TV is to sell audiences to advertisers. Each show is intended to attract a **target audience** of viewers, who will then watch commercials specially designed to appeal to their desires.

Programs are shown in **time slots** during which the target audience will be available. That way the advertiser knows that its commercials will be seen by the people who are most likely to buy the product.

Each television show is carefully structured around its commercials. The story presented in a drama, for example, is specially written so that an exciting development occurs just before a commercial break. The audience sits through the commercials, knowing that something important will happen as soon as the show starts again.

Issues and Controversies

Many people are concerned about the effects of TV, especially since it reaches so many people and is so popular. Here are some of the most controversial issues.

Values. Every television program and commercial expresses certain values. Some people strongly object to the values they perceive. For example, environmentalists might argue that few commercials or programs present the negative aspects of our reliance on automobiles.

Violence. Violence is a part of many programs, and is rarely shown in a realistic way. Parents and others worry that television encourages children to solve their problems through violence.

Consumerism. Through television we are bombarded with messages that tell us we can be happy by buying the latest product. Some people object to this narrow view of what makes people happy. Others are concerned about the environmental impact of consumerism.

Let's Practise

Use the following tips as you evaluate a film, video, or TV program. Write your responses on a piece of paper or in a notebook computer.

1. **Watch the film, video, or TV program.** Does the beginning draw you in? Does the rest of it hold your attention? What works well? What doesn't? Be aware of the various aspects of the film, video, or TV program as you evaluate the acting, directing, camera work, sound quality, musical score, special effects, animation, lighting, costumes, make-up, and editing.

2. **Take notes.** Jot down short phrases to remind you of key thoughts. Watch the opening and closing credits. Record the names of the director, actors, writer, and anyone else you want to single out.

3. **Develop your notes in detail.** As soon as possible after viewing the film, video, or TV program, expand and clarify your thoughts in writing while they're still fresh.

4. **Write the review.** A review of a film, video, or TV program should mention its title, year (unless it's new), director, and cast. It should tell a bit about the plot—without giving away anything important. Your overall recommendation (see it, don't see it) has to be supported with convincing reasons. They don't have to be brilliant reasons. Sometimes the best reasons are common sense: "If a comedy keeps you laughing, it must be good" or "I didn't like it because I never believed the main characters cared about each other."

5. **Share your review.** Give it to some friends to read. Post it in your classroom, or submit it to your school paper. If you enjoyed writing the review, offer to do more of them for your school paper. Or offer to review young people's films, videos, or TV programs for your local newspaper.

Advertising

Ads: Purposes and Targets

An advertisement's purpose may be to sell a product (cereal ad), a service (house-painting ad), an idea (ad against drug abuse), or a person (political ad). A successful ad grabs your attention and then persuades you to buy or act.

You see ads in print media such as magazines, newspapers, direct mail, and billboards. You wear them, and also see them on web sites and TV commercials.

Actually not all advertising on TV is in commercials. Music videos help sell CDs and concert tickets. A product may be mentioned or displayed on a show. Actors appear on talk shows to promote their newest film. Infomercials are programs devoted to selling a product or service.

Focus Your Learning

- Identify purpose of advertising
- Examine design techniques that communicate meaning
- Identify structural features of ads

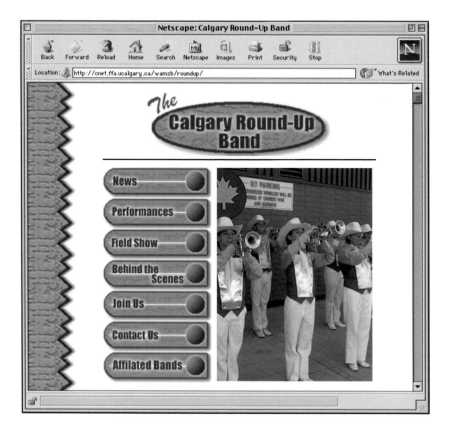

Who looks at all these advertisements? You do, for one. You don't see them all, of course. Advertisers just hope you'll see the ones targeted specifically at you, and you probably will. Advertisers make it their business to find out all they can about people like you: what you watch on TV and when, where you shop and why, what you listen to and when, what you read and why.

Using such information, advertisers target ads to specific audiences, or *markets*, such as teens. It's no coincidence that the commercials aired during your favourite TV program advertise things *you* might buy: jeans, shampoo, snacks. It's also no coincidence that travel magazines advertise luggage, or that gardeners' web sites advertise rakes.

Persuasion, Emotions, and Design

Canadian Dairy Products
The Taste Of Home

If someone covered the label on your usual brand of shampoo or soft drink, could you tell it from another well-known brand? Sometimes it's hard to tell the difference (if there is one) between various brands. That's why ads often make emotional appeals, associating a product with something the target audience wants: popularity, beauty, security. If you stop to think about an ad, you can often see it's offering something a product could never actually provide—happy relationships, or a trouble-free life. It's when you don't think, but simply respond to the ad's emotional appeals, that an ad has the most power to persuade.

Think about the words used in ads: "Just do it." "Take the plunge." Do they suggest buying on impulse without thinking carefully about the ad—or the product? Consider the visual images used: slam dunks, business suits, mountain streams, cosy fireplace settings. They associate a product with qualities such as success, freshness, and security. Advertisers choose words, colours, and photos very carefully. Each word and design element focusses on the message. Type and photography reinforce each other to give the message maximum impact. Design features such as the following help get a message across:

- A striking contrast between a dark and light colour is easy to see.

- Simple, uncluttered shapes and letters are easy to identify and read.

- Complex uses of type and image become a puzzle that the viewer must solve. Most ads follow the "keep it simple" principle.

- Photographs of people can make a message seem more real and believable.

- Use of colours—warm or cool—can bring out specific emotions.

The NUTRAM Performing Dogs
Powered by NUTRAM Super Premium Pet Food

Let's Practise

Either use some ads in this book, or choose three of your own for this exercise.

1. What is the purpose of each ad?

2. For each ad, state who you think the targeted viewers are. How do you know?

3. Explain what tricks you think **one** of the ads uses. How persuasive do you find them?

4. Explain how **one** of the ads uses emotions.

5. Which ad do you think has the best design? Why?

6. Will you buy or use the goods or services advertised? Why or why not?

What advertising tricks are on this cereal box? What ones does your favourite cereal use?

Measure Your Growth

Write the numbers 1–14 in your notebook. Beside each, rate yourself according to the following scale:

A Excellent

B Good

C Fair

D Needs a lot of work

1. I can list and classify various types of visual presentations.

2. I can identify features of various types of visual presentations.

3. I recognize strong and weak points of various media.

4. I can detect stereotypes and violence in the media.

5. I know and apply strategies to combat stereotypes and violence in the media.

6. I can explain the elements of art and reasons for people's responses to it.

7. I can respond to and compare works of fine art.

8. I can identify producers' purposes in making films, TV programs, and videos.

9. I can document the kinds of films, TV programs, and videos I watch, and detect trends in my viewing habits.

10. I can give examples of ways modern technologies meet communication needs.

11. I evaluate the films, videos, and TV programs I watch.

12. I recognize that ads are targeted to specific purposes and viewers, and can give examples.

13. I understand some of the strategies advertisers use to inform and persuade.

14. I evaluate and respond critically to ads.

CHAPTER *five*

Representing

CONTENTS

Principles of Design

Focus Your Learning
- Use imagery
- Use composition
- Use balance

In this chapter you'll learn about creating sculptures, charts, spreadsheets, mini-lesson demonstrations, videos, multimedia documentaries, and other creative representations of the world, using design principles. You probably already follow design principles in the way you dress or arrange photos on your wall or locker door. Here's a list to help you recognize some you already follow—and learn about more.

❊ **Imagery.** The use of figures, objects, or other design elements to represent ideas and emotions.

A budding tree could represent hope.

❊ **Symbolism.** The use of symbols to represent ideas and emotions.

A plus symbol represents addition.

❊ **Juxtaposition.** The placing of figures, objects, or other design elements close together to convey an impression.

A border of teapots or snowshoes at the top of a page could convey a sense of harmony. It could also tell viewers at a glance that the page or chapter is about tea or snowshoes.

❊ **Contrast.** Design elements are placed close together to draw attention to differences. Sometimes contrast is used to cause an emotional reaction.

A bomb beside a baby might make viewers feel concern or shock.

❊ **Balance.** The arranging of design elements to create a pleasing overall impression.

A painting in which a blue sky at the top is balanced with a golden wheatfield at the bottom. The focal point, or point of greatest visual interest, could be a green pickup truck, which draws the viewer's eyes first to it and then to every other part of the picture.

Design principles are related to elements of art. **For elements of art see page 182.**

Let's Practise

1. Rearrange a shelf or table of objects using design principles.

2. Make a labelled sketch showing how you would apply design principles to an outfit or garden design.

3. Compare this photograph to the stereotyped photograph of a Mountie on page 179.
    a) In your opinion, which one shows more elements of good design? Explain.
    b) In a group, discuss why the photographs might have captured the same subject in such a different manner.

Collages, Sculptures, and Prints

Maybe you thought fine art included only works by famous artists such as Emily Carr or Henry Moore. Actually you can create works of fine art yourself—collages, sculptures, prints, and others. Maybe you won't see your works in an art gallery in the near future. On the other hand, fine art is a great way to express yourself and communicate with people. **For information on viewing fine art, see pages 189–191.**

Focus Your Learning
- Make a collage
- Make a sculpture
- Create prints
- Experiment with techniques

Make a Collage

Collages are just as creative as drawings but done in a different way. You make a collage by pasting (or otherwise attaching) various materials to a firm, flat surface. You can use almost anything you can find—calendars, coloured yarn, ribbons, leaves, pennies, paper clips, buttons, feathers, bones, labels, orange peelings. These items add a variety of textures (smooth, rough, hard, soft) and colours to your collages.

Without knowing it, you may have started a collage at home or school. Do you have a bulletin board to which you pin photographs, ticket stubs, comic strips, or other personal items? In a way a bulletin board is a collage. It's a collection of existing or "found" items that combine to express something about the person who assembled them. **For more on collages, including a photo of one, see page 191.**

Here's How to

Make a Collage

You can make a collage with almost any materials you can attach to a flat surface—whatever helps get your ideas across.

1. **Choose a person, idea, or topic as your subject.** You might choose your grandmother.

2. **Think about what makes up your subject.** What does your grandmother wear?

3. **Think about colours and textures.** Which ones best express your subject?

4. **Collect magazines, newspapers, and other objects.** You'll want materials you can cut up or add to your collage.

5. **Make a few sketches about your subject, or arrange a few photographs of your subject.**

6. **Make a final sketch of your subject on heavy paper.**

7. **Cut up your materials to the size and shape you want.** Attach them to your sketch, overlapping layers as needed.

Make a Sculpture

Since ancient times, people have had the urge to make art that imitated the solid nature of things. Sculpture is the art of doing just that: creating in 3-D. There are two main ways to make a sculpture. One is to start with a block of material and carve, chip, or scrape away at it until only the shape you want remains. This kind of sculpture is often done in stone or wood. The other way is to start with soft material and mould it into the shape you want. This way of sculpting is often done with clay, or with liquid metal or plastic that hardens inside a mould.

You might decide to create an exact model of something, such as a horse or a pyramid. Or you might want to make something that does not look real but instead expresses an emotion, like playfulness or anger. If you've never tried sculpting before, you might try something simple—just to get the hang of the process. You could experiment with modelling clay or try creating a plaster sculpture.

Joseph Deborah Butterfield, 1988

What sculpting method do you think the artist used to create this sculpture? What do you think the artist is expressing about horses? Why?

Courtesy of Edward Thorp Gallery.

Here's How to

Create a Plaster Sculpture

Here's one way to make a plaster sculpture using a balloon. As you work with the material, see what feelings you can express and what shapes you can produce.

Materials

Plaster mix	Water	Funnel	Bucket
Balloons	Twine	Tempera paints	Carving tools

1. **Mix up a batch of plaster.** Follow the directions on the package. You'll need about 750 mL to 1 L of plaster per balloon.

2. **Stretch your balloon.** Blow it up and let the air out a few times.

3. **Pour the plaster into the balloon using a funnel.** Fill it as full as you can.

4. **Tie a knot in the open end of the balloon.**

5. **Shape your balloon sculpture while the plaster is still soft.** Think of different ways you can alter the shape of the plaster-filled balloon. Tie it in several places with twine, stretch it, squeeze it, drape it over a ledge, press heavy objects into it. Be careful not to pop the balloon.

6. **Let the plaster harden overnight.**

7. **Cut away the balloon and admire your sculpture.** Be sure the plaster has thoroughly hardened first.

You may want to add to your sculpture by carving into it or by painting the surface with tempera paints.

Try Printmaking

Sometimes you want to have a number of copies of the same work of art. Today a photocopier, fax machine, or scanner can be used to make lots of identical copies of any flat image or text. But another method, called printmaking, has existed for over a thousand years. It allows you to make many copies of your work, and each print—unlike a photocopy or scanned image—is considered an original work of art.

There are many different methods for making prints. Most methods start with a firm surface of wood, metal, or linoleum, on which carving is done. This carved surface is called the plate. Ink is applied to the surface of the plate. The plate is then pressed against paper, leaving the image on the paper. The paper with the image is the print. Rubber stamps use this same method.

Another method of printmaking is called silk-screening. In this process an artist first makes a fine screen by stretching silk or other material across a frame. The artist then applies a stencil of a design to the screen. The stencil masks out parts of the design that are not to be printed. The paper to be printed on is placed beneath the stencilled screen. The artist then rubs ink across the top of the screen. Because of the stencil, the ink can only pass through certain areas, creating the design.

Flowers
Andy Warhol, 1970

This flower print was silk-screened by artist Andy Warhol. Each colour was printed separately. How many screens did Warhol use?

Make a Potato Print

You can carve a simple potato print, then use this potato "plate" to make prints.

1. **Get a large, firm, raw potato.**

2. **Think of a simple figure or design you'd like to print.** Make practice sketches. Your figure should not be too detailed and should be smaller than the potato's diameter.

3. **Slice the potato in half.** Then carve on the flat, cut surface. Carve away what you *don't* want to show of your figure and leave protruding what you *do* want to print. The figure should be standing out at least 6 mm from the area that has been carved away.

4. **Blot the surface of your potato plate after carving.** Use a rag or paper towel to absorb any potato juice.

5. **Coat the raised surface of your plate with ink, food colouring, or tempera paint.**

6. **Press the plate surface on paper or cardboard.**

7. **Stand back and admire your spud art!**

Let's Practise

Think about ways to use collages, sculpture, and printmaking. Examples: Make a collage birthday card for a relative. Sculpt a toy for a child. Use printmaking to create your own letterhead, fax sheets, or wallpaper border. When you think of something that appeals to you, do it. Apply what you've learned and add your own ideas.

Illustrations: Drawings and Diagrams

There you are, minding your own business, doodling on a poem about skating that your best friend has sent you for the school paper. Gradually a pair of ice skates emerges from your doodling. Though you may not realize it, you've become an illustrator. What is an illustrator?

Illustrators are visual artists who create visual representations to go with written information. Illustrators often work on assignments from publishers and writers who ask them to create art for books, magazines, newspapers, instruction booklets, and other printed material. Here are some sample assignments:

★ Create drawings for a children's storybook.

★ Draw the surface of the planet Venus based on scientific data.

★ Draw a crime suspect based on an eyewitness description.

Drawing Illustrations

Drawing can be an end in itself. On the other hand, you can use drawing to illustrate stories, articles, science experiments, or history reports.

Even when you're drawing for a very practical purpose—to illustrate—you can express your own feelings and opinions. For example, you can draw a house in a way that expresses how you feel about it, not how it actually looks. Maybe the house has a happy look, or maybe it seems to shrink back from the street as if embarrassed. Or you might draw something that exists only in your imagination, such as a house made of pizzas.

What is the purpose of diagrams such as this?

Here's How to

Draw Illustrations

Try following this procedure:

1. **Pick drawing tools.** Choose tools that seem to suit what you're illustrating. For example, a fine-point pen works well for a detailed illustration; felt markers can make great cartoons.

2. **Focus on how you feel about your subject.** Ask yourself what it means to you.

3. **Close your eyes and imagine** where your first line will begin and end. Do this before you start drawing.

4. **Make a few sketches of your illustrations in pencil.** Use fresh sheets of paper for the final copy.

Illustrating with Diagrams

A diagram is a simple line drawing, often with labels. You can use diagrams in many subject areas. They have many purposes. They may show:

★ parts of something, such as a tree.

★ how something works; for example, a compass.

★ how to do something, such as make paper snowflakes.

Bright Ideas

for Diagram Drawing

❉ Look at other diagrams. They can give you ideas for creating your own.

❉ If you have trouble starting, get a stack of scrap paper and just draw quickly without worrying about details.

✳ Keep trying until you find an idea that works.

✳ You might use computer clip art for some objects in your diagram. Try clicking *Insert* at the top of your screen, if you are using software that has it. Choose *Object* from the drop-down list and then *ClipArt Gallery*. (Since software programs vary, you may need to do it slightly differently.) Print out your clip art and glue it to your diagram.

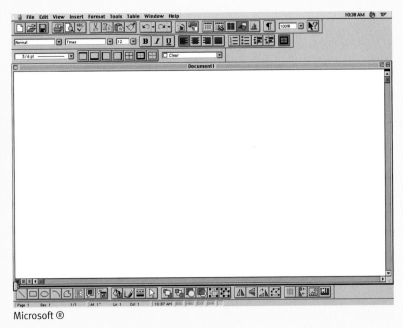

Microsoft ®

✳ Keep your diagram simple. Too much detail can confuse viewers.

✳ Add labels unless viewers can easily understand your diagram without them. It's usually clearer to *print* or *type* rather than *write* labels.

Let's Practise

1. Write down two ways you could use drawn illustrations.

2. Write down two ways you could use diagrams.

Tables, Graphs, & Spreadsheets

Focus Your Learning
- Use tables and graphs
- Use spreadsheets
- Use computer-generated charts to convey information

A chart is an arrangement of information showing how the pieces of information relate to each other. Kinds of charts range from TV listings to family trees. One of the most useful kinds of chart is the *table.* A table has columns (vertical) and rows (horizontal).

Wall calendars use columns to show the days of the week. Rows give the actual date. If you want to know the dates of all Wednesdays in a month, look at the Wednesday column.

You can use tables to illustrate key information in a mathematics assignment, article, or other work. A table draws viewers' eyes to the key information and helps them grasp it quickly. In the following excerpt from a class report, how does the table convey information?

The Raven Gallery, which our class visited, has many works by Canadian Aboriginal artists. See the table below.

Alan Sapp	5
Donalda Grassie	3
Jessie Oonark	8
Bill Reid	1
Daphne Odjig	7

Numbers of works by Canadian Aboriginal artists in the Raven Gallery

This table has a caption below rather than a title above. You can use either a caption or a title to tell what a table is about. Titles are usually short, while captions can be longer.

You can make a table by hand, drawing your own columns and rows. Graph paper and a ruler are helpful tools. You can also create a table on a computer.

Create a Table on a Computer

Here are the instructions for creating a table using Microsoft Word 6.0.1. Since software programs vary, you may need to do it slightly differently.

1. Decide how many columns and rows you want.

2. Look at the bars at the top of your computer screen. Find *Table* or a button with a table symbol. Click on it.

3. You'll see a grid of squares. Holding the mouse button down, move the cursor to highlight four rows and three columns. They'll turn dark when you've highlighted them.

4. When they're highlighted, let go of the mouse button. You should see the following on your screen.

5. Now type in your information. To move from one table cell (box) to another, use your keyboard arrows → ← ↑ ↓ (right, left, up, down) or the tab key.

6. If your information is brief, your table may have too much empty space. You can shrink it by moving vertical lines. Use your mouse to move the cursor on top of a vertical line; you will see a symbol something like this +. Then hold the left mouse button down and "drag" the line to where you want it.

7. To delete part of your table, highlight it by moving your cursor over it while holding down the left mouse button. Then press *Delete* on your keyboard.

Graphs Show Relationships

A *graph* is a chart that shows relationships between pieces of information. When you prepare a report or other assignment, a graph can help convey important information. A graph draws viewers' eyes to key information and helps them grasp it quickly. How does the bar graph convey information in the following excerpt from a class report?

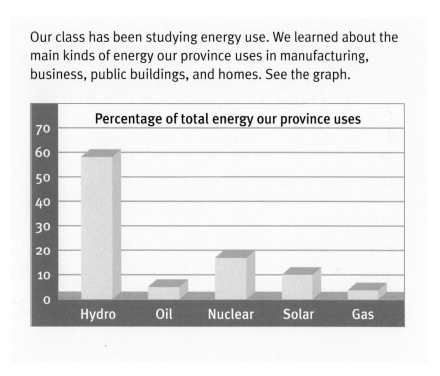

Our class has been studying energy use. We learned about the main kinds of energy our province uses in manufacturing, business, public buildings, and homes. See the graph.

You can make a bar graph by hand. You can draw the lines and boxes and write in the information. Useful tools include graph paper, ruler, pocket calculator, compass to draw circles, and protractor to measure angles. You can also create a graph on a computer.

Spreadsheets

A spreadsheet is a special kind of table used to record information and make calculations. A spreadsheet is often bigger than a regular table.

Three families on Armin Street did a waste management study. They were trying to reduce the amount of garbage they threw out. What does their spreadsheet tell about the study? Answer the questions that follow it.

Families	Week 1 Garbage thrown out	Week 1 Recycled cans, paper,etc.	Week 1 Compost	Week 2 Garbage thrown out	Week 2 Recycled cans, paper,etc.	Week 2 Compost
			Waste Management Study			
Griff	4.5	–	3.6	3.7	2	3.9
Stasz	8.25	5.1	9.4	–	5	10.7
Cardinal	3.3	2.5	–	3.1	2.9	12.6
Totals	16.05	7.6	13.	6.8	11.9	27.2
Families Reporting	3	2	2	2	3	3
Averages (totals divided by families reporting)	5.35	3.8	6.5	3.4	3.9	9.1
Changes Week 1 to Week 2				-1.95	+0.1	+2.6

Note: Weights are in kilograms.

1. What three kinds of waste did the families study?
2. How long did their study run?
3. What was the total amount of garbage in Week 1? in Week 2?
4. What was the average amount of compost in Week 2?
5. By how much did the average amount of garbage go down from Week 1 to Week 2? By how much did the average amount of compost go up?

You can use spreadsheets in many ways, including:

★ Budgeting your allowance

★ Keeping track of baseball statistics

★ Calculating how much food you'd need to feed 10 or 50 people at a party

You can make a spreadsheet by hand. You can draw the boxes, write in the information, and do the calculations. Useful tools include graph paper, a ruler, and a pocket calculator. You can also create a spreadsheet on a computer.

Let's Practise

1. Think about how you might use a table, graph, and spreadsheet. Examples: For a geography article, you could use a table to list cities and their populations. For a science report, you could make a spreadsheet recording temperatures, wind speeds, humidity, and pollution indexes for a week.

   When you think of ideas that particularly interest you, put them into practice by using what you've learned in this section. If possible, use a computer.

2. Interview someone who uses spreadsheets on a regular basis. This could be a scientist, accountant, or other professional. Find out what spreadsheet software programs are most popular—and how to use one.

Mini-Lesson Demonstrations

Focus Your Learning
- Deliver an effective demonstration

You can probably do things some other students can't. Examples: make cocoa, use a wrench, write Chinese letters, take pictures with a digital camera. You could use a mini-lesson to demonstrate (show and explain) your skill.

Here's How to

Give a Mini-Lesson Demonstration

1. **Note your expected outcome.** Briefly note the result you want. Example: *Students will be able to take low-angle shots with a camera.*

2. **Plan introduction.** Briefly note a way to interest students, perhaps by telling how your lesson will improve their lives. *A low-angle shot makes your subject appear larger than life. A low-angle shot of your dog could look dramatic on your locker.*

3. **List steps.** Think through the skill you will teach and briefly note its steps. Example:
   - Holding camera, crouch or lie down.
   - Aim camera up at subject (what you're photographing, such as a dog).
   - Take picture.

4. **Plan demonstration.** Plan and practise demonstrating the skill you will teach.

5. **Follow plan.** Teach the mini-lesson.

6. **Invite students to show their understanding.** Ask two or three students to demonstrate the skill you have taught. If they don't do it right, correct them in a kind way.

7. **Answer any questions students may have.**

Let's Practise

1. Think of something you can do that could be used as a topic for a mini-lesson. For example, do you know how to make a photocopy or do a grammar check on a computer?

2. Use the Here's How above to develop a mini-lesson about your skill.

Students teach each other how to do a litter survey. What are the advantages of learning from a peer?

Graphic Design

Graphic design uses visual forms, often along with type, to send clear messages to specific audiences. It *shows*, as well as telling.

Focus Your Learning
- Enhance artistry and create mood by experimenting with techniques
- Produce a poster

Graphic Designers Show and Tell

Imagine yourself on the committee that creates information signs for the Olympic games. Thousands of people are coming from all over the world. Which languages would you use? Even if you used a hundred languages, they still wouldn't be enough. Instead of language, you could create symbols that all viewers could understand. In other words, you could *show* rather than *tell* them things like where the bicycling, skiing, and other events are taking place.

You're almost always surrounded by the work of graphic designers. Here are some things graphic designers create:

★ Movie posters

★ Subway maps

★ Book covers

★ Videos

★ Brochures

★ Product advertising

★ Fashion illustration

4-H uses words and a symbol to attract members. The Olympic symbol and the CBC (Canadian Broadcasting Corporation) symbol communicate without words. Depending on the audience you want to reach, you might use symbols or a combination of symbols, words, photographs, and illustrations.

4-H Looks Good On You

Typefaces and Fonts

Designers work with printed words and images the way painters work with paint or sculptors work with stone. When a design includes words, the designer must choose a style for the printed type. A *typeface* (or *face*) is a family of letters and numbers all having the same design. There are three kinds of typefaces—*serif, sans-serif,* and *script.* Examples:

1. This typeface is called Times Roman. It is a serif typeface. This means it has *serifs* (little strokes and "feet" extending beyond the letters).

2. This typeface is called Helvetica. It is a sans-serif typeface. This means it is without (sans) serifs.

3. *This typeface is called Carlotta. It is a script typeface. This means it looks like handwriting.*

Many of the most common typefaces used today are hundreds of years old. Garamond was designed by Claude Garamond, who died in 1534—the year Jacques Cartier first came to the New World. Times New Roman was designed in 1932.

The term *font* refers not only to a typeface, but also to its size and style. For example, each of the following is a different font.

❋ This is 14-point Times Roman.

❋ *This is 18-point Times italic.*

❋ **This is 20-point Times bold.**

You can create your own typefaces with a calligraphy pen or a regular pen. If you work on a computer, you have many faces and fonts at your fingertips. Try clicking *Format* or *Layout* at the top of your computer screen. Choose *Font* from the drop-down list. You'll see a chart that lets you choose a face and its size and style. Click your choices and then click OK.

You can express your own personality through your choices of typeface, size, and style.

Design a Poster

Many posters use words and images to really get a message across. Designers look for the combination of words and images that communicate most effectively.

Poster for movie *Godzilla: King of the Monsters*, 1954

1955 TOHO/MPTV

Once you've chosen your type and some images to go with it, check how everything looks together. You can make a full-size sketch or a "thumbnail" (miniature sketch). You can do it by hand or on a computer. Look at your sketch. Ask yourself:

👁️ Are my words clear and easy to read?

👁️ Are my images clear and easy to see?

Make any improvements that seem to be needed.

Thumbnail sketches are also useful for designing other works, such as how-to manuals with many illustrations, magazine pages, and brochures.

Bright Ideas

for Making a Poster

✳ **Do research.** Read books or magazine articles about your subject. If possible, view the subject directly.

✳ **Let your mind process the information you've found.** It takes time for great ideas to flow.

✳ **Start with a thumbnail sketch.** This will show you what viewers will see of the poster from a distance.

✳ **Make many thumbnails.** Try more than one design. It's not uncommon for a designer to make 50 to 100 thumbnails.

✳ **Create a final layout.** A layout is a design that is the same size as the finished poster will be. Make sure the typefaces and photos or illustrations work well together and are large enough to be seen from a distance.

Let's Practise

Use what you've learned in this section to make a poster. Perhaps it could advertise a film or show pictures of birds with names in both French and English. Choose a topic that interests you.

Create a Video

Focus Your Learning
- Make a storyboard
- Produce a video
- Use and examine techniques that communicate meaning and enhance effects

Have you been bitten by the video bug? Maybe you'd like to make a short film or video about a person or a place—or even about a feeling. Maybe a music video would be more your style—or a documentary about your school. Since you are the director, the choice is yours! Once you decide, this section can help you with the technical aspects of making a video.

Plan Your Video

Make a storyboard. A storyboard is a series of sketches with captions that describe what scenes you plan to shoot, what camera techniques you'll use, how long the parts of each scene will last, and where the dialogue will go. (Not artistic? Don't worry. Stick figures are fine.) The following example could be part of a storyboard for a TV ad.

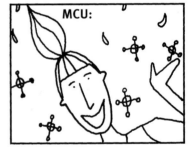

V/O: *It feels as if it's 50 degrees. You're hot and tired. You thought you hated winter. Right now you wouldn't mind a little snow and cold.*

V/O: *We can't make it snow in summer, but we can help cool you down.*

Terms

Use these abbreviations to indicate what is to happen in each scene:

LS: long shot (shows the setting)
MS: middle distance shot (shows persons in the setting)
CU: close-up (head and neck of one person)
MCU: medium close-up shot (body of one person)
POV: point of view (where—or who—camera eye seems to be)
V/O: voice-over (unseen narrator)
SFX: special effects

Write a shooting script. Unlike a storyboard, a shooting script doesn't use any drawing. However, it includes the same technical terms and information about each scene as a storyboard. **The following example shows part of a shooting script for the TV ad planned in the storyboard on page 228.**

> **Scene:** Exterior; driveway, middle-class neighbourhood. Soapy car in driveway, hose, pail, etc.; woman leaning against car—hot, exhausted.
>
> **V/O:** *It feels as if it's 50 degrees. You're hot and tired. You thought you hated winter. But right now you wouldn't mind a little snow and cold.*
>
> **MS:** We see child pick up hose and start to spray mom. Zoom in to CU of woman's face—smile appears as water turns into flakes of snow.
>
> Dissolve and slow zoom-out to MCU: Woman lying in snow making snow angel.
>
> **V/O:** *We can't make it snow in summer, but we can help cool you down.*

Keep in mind that your storyboard or shooting script is just a guide to help you keep track of where you're going. You're not stuck with it. You may find you can't shoot a scene exactly as planned. Or you may get a better idea while "on location." In that case—go for it! (Just don't forget the big picture: keep in mind what comes next.)

Shoot Your Video

Make your movie move. Movement shouldn't be only *in front* of the video camera. Try moving your camera too.

Pan It. Panning reveals a panorama or builds suspense.

> A terrified girl edges into the shadowy room and looks around. The camera pans slowly, showing you what she sees.

Zoom It. Move in close or back away. Use the automatic zoom button to do this slowly and steadily. For a sudden zoom, you'll have to move the lens yourself.

The detective is looking for clues. The camera zooms in on a gardening glove on the sofa.

Track It. Tracking means staying with a moving person or thing. This is easiest to do by putting your camera on a cart or by sitting on a moving vehicle.

The camera tracks beside the runner. The background is just a blur. But we can see the runner clearly—her face determined, arms pumping, legs churning.

Tilt It. Tilting the camera creates interesting angles and effects.

A little boy, running around a corner, crashes into a man. The camera tilts to show what the boy sees as he looks up.

Switch scenes with style. Scene changes, or transitions, can be done in various ways.

1. **Use the On/Off Switch**. To make a transition from one scene to the next, simply turn off the camera and turn it on again for the new scene.

2. **Fade Out and Fade In**. If your camera has a fade-in/fade-out dial, turn it to darken the picture until the image disappears. Turn it the other way to slowly lighten the picture until the image of the next scene is clear. You can get similar effects using the exposure setting of your lens.

3. **Use a Blackout.** To do this variation on a fade-out, use the fade dial or the exposure part of the lens to darken the scene. Return to normal light before shooting the next scene.

4. **Do a Dissolve.** Make one scene blend into another. Turn the focus ring on your camera lens to blur the last image in a scene. Keep the focus where it is while you position your camera for the next scene. Then start shooting, turning the focus ring until the new image is clear.

Edit Your Video

The final process in making a video is selecting and arranging your scenes so they create the effects and the message you want. Here are two ways to edit:

Field editing: edit as you go. You shoot each part of your video in order beginning with shot 1, scene 1. This method requires careful planning. You'll need to think through every shot *before* you start filming, to make sure you'll be satisfied with the way the scenes flow into one another. Suppose you're doing a documentary about your school. **(For information on documentaries, see pages 232–233.)** You want to open with a shot of the school building before anyone has arrived, and dissolve to a stream of students entering. You know your first shot will have to be on a weekend or early in the morning. You'll wait for your next shot until school opens.

Post-production editing: edit after shooting. With this method, you're free to experiment with shots, using your storyboard or shooting script as a guide. For example, to create your school documentary, you might shoot all or most of your outside shots at the same time. You can experiment with shooting from different angles, maybe using different lighting. When you've finished shooting, you use an editing machine to select your shots and arrange them in the order you think works best.

Title Your Video and Show It

Shoot the title and a list of the people who worked on the production. You can write the information on a poster and film that. Or you might spell it out in pebbles on the sidewalk and shoot that. Any format is possible, so be creative!

Now for the best part. Once your video is finished, you can show it. Your audience might be your friends, your family, or your class. Maybe they're a group you filmed. Afterward, invite them to let you know what camera effects they liked best or what message they thought your video expressed. (And don't forget the popcorn!)

Let's Practise

Use what you have learned in the preceding section to make a video. You could work alone, with a group, or with your class to video a class field trip, a school fund-raiser, or a community event.

Multimedia Documentary

Focus Your Learning

- Discuss choices made in planning and producing media texts
- Use appropriate visual media to inform and engage audience
- Produce a multimedia documentary
- Explain how sound and image work together to create effects

You may not have realized it, but your video was a media presentation. *Multimedia* presentations combine various media. They usually appeal to more than one of the five senses (usually sight and hearing). **For more on media and multimedia, see pages 174–178.**

In this section you'll learn how to make a multimedia *documentary*. A documentary is a factual presentation on a topic of current (up-to-date) interest. Examples: homeless people, cancer, or diamond mining. A documentary often includes actual news and interviews. Usually one main speaker, called the *narrator,* introduces the documentary and explains its various parts as it proceeds.

Here's How to

Make a Multimedia Documentary

Here's one plan that you can change to suit your topic.

1. Look for slides or big pictures and maps on your topic. Friends or relatives may have slides. Some libraries have big pictures and maps you can borrow.

2. If possible, interview someone on the phone or in person about the topic. Tape-record the interview.

3. If possible, tape-record radio coverage of the topic. Or use a VCR to record TV coverage.

4. Find sound effects or music to accompany your documentary. A library may have suitable recordings.

5. Do any other necessary library research. **For information on library research, see page 241.**

6. Make overhead projections or slides of the documentary's title and any charts you are using. Or put these on a flip chart, or on sheets of Bristol board.

7. Once you've gathered material, plan how to put it together. Make notes on what the narrator will say and where to use various media. Examples:

   ❋ Narrator introduces topic as title is shown and background music plays.

   ❋ Narrator discusses first subtopic as two pictures and a map are shown.

   ❋ Narrator introduces second subtopic. Part of a recorded interview or video is played.

   ❋ Narrator introduces third subtopic. More of the recorded interview or video is played.

   ❋ Narrator concludes documentary as two pictures and a chart are shown. A few seconds of music end the documentary.

8. Practise the documentary live. You'll probably try it several times before everything works well together.

9. Present your documentary live in front of an audience. Or make a video of it and show it to different audiences. **For information on making a video, see page 228.**

Let's Practise

Make a multimedia documentary, working alone, with a group, or with the class. Use a topic of current interest. You may get ideas from television documentaries or news programs, magazines, radio news and commentaries, or real-life situations in your school or community. Examples: the changes in your friends between the ages of 11 and 14, the level of purity or pollution of your area's water, or your favourite Olympic athlete or team.

Create an Advertisement

Focus Your Learning
- Create an advertisement
- Explore how language use conveys meaning in popular culture
- Prepare eye-catching visuals

Which of the following is more persuasive?

★ Our new robot is lively.

★ Our new robot is livelier than fifty crickets.

The second example compares the robot to crickets. Ads often use comparisons because comparisons appeal to people's senses. Most people know how crickets look and sound, so they quickly understand that the robot is lively. To which senses do the following comparisons appeal—sight, hearing, touch, taste, smell, or a combination?

★ This detergent is lemon-fresh.

★ Our palmtop computer is wafer-thin.

★ Try a jacket in ruby red, fashion's latest colour.

★ Try our woodsy new fragrance.

Think of something you'd like to advertise. How might you use comparisons to persuade? To which senses would your comparisons appeal? **For more on persuasion in advertising, see pages 201–202.**

Language That Includes Everyone

Which of the following includes both males and females? In other words, which is gender-inclusive?

❋ Every chef needs these widgets in his kitchen.

❋ Every chef needs these widgets in her kitchen.

❋ Every chef needs these widgets in the kitchen.

Gender-inclusive language is fair. It encourages equal treatment and opportunities for both males and females. Gender-inclusive language is also likely to sell more goods and services. If you were

a female chef, how would you regard an ad that says "his kitchen"? If you were a male florist, how would you regard an ad that says "her florist shop"?

Which of the following give more positive impressions of people and groups?

❋ This magazine is for senior citizens.

❋ This magazine is for old people.

❋ She speaks a foreign language.

❋ She speaks a language other than English.

Unbiased language is fair. It encourages equal treatment and opportunities for all groups in society. It's also likely to sell more goods and services. If you were over 65, why might you be more interested in a magazine for "senior citizens" than one for "old people"?

Here's How to

Create an Advertisement

1. **Choose a product or service to advertise.** Give it a catchy name. Examples: Marmot Mountain Minibikes, Rush Courier.

2. **Decide on a target audience.** Who would be most interested in your product or idea?

3. **Choose a medium.** What is your target audience most likely to see: advertising flyer, newspaper ad, magazine ad, billboard, hockey arena ad, web site?

4. **Plan a strategy.** Keep your plan simple. The best ads are often those that create a simple, appealing image for the product.

5. **Think of an attention-getting headline.** If your ad's large headline attracts people's attention, they may take time to read the smaller type. Try using comparisons. **(See page 34.)**

6. **Write strong, persuasive body copy.** Body copy is the small type in an advertisement. It gives the details, explaining why and how to follow through—where the store is located, for example, and when the sale begins. **Need some tips on being persuasive? See pages 103 and 143.**

7. **Prepare eye-catching visuals.** Visuals include photos, images, designs, sketches. This a good way to catch the reader's attention.

8. **Check your text and visuals.** Make sure they're gender-inclusive and unbiased. **See page 80.**

9. **Use your design skills.** Experiment with the impact of larger type, lots of white space, bold contrasting colours. **See the design ideas on page 206.**

10. **Does your ad persuade?** Test it on friends. Does it get their attention? Is it clear? Experiment with your ad until it works.

Let's Practise

Prepare an ad, applying what you've learned in this section. Use your own idea or advertise your ability to baby-sit, keyboard, or walk dogs. As you design your ad, consider the following:

- a name for your product or service
- an appealing image
- the best words to convince people to use your product or service

Measure Your Growth

Focus Your Learning

• Reflect on personal growth to set goals

Write the numbers 1 through 12 in your notebook. Beside each, rate yourself according to the following scale:

A Excellent

B Good

C Fair

D Needs a lot of work

1. I recognize and use principles of design.

2. I can express myself and communicate with others through one or more fine art forms.

3. I can prepare drawings and diagrams, and use them as illustrations.

4. I understand the characteristics and purposes of tables, graphs, and spreadsheets.

5. I can create and use tables, graphs, and spreadsheets.

6. I can prepare and give a mini-lesson demonstration.

7. I can define the terms *typeface* and *font,* and use different ones.

8. I can apply graphic design principles to a project such as making a poster.

9. I can identify basic processes in video making and editing.

10. I can prepare and present a multimedia documentary.

11. I can use comparisons and other persuasive techniques to create an ad.

12. I recognize and use gender-inclusive and unbiased language.

Researching

CONTENTS

The Research Process

The research process is a focussed investigation. Like many processes, researching will be more manageable if you break it down into steps or stages.

Stage One: Planning

Select your topic and narrow it down to a size that fits your assignment. Even if your teacher selects the topic, you will probably need to narrow it down and decide what point of view you will take.

As you think about your topic, use questions to keep yourself focussed on your task. What is the purpose of your research? Who will your audience be? How much will your audience already know about your topic? How will you present your findings: an oral presentation, a multimedia production, or a written report?

A KWL chart (see page 21) or a web diagram (see page 32) will help you figure out what you already know about the subject and what further information you need.

Stage Two: Gathering Information

Identify some possible resources for your information gathering. You'll find many suggestions for these in the rest of this chapter. Talk to your teacher and other knowledgeable people about your topic. Plan to use a combination of print and other media sources (including the Internet). It's also a good idea to create a list of key words related to your topic; you can use these for electronic searches and for print indexes.

Stage Three: Collecting Information

To find out which information is relevant to your topic, start by skimming and scanning the source. **For more on skimming, see page 24.**

Technological resources such as CD-ROMs and the Internet can be wonderful research tools as long *as you keep yourself focussed*. Write your purpose down—and keep it in front of you at all times. Use the opening pages of CD-ROMs and home pages of web sites to get your bearings. Check out the icons on each new web page you visit.

Keep track of where you've been. Either "bookmark" useful web sites or note their URLs (addresses), so you can come back later. Make notes as you go.

Evaluating your information is also very important. **For more on this subject, see "Evaluating Information" on page 116.**

Stage Four: Organizing and Recording

Draw up a tentative outline for your presentation. You will revise this outline a number of times before you are finished.

Keep careful note of everything *as you do your research*. Don't assume you will remember what you read, especially when you are on the Internet. We all like to think we can remember—the book, the article, the web site—that the information comes from. But we can't! **For help on taking notes, see page 4.**

Once you have completed your research, sort out your notes and decide what is relevant to your topic. You may need to go back and fill in some blanks if you have more questions. Revise your outline again and refocus your main idea if you need to do so.

Then, with your revised outline as a guide, start drafting your research presentation. Earlier chapters of this book offer suggestions on how to draft, revise, and edit a wide variety of written, spoken, and representational presentations.

Stage Five: Presenting Findings

As you present your research findings, don't forget that you are presenting *your* ideas on the research topic, not just a collection of information and other people's ideas. These are your findings, your concerns, and your conclusions.

Planning a Library Visit

A library is a collection of printed materials (like books) and recorded or electronic materials (like CD-ROMs). In a library you have a chance to discover new interests, visit new worlds, and find answers to many questions.

Before you visit the library, ask yourself:

❋ Why am I going to the library?
Do you have a specific assignment or are you satisfying your own curiosity about a topic of interest? If you know what your goal is, you won't get side-tracked when you get there.

❋ How much time do I have?
If you plan your library visit well, you won't spend too much time on one stage of the research process and have to rush to finish your project.

❋ How much leeway do I have to change topic if research proves too difficult?
If you're working on an assignment, but you're not sure how closely you have to stick to your original plan, check with your teacher. **For help in zeroing in on a topic that will inspire the researcher within you, see page 113.**

❋ What will I do with my research?
Will you turn it into a written report or an oral presentation? Think about the format you will want to use. Planning ahead may save you a return trip to the library—when you decide to present a slide show and all you've collected are newspaper clippings. **For more advice on giving presentations, including tips on how to wow audiences with your incredible performances, see pages 137 and 149.**

Plan Ahead

As you do your research, consider how you're going to present it. That will help you zero in on what you need. Consider these presentation ideas.

Posters—Use splashy headings, colourful drawings, and even 3-D objects. Make every word count.

Mini museum—Put interesting objects on tables, or hang up artwork and let people walk around while listening to an audiotape. You can record explanations of what they're seeing, interviews with experts, sound effects, and music.

Docudrama—Take an actual event (the *documentary* part), and write a short play about it (the *drama* part).

Monologue—Take on the role of someone you've researched, and talk about yourself, your times, or your culture. While you're at it, wear a costume.

Model—Build a model and caption the parts. Your model could show the earth cut in half, a bee flying with its tiny wings, or the parts of a pulley working together.

Here's How to

Research in a Group

The key to researching in a group is making sure everyone participates. Combining brainpower can produce great ideas that might not surface if group members were working on their own. It can reduce the workload, too.

1. **Team up.** You may find that a manageable group has three to five members, including a leader to track jobs and keep discussions moving.

2. **Brainstorm for areas to investigate.** Make a giant list of questions about the topic—welcome all suggestions. **For more on searching for ideas, see page 71.** Then choose three or four questions to research.

3. **Discuss presentation possibilities.** The way you'll gather information may depend on your presentation plan, so shape some ideas now. Perhaps all the group members should look for photographs or for relevant quotations, as well as their particular part of the research.

4. **Set up a research strategy.** You could divide the team according to the sources you plan to use (one person covers newspapers, another checks magazines, and so on), or each person could pursue one of the research questions the group has chosen.

5. **Make a schedule.** Write down each person's job, and arrange a few meeting times to review progress; list what should be completed by the time of each meeting.

Let's Practise

Think about a topic you would like to research. When you have made a decision, plan your trip to the library, using what you have learned in the preceding section.

Library Services and Resources

Focus Your Learning
- Use a variety of tools to access information
- Obtain information from a variety of sources

In addition to books, magazines, and newspapers, modern libraries may contain a wide range of other materials, including pamphlets, posters, photographs, maps, videotapes, audio tapes, and computer databases.

One of the most helpful library resources is the living, breathing person who is there to assist you: the librarian. Librarians won't do your work for you, but they can help you determine what you need and how to find it—especially when you've thought ahead and know what you're looking for.

The map below gives a general idea of services and sources that can be found in many libraries.

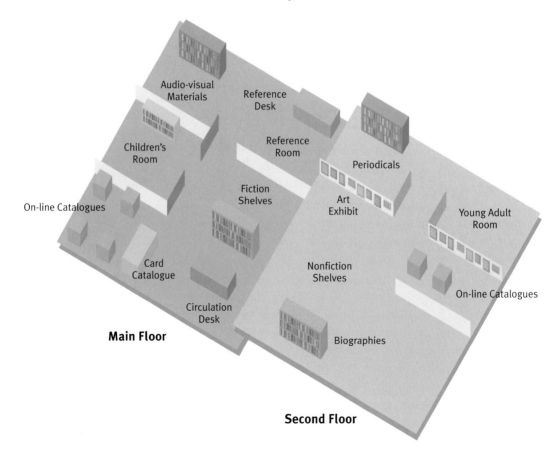

Main Floor

- Audio-visual Materials
- Reference Desk
- Children's Room
- Reference Room
- Periodicals
- On-line Catalogues
- Fiction Shelves
- Art Exhibit
- Young Adult Room
- Card Catalogue
- Nonfiction Shelves
- On-line Catalogues
- Circulation Desk
- Biographies

Second Floor

Libraries have more than just books. They also have:

Periodicals such as newspapers, magazines, journals, and newsletters.

Non-print materials such as **photographs, prints, painting reproductions, and computer software.**

Special collections that include original documents, letters, rare books, manuscripts, and maps.

Audiovisual materials such as documentaries, films, videos, television programs, newscasts, cassette tapes, and CDs.

How Library Resources Are Arranged

Even though it may not be obvious at first glance, library books are arranged in categories that make a lot of sense. The quickest way to decode the system is to look at a library floor plan. If the floor plan isn't posted, ask the librarian for one. The floor plan will show you where the different resources are and how they are arranged. If the shelves are labelled on the map with letters only (for example, *E–F*), that means the books are arranged in alphabetical order by authors' last names. Fiction books—such as mysteries, romances, and adventures—are usually shelved that way.

Numbers or number-letter combinations (known as call numbers) indicate nonfiction books. Nonfiction books are organized by subject, so once you find the category you want, you can camp there without having unrelated books in your way. Biographies (nonfiction stories about people's lives) are sometimes kept in a separate section, alphabetized by the subject's last name.

Most Canadian and U.S. libraries use the Dewey decimal system to organize their nonfiction books.

Dewey Decimal System

000	General works	**500**	Science
100	Philosophy	**600**	Technology
200	Religion	**700**	Fine arts
300	Social sciences	**800**	Literature
400	Language	**900**	History and Geography

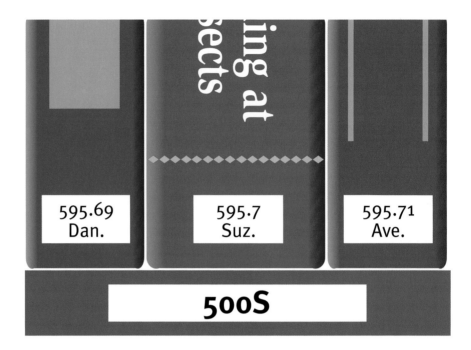

| 595.69 Dan. | 595.7 Suz. | 595.71 Ave. |

500S

To find *Looking at Insects* by David Suzuki, you would look in numerical order among the **500** shelves for **595.7** (The numbers after the decimal are ordered digit by digit; 595.7 would come after 595.69 or 595.613.) Then you would look in alphabetical order among the listings under **595.7** for **SUZ**.

Let's Practise

Visit your library and explore the services and resources available. Draw a floor plan to help you find what you need. Locate the following:

- nonfiction section
- fiction section
- periodicals area
- A–V section
- computer area
- reference area

Searching Library Catalogues

Today most libraries are equipped with on-line catalogues accessed by a computer terminal. Some smaller libraries may still have card catalogues. Card catalogues consist of index cards arranged alphabetically in rows of small drawers.

Whether you're using the computer keyboard or flipping cards in the card catalogue, you always have three ways to begin your search: by subject, by author, or by title. You will probably start with your subject, unless you already have the names of authors or titles of books.

The Computer Catalogue

Computer catalogues, with simple commands that carry you from screen to screen, have a number of features that are not available with card catalogues.

Keywords—These enable you to focus your search by using more than one identifying term at a time. Typing *Bees and Hum* will bring up Hum Bug's book entitled *Bees I Have Known*. Typing *insects and habitats* will bring up all the titles with those two words in their entries. Sometimes you'll need to fish for a keyword. If your topic is "Getting Power from the Sun," you may not find much until you stumble upon the magical combination *renewable and energy and sources.* Don't give up—keep trying all related words that come into your mind. Don't get too specific, though; remember that you're looking for entire books.

Alternative suggestions—When you arrive at a list of sources on one topic, a "see also" list will often appear on the screen, recommending related categories to search. You can also use the way books are organized to help you narrow your research topic. First look up two or three books about a subject that interests you.

When you go to the shelves that carry those titles, you will find many other books covering different aspects of the same topic. Look through these until you find the books you like.

Location identification—Computer catalogues tell whether your library owns the book and whether it is on the shelf or out on loan. If the book is out on loan, you can ask the librarian to reserve the book for you when it is returned.

Library listings—Some computer catalogues list nearby libraries that have books your library doesn't own. Often you can ask the librarian to request the book from another library, and the book will be delivered to your library within a few days.

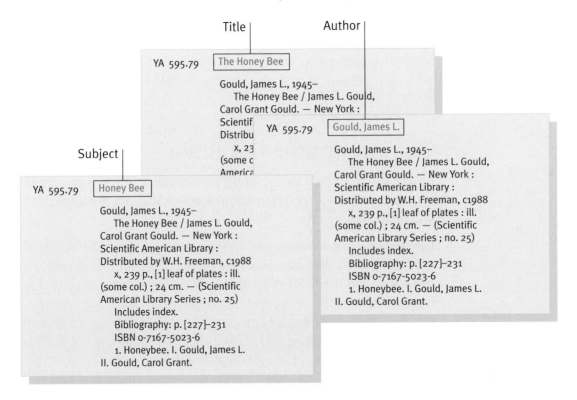

Let's Practise

Use the on-line catalogue to look for a book. If you need it, ask the librarian or a peer for help.

Using the Reference Section

Focus Your Learning
- Obtain information from a variety of sources

Many students know where the reference section of their library is because that's where the encyclopedias are found. There are many other research tools, including:

Indexes: Encyclopedias have a special volume called an index. If you are interested in bees, check the Index volume. It will list all the references to bees in the entire encyclopedia.

Biographical dictionaries: Many are specialized, offering biographies of authors, artists, musicians, scientists, and so on. *Current Biography* and *Canadian Who's Who* give short biographies of notable living people.

Almanacs and yearbooks: Books such as the *Information Please Almanac* or the *Canada Year Book* collect amazing varieties of information, ranging from census results to world records.

Specialized encyclopedias: How about an entire encyclopedia devoted to your topic? See if something like the *Penguin Encyclopedia of Popular Music* exists for your topic.

Directories. Directories list addresses, associations, members, or other types of information about a topic. *Bowker's Complete Video Directory* lists all kinds of videos and tells what they're about and where to get them.

Readers' Guide to Periodical Literature: This is the most commonly found index to magazine articles. It covers about 200 popular magazines, beginning with the year 1900. This index is also available in electronic form. Electronic indexes allow you to search for articles by subject, author, or title. Prompts appear on the screen at every step to make it easy. The computers often come with printers, so you can print out each helpful entry.

Note the publication date when consulting reference books.
Entries can sound as if they were written a week ago even though they are years old and out of date.

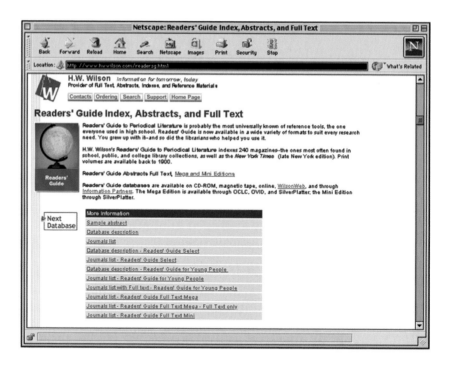

Here's How to

Use a Magazine Index

1. **Decide which time period you want to explore.** The most recent? The time when a particular event occurred? A five-year time span? Select the volumes covering the period you want.

2. **Choose a word that covers your topic and look it up.** If you already have an article title or author, you can use that to find where and when the article appeared.

3. **Make note of each listing.** Use the directions at the beginning of the index to interpret abbreviations you don't understand.

4. **Follow up on any "see also" listings that appear.**

5. **Repeat steps 1 through 4 for each question or subtopic you are researching.**

Newspaper Indexes

Newspapers are not as well indexed as magazines. Most small newspapers are not indexed at all. Larger papers may be indexed through computer services such as Infomart or CBCA (Canadian Business and Current Affairs), or through databases produced by individual newspapers (such as the Toronto *Globe and Mail*'s Info Globe). Some computer indexes show where articles appear, while others display entire articles. Ask your librarian which indexes are available in your library.

Bright Ideas

for Finding Useful Newspaper Articles

Try the *Canadian News Index*. CNI has been indexing seven large Canadian newspapers since 1977 and is available at most libraries in Canada.

Look in computerized periodical indexes. Some may include a few major newspapers in their listings.

Ask for a newspaper index. Some newspapers have created their own indexes. Your library may have indexes for one or two major newspapers.

Find Your Article

When you have located the magazine or newspaper articles you want to read, be sure to write down the name of the periodical, date, and volume number, as well as the article title and page number for each article you hope to find.

Look for a listing of the periodicals the library holds, and find out in what form they are stored. With library floor plan in hand, head toward the appropriate area.

Vertical files are file folders containing clippings of magazine and newspaper articles and illustrations. The files are arranged in alphabetical order by topic or by proper name and are usually kept in filing cabinets. Older issues might be bound into books or saved as miniaturized photographs, called microfilm or microfiche, to be read on a machine that magnifies the photographs. Once you find the pages you need, you can usually print a copy for a small fee.

If your list contains periodicals that the library doesn't own, you may be able to request the articles from other libraries. Your librarian can help you do this. Be sure to find out when you can hope to receive the articles.

Let's Practise

Look for a magazine or newspaper article with current information relating to your topic. Begin by locating the *Reader's Guide to Periodical Literature* either in hard cover or electronic form. Find your article using what you have learned in the preceding section.

Choosing Sources

A good researcher has to be selective. Knowing how to shop for sources can save hours of time as you pass over irrelevant information and pull out only what you need for your report.

Previewing Resources

When you're researching, why read an entire book when you may need only some of what it offers? By looking first at five key parts of a book, you can figure out how much of it will be useful for your research. Then you can rearrange your collection of resources while you're still at the beginning of your project.

Copyright Page—This is usually the reverse of the title page at the beginning of the book. The date after the © symbol indicates when the book was published.

Table of Contents—This outlines how the book is organized, which aspects of the topic are covered, and how much space is devoted to each aspect. It's at the beginning of the book.

Index—Found at the back of the book, this is a detailed alphabetized list of the topics covered with a page number for each item; it is much more thorough than the table of contents.

Author Information—Often found inside the back cover of a book, this description usually provides the author's qualifications for writing on a specific topic.

Scan the rest of the book to see if it has any other features that could be useful to you. These include:

❋ **Notes** that explain certain points in a book

❋ **Bibliography** lists that show the sources the author used

❋ **Recommended Reading** lists that suggest other research sources

❋ **Maps and Charts** that help you picture information

For more on previewing, see page 23.

Henry Michel teaches English and Native Studies at the En'owkin Centre in Penticton, British Columbia. Born of Shuswap ancestry on the Sugar Cane Reserve in Central British Columbia, he has published several poems.

Focus Your Learning
- Identify key words to locate information
- Determine information needs and select resources to suit topic and purpose

Using Computer Resources

Not long ago, a researcher probably would not have sat at a computer until it was time to begin writing. Then card catalogues went on-line and computers helped speed up library catalogue searches. Now computers are helping researchers gather facts, too.

CD-ROMs

CDs can hold more than your favourite tunes; they can also hold books, pictures, indexes, educational programs, cartoons, and much more. Called CD-ROMs, most of these CDs won't sound like much in your CD player. They work like computer disks, except that you cannot change or add to their information—hence the initials ROM (Read-only Memory). The most popular library CD-ROM holdings are encyclopedias and indexes to articles.

The Internet

Even more databases and other kinds of information can be found on the World Wide Web. The Web is part of the Internet, a world-wide computer network of web sites, newsgroups, e-mail, and other on-line facilities. Many organizations—companies, government agencies, universities, and so on—publish information on their web sites.

Most libraries and many homes have computers connected to the Internet so that you can surf the Web there. But the Web consists of millions of sites, so it's hard to know where to begin.

The best way to start looking for information on your subject is to use a search engine. There are dozens of them available, such as Yahoo!, AltaVista, Lycos, WebCrawler, InfoSeek, Magellan, Excite, Thunderstone, Planet Search, and GoTo.com.

But before you start searching with one of these engines, read their help files. Most search engines allow you to search for several keywords at once, which can help you search as specifically as possible.

Suppose, for example, you're looking for information on John Ford, the film director. If you typed "John Ford" into a search engine and clicked the search button, you would end up with a list of dozens, perhaps thousands, of "hits"—web sites or documents the engine has found—mostly concerned with Ford automobiles. Searching through pages of hits that aren't what you're looking for is frustrating. So making your search as narrow as possible will save you time. Try searching for "John Ford" *and* the title of a film he directed, or *"John Ford" and film.*

Also, keep in mind that not all the information presented on the Internet is reliable and well researched. Be sure that any information you take from the Internet to use in school projects comes from an organization such as a well-known publisher or other company, a university, or a government agency. If you're not sure about the reputation of a source you plan to use, your librarian may be able to help you.

The best way to learn to use the Internet is to practise. Don't get discouraged. Each search engine operates differently, but in time you'll learn which ones work best for you.

On-Line Research Options

Encyclopedias
Consumer Reports
Weather Maps
News Summaries
Newspaper Articles
Magazine Articles
Biographical Profiles
Country Profiles

Using Audiovisual Resources

As video cassette recorders (VCRs) become more common, opportunities abound for you to learn about a topic in new ways. Even if you don't own a VCR, many libraries and schools do, so there's no reason to limit yourself to books and periodicals when researching.

Videotapes

Interested in travelling with a mountain climber through the Himalayas? Want to watch a beekeeper collect honey—from a safe distance? Check at the library or the video rental store. Some videotapes show experiences or discoveries in science, history, foreign cultures, or the arts. Others fall into the "how-to" category and can teach you about anything from playing basketball to setting up computer software. Take a look at video catalogues to see what you might be able to borrow, rent, or order.

Television Programs

TV can occasionally be a good source of information, especially if you watch public broadcasting. Check listings to see if any programs might meet your research needs. Keep an eye out for travel stories, science programs, special news reports, and documentaries. If you decide to take notes, write down the station, date, and time of the program you watched, including the title, if there is one. This information can be difficult to track down later.

Maps

Maps can communicate in one glance ideas that would require pages of description. Maps can also be studied. For example, you might compare different types of maps (a political map for national boundaries and a population map for bee populations) and combine the facts gathered from each one. You can also use maps as a visual aid when it's your turn to communicate information.

Political maps show boundaries inside and between nations.

Road maps show how to get from here to there.

Specialized maps show particular features, such as mountains, climates, or populations.

Charts and Graphs

Drawings can sometimes show connections among pieces of information far more clearly than words can. If you hear that the number of bees living in the Northwest Territories has decreased by twenty percent, this might not impress you as much as a drawing would. How many bees were there before? Is this a noticeable change? If you saw a line on a graph slanting down sharply from last year to this year, you'd understand more quickly.

In **pie charts**, also known as circle graphs, the whole circle represents 100 percent of something. This total is divided into wedges that represent the different parts of the whole. You can see immediately how much space each part takes up. **For more on graphs and charts, see pages 217–221.**

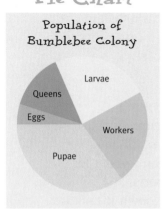

Pie Chart

Population of Bumblebee Colony

Larvae

Queens

Eggs

Pupae

Workers

Line graphs often show trends over time. Segments of time are marked along one side of the graph, and amounts of a certain item are marked across an adjoining side. Points are marked where the two categories meet. A line drawn to connect the points will reveal trends.

Bar graphs show several thick lines that represent amounts. Seeing the bars lined up allows you to compare them easily. To understand what a bar graph is showing, you need to read the title and the information along the sides of the graph.

Pictographs are similar to bar graphs, except that they use symbols (instead of bars). Instead of measuring the bars, you add up the symbols. Each symbol stands for a given amount, usually specified on the graph.

Line Graph

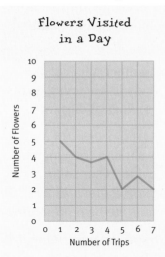

Flowers Visited in a Day

Bar Graph

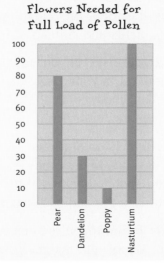

Flowers Needed for Full Load of Pollen

Pictograph

Flowers Needed for Full Load of Pollen

✿ = ten flowers

Let's Practise

Think of ways to illustrate your topic. Draw some simple examples using what you have learned in the preceding section.

Taking Field Trips

What if you could walk inside a book and experience all of its sights, sounds, smells, and surfaces first-hand? Visiting places that relate to your topic is like having that chance. Check out the following places:

Museums: Ask any nearby museums to mail you notices of the different exhibits they have throughout the year. You can visit shows that interest you and turn them into the beginnings of research projects.

Zoos and Botanical Gardens: The exhibits and staff at many zoos and botanical gardens provide information about the care and handling of plants and animals.

Tourist Attractions: Call your town or city hall for a listing of points of interest in your area. You might find old photographs of your neighbourhood, collections from archaeological digs, or famous landmarks under your very nose.

Radio and Television Stations: Most radio stations are happy to host student tours. Many cable stations provide tours. Some allow students to handle equipment. Other television stations allow students to sit in the audience while programs are being recorded.

Homemade Tours: If you're interested in a specific type of job, or in how a product is put together, arrange a behind-the-scenes tour. You could ask to visit a factory, a bank, or a specific store.

Interviewing Experts

Focus Your Learning
• Obtain information from a variety of sources

As a researcher absorbed in your books and other sources, you can easily forget that there are people in the world who are interested in your topic and have devoted even more time to it than you have. These people may work in a job related to your topic, or they may have made a hobby of it, or in some other way they may pursue their interest in it. Why not talk with them and enjoy a new view on what you're researching?

When looking for people to interview, the telephone yellow pages can be your research assistant. Use your imagination to think of experts you might call. Are you researching plants and trees? Look up *Garden Centres* or *Nurseries.* Researching garbage and recycling? Look up *Rubbish Removal.*

People to Interview

Professionals have special knowledge and experience. Who would know something about your research topic—a veterinarian? a firefighter? a journalist? an artist? Even someone who can't talk for long might suggest other resources.

Travellers often enjoy telling about their experiences. If you are researching a place, do you know of people who have visited there? Do they have slides or photographs? You can learn a lot by looking at pictures of a place and hearing it described.

Narrators are simply people who like to tell stories. A narrator could be anyone—from a citizen who has served on a jury to an person who came to this country at the age of ten. If you were researching bee stings, you might look for a bee keeper with stories to tell.

Members of organizations have reasons for being members, such as support for a cause or enjoyment of membership activities. Find out what types of societies and organizations meet in your area, and see if any relate to your research topic. You might find a whole group of people to interview.

For more on interviewing, see page 132.

Let's Practise

1. Call an expert to arrange for an interview or visit. Explain what you want and ask who is in charge of handling your request. Get the name and address (correctly spelled) of that person.

2. Draft a short letter explaining who you are, what you'd like to learn, and why. If you have a deadline, include it.

3. Have a peer make revision suggestions, then proofread your good copy. **See pages 101 and 104 for sample business letters.**

4. Send the request by mail, fax, or e-mail.

5. If you receive no reply within two weeks, follow up with a phone call.

6. While you're waiting, prepare a series of questions to ask during your interview.

Making Research Notes

Focus Your Learning
- Prepare references and documentation

As you collect research material on your topic, write careful notes. Your notes will coax your brain to remember what you read. The harder you make your mind work, the more you'll remember. You could decide which parts of your research material are the most important and copy them; this forces you to think about them longer. Better yet, you could put the important parts into your own words. This involves your brain even more.

If you like the way something is worded and you want to quote the author, go ahead! Just make a note of the source and the page number (to be included in the research essay), and put quotation marks before and after the quoted words to make clear that you're repeating someone else's writing.

Use Your Own Words

Being able to repeat what you've heard or read doesn't mean you understand it; it only means that you can repeat the words, just as you might repeat a bird call. However, to put information into your own words, you really have to understand it.

The following information about bees' dances comes from an article in *Scientific American* written by Karl von Frisch in 1962. The researchers marked the bees with coloured dots and put them in a glass hive so they could watch them. A bee that has found food performs a "round dance" for the other bees. They soon fly off.

A bee that has discovered a rich source of food near the hive performs on her return a "round dance." (Like all the other work of the colony, food-foraging is carried out by females.) She turns in circles, alternately to the left and to the right. This dance excites the neighbouring bees; they start to troop behind the dancer and soon fly off to look for the food. They seek the kind of flower whose scent they detected on the original forager.

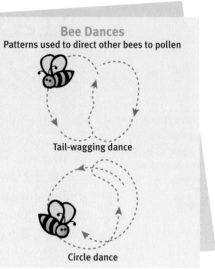

Bee Dances
Patterns used to direct other bees to pollen

Tail-wagging dance

Circle dance

Make Notes

There are many ways to make notes about research such as this.

1. Use file cards with your own personal shorthand.

> DANCE -- when fnd rich source fd
> -- turn in circ
> -- alt left & right

2. Develop a chart.

> "Dialects in the Languag e of the Bees"
> by Karl von Frisch, 1962
>
> | Round Dance (for food closer than 84 m) | • B turns in circles, other bees watch, smell flower type, go look
 • Richer the food, rowdier the dance
 • When others return, they do same until source runs out |
> | --- | --- |

3. Write an outline of what the article explains. **For a sample outline, see page 114.**

Create a Bibliography

A bibliography is a list of books and other reference materials used to research your topic. It is usually placed at the end of your written project.

Here's How to

Make a Bibliography

❋ Arrange the sources so they are alphabetized by the authors' last names. If there is no author, alphabetize by the first main word of the title. If you're working on a computer, your word-processing program can probably alphabetize your sources for you.

❋ List your sources according to the styles below.

1. Book with one author:

   Blodgett, E. D. <u>Alice Munro</u>. Boston: Twayne, 1988.

2. Book with more than one author:

   Elwood, Ann, and Linda C. Wood. <u>Windows in Space</u>. New York: Walker, 1982.

3. Article in a magazine:

   Daglish, Brenda. "A Matter of Interest." <u>Maclean's</u>, February 15, 1993, pp. 36–37.

4. Article in a newspaper:

   Smith, Beverley. "Canadians Skate to Gold Medal." <u>The Globe and Mail</u>, March 11, 1993, p. A1.

5. Article in an encyclopedia:

   Humber, William. "Bicycling." <u>The Canadian Encyclopedia</u>, 1988.

6. Video or film:

   <u>Shooting Stars</u>. videotape. National Film Board of Canada (Toronto), 1987. 49 min., 30 sec.

7. Radio or television program:

   "Haida Gwaii—Islands of the People." <u>Nature</u>. PBS, December 19, 1992.

8. Interview:

   Delaney, Daphne (musician). Personal interview. Toronto, April 10, 2000.

9. Information from the Internet:

   Include the web site address and the date the information was researched.

   http://www.cableducation.ca (January 1, 2001)

Let's Practise

1. Use the above style in developing a bibliography for your project.

2. Find a piece of information on the Internet. Note the web site address and the exact web page address.

Measure Your Growth

Focus Your Learning
- Reflect on personal growth to set goals

Write the numbers 1 through 5 in your notebook. Beside each, rate yourself according to the following scale:

A   Excellent

B   Good

C   Fair

D   Needs a lot of work

1. I can plan a useful library visit.

2. I can find a variety of resources in the library, including print and non-print materials.

3. I can preview resources and decide which ones best fit my research topic.

4. I can keep useful research notes.

5. I can develop a bibliography using a standard format.

Language
Handbook

CONTENTS

Focus Your Learning

- Use reference materials
- Revise and edit
- Attend to grammar and usage
- Attend to spelling conventions
- Check spelling
- Attend to capitalization and punctuation
- Explore how new words enter a language

Parts of Speech

Words fall into eight different categories, called parts of speech. Nouns are parts of speech—as are pronouns, adjectives, verbs, adverbs, prepositions, conjunctions, and interjections. Let's explore each part of speech in turn.

Nouns

Nouns name persons, places, things, and ideas so you can identify and talk about them. Example: Say you ask someone, "What's that?" The answer you get is usually a noun—"a hippopotamus," "Lake Winnipeg," "music," "an earthquake," "the band."

Types of Nouns

Nouns can be grouped in different ways, depending on what they name or how they're written.

Common Nouns

Common nouns name kinds of persons, places, things, or ideas. Common nouns do not use capitals.

band	province	car
month	magazine	

Proper Nouns

Proper nouns give particular names of persons, places, things, or ideas. Proper nouns start with capitals.

Metal Heads	Alberta	Corvette
April	Teen Beat	

Compound Nouns

Compound nouns are made up of two or more nouns. Some are written as one word, some have a hyphen, and some are separate words. Check the dictionary for the correct spelling of each type.

One word	keyboard
	grandmother
Hyphen	yo-yo
	sister-in-law
Separate words	Duchess Dee
	high school

Collective Nouns

Collective nouns name groups of people, animals, or things that act together.

people	band	team
herd	family	audience

Concrete Nouns

Concrete nouns name something or someone that can be seen or touched. (They can also be either common or proper nouns.)

drum	guitarist	Lake Erie
aunt	smoke	

Abstract Nouns

Abstract nouns name ideas, qualities, or feelings—things that can't be seen or touched. (They are usually also common nouns.)

freedom	beauty	love
courage	time	nation

Features of Nouns

Gender

Gender tells whether a noun is referring to a male (such as *boy*), a female *(Sheryl,* for example*)*, or a thing *(ticket,* for example*)*. A noun is masculine if it refers to a male, and feminine if it refers to a female. In English, all other nouns are not associated with a gender.

Number

Number tells how many people or things there are. A noun is singular if it names one item, and plural if it names more than one. Most nouns are spelled differently when they name more than one item.

Singular nouns
The **singer** had a terrific **voice.**

Plural nouns
The **singers** had terrific **voices.**

Here's How to

Form Noun Plurals

When you use the plural form of a noun, you're telling your listener or reader that you are talking about more than one thing. For most nouns, you form the plural just by adding *-s*. Some nouns have special plural spellings. You have to memorize these or learn when to check your dictionary.

1. For most nouns, just add *-s*.

   band + s = bands

2. For nouns ending in *s, sh, ch, x, z,* add *-es*.

   glass + es = glasses

3. For nouns ending in *y*:
   - If a vowel comes before *y*, add *-s*.

     toy + s = toys
   - If a consonant comes before *y*, change the *y* to *i* and add *-es*.

     sky + es = skies

4. For nouns ending in *f* or *fe*:
   - For some nouns, change the *f* to *v* and add *-s* or *-es*.

     life + s = lives
   - For other nouns, add *-s*.

     roof + s = roofs

   Check your dictionary.

5. For nouns ending in *o*:
- If a vowel comes before *o*, add -*s*.   studio + s = studios
- If a consonant comes before *o*, add
  -*es* to most words.   potato + es = potatoes

6. If the noun is a musical term, add -*s*.   piano + s = pianos
    Check your dictionary.

Special Plurals

Some nouns have only plural forms.

jeans
scissors
eyeglasses

Some singular nouns end in *s* and have no plural forms.

news
mathematics
measles

Some nouns have special plural forms.

person—people
woman—women
child—children
mouse—mice
foot—feet
goose—geese

For a compound noun written as one word, make the last part plural.

newspapers
bookshelves
grandchildren

For other compound nouns, make the most important word plural.

music boxes
rock bands
sisters-in-law
governors general

Some nouns do not change forms in the plural.

sheep
deer
salmon
moose
Métis

Endings

Some word endings are typical of nouns. Example: -er, -or, -ment, -ion, -hood, -ity, -ness, -ist, -ship. Spot one of these endings or suffixes, and you've probably found a noun.

Base word		Ending		Noun
sing	+	er	=	singer

Let's Practise

List two or more nouns with each of the endings listed above.

Case

Case tells you how a noun is used in a sentence. Nouns can be used as subjects, as objects, and as possessives. **For more about nouns in sentences, see page 288.** Pronouns have different forms for the different cases. **See Pronouns, page 272.** Nouns, however, have special forms used only in the possessive case. The possessive form shows that the noun owns, or is closely related to, the noun that follows it. Often a possessive noun is used instead of a phrase that uses *have* or *of*.

1. **Subjective**
   - Noun as subject of sentence:
     Lucas *is a member of the Me2s.*
   - Noun as subject complement:
     He is an awesome **drummer***.*

2. **Objective**
   - Noun as object of verb:
     Duchess plays **keyboard***.*
   - Noun as object of preposition:
     The band is going to **Edmonton.**

3. **Possessive**
   - Noun shows ownership:
     Those are **Lucas's** *drums.*
   - Noun shows close relationship:
     Is that the **band's** *favourite song?*

Here's How to

Form Possessive Nouns

1. For a singular noun, add an apostrophe plus -*s*:
   voice of the singer → singer**'s** voice
   voice of Janice → Janice**'s** voice

   Exception: A singular noun that ends in -*sus* or -*ses* sounds better if you add only an apostrophe, not apostrophe plus -*s*.

   Hercules' adventures
   Marcus' leadership

2. For a plural noun ending in *s*, add only an apostrophe.
   The musicians have a schedule → musician**s'** schedule

3. For a plural noun not ending in *s*, add an apostrophe plus -*s*.
   cheers of the people → people**'s** cheers.

   Things can get a little tricky when you're talking about two people owning something:

   - If two people own one thing, add an apostrophe plus -*s* to the last noun only.

     Julie and Jim's kitten

   - If two people own things separately, add an apostrophe plus -*s* to each noun.

     Julie's and Jim's kittens

Let's Edit Nouns!

Here are some noun errors. Read about why they're errors and how to fix them. It will help you do a better job of editing your own nouns.

Know when to cap and when not to cap.

DRAFT	*I interviewed them after their concert on **tuesday**.*
WHAT'S WRONG?	*Tuesday* names a particular day. It's a proper noun and should begin with a capital letter.
EDIT IT	*I interviewed them after their concert on **Tuesday**.*

Know where the apostrophe goes.

DRAFT	*Lucas Labelle is the **groups'** drummer.*
WHAT'S WRONG?	To make a singular noun possessive, add -'s, not -s'.
EDIT IT	*Lucas Labelle is the **group's** drummer.*

Check plurals in a dictionary.

DRAFT	*He said "Our **lifes** are nothin' like what **peoples think**."*
WHAT'S WRONG?	The *f* in *life* changes to *v* in the plural. *People* is already a plural form and doesn't need -s added.
EDIT IT	*He said, "Our **lives** are nothin' like what **people** think."*
DRAFT	*"Mostly we gotta hang out in cold **studioes** and crummy dressing rooms."*
WHAT'S WRONG?	*Studio* ends in 2 vowels; the second vowel is *o*. The plural form adds -s, not -es.
EDIT IT	*"Mostly we gotta hang out in cold **studios** and crummy dressing rooms."*

Check compound nouns in a dictionary.

DRAFT	*She's the **key-board** player.*
WHAT'S WRONG?	*Keyboard* is listed as a single word in the dictionary.
EDIT IT	*She's the **keyboard** player.*

Know the difference between a plural and a possessive.

DRAFT	*"... when we hear the **crowds** applause, it all seems worth it."*
WHAT'S WRONG?	*The crowds applause* stands for *the applause of the crowd. Crowds* is not a plural here but a possessive. Change -s to -'s for the possessive form.
EDIT IT	*"... when we hear the **crowd's** applause, it all seems worth it."*

Pronouns

Pronouns replace or "stand in" for nouns or for other pronouns. They keep nouns from being overworked. An *antecedent* is the word that the pronoun replaces. It can be a noun or another pronoun and usually comes before the pronoun that refers to it.

Types of Pronouns

There are several different kinds of pronouns, and each has a different job to do.

Personal Pronouns

These pronouns stand for persons or things. They are the pronouns you use most.

I, me, my, mine
we, us, our, ours
you, your, yours
he, him, his, she, her, hers, it, its
they, them, their, theirs

Reflexive and Intensive Pronouns

These are the pronouns that end in *-self* or *-selves*. They never stand alone. They always have antecedents in the same sentence.

myself, ourselves
yourself, yourselves
himself, herself, itself, themselves

Interrogative Pronouns

These pronouns ask questions. They do not always have specific antecedents.

what, which, who, whom, whose

Demonstrative Pronouns

These pronouns point out specific people, places, or things. The antecedent usually comes after a demonstrative pronoun.

this, these, that, those

Use *this* and *these* to point out people or things nearby.
Use *that* and *those* to point out people or things not nearby.

Relative Pronouns

These pronouns begin subordinate clauses and connect them to independent clauses. **For more on clauses, see page 330.** All of the relative pronouns, except *that*, can also be used as questions. What? Who?

Refers to people: who, whom, whose
Refers to things: which
Refers to people or things: that

Indefinite Pronouns

These pronouns refer to people, places, or things, often in a general, unspecific way. They usually don't need antecedents.

Singular: another, anybody, anyone, anything, each, either, everybody, everyone, everything, little, much, neither, nobody, no one, nothing, one, other, somebody, someone, something

Plural: both, few, many, others, several

Singular or plural: all, any, more, most, none, some

Using Personal Pronouns

The following six guidelines will help you use personal pronouns.

1 *Know the different features of personal pronouns.*

Personal pronouns show the features of case, person, gender, and number.

Case	Person	Gender	Number	
Case tells you how a pronoun is used in a sentence.	Person tells you who is speaking (first), being spoken to (second), or being spoken about (third).	Gender tells you whether a third-person singular pronoun is referring to a male, a female, or a thing.	Number tells you how many people or things there are. **Singular**	**Plural**
Subject pronouns	first		I	we
	second		you	you
	third	masculine	he	
		feminine	she	they
		neuter	it	
Object pronouns	first		me	us
	second		you	you
	third	masculine	him	
		feminine	her	them
		neuter	it	
Possessive pronouns	first		my, mine	our, ours
	second		your, yours	your, yours
	third	masculine	his	
		feminine	her, hers	their, theirs
		neuter	its	

2 Make the personal pronoun agree with its antecedent.

A pronoun should have the same features as the noun or pronoun it stands for. Make a pronoun agree with its antecedent in person, number, and gender.

antecedent   pronoun
↓   ↓

*Does your **sister** have **her** ticket?*

Third person, singular, feminine

3 Make sure the antecedent is clear.

Don't confuse your reader with an unclear pronoun reference. You may need to name a noun again or rewrite the sentence so your meaning is clear.

No
*Toby told Alex **he** had won a box of candy.*

Yes
Toby told Alex that Alex had won a box of candy.

Yes
"Alex, you won a box of candy!" exclaimed Toby.

4 Use the right case.

Use a subject pronoun when the pronoun is a single or compound subject, or a subject complement. **See page 327 for more about subjects.**

Subject
***She** watched a video with the Browns.*

Compound subject
***He** and **I** thought Chilly Billy was silly.*

Subject complement
***It** is I.*

Use an object pronoun when the pronoun is a single or compound direct object, an indirect object, or an object of a preposition. **See page 327 for more about objects.**

Direct object
*My parents drove **us** to the movie.*

Compound direct object
*My parents drove **him** and **me** to the movie.*

Indirect object
*Did Toby tell **her** about that scary movie?*

Object of a preposition
*She gave it to Lee and **me**.*

Use a possessive pronoun to show ownership or a close relationship. Some possessive pronouns are used before nouns; others are used alone.

Possessive used with a noun
*Is that **your** jacket on the seat?*

Possessive used alone
*Is that **yours**?*

5 Leave out the apostrophe.

Possessive pronouns are often confused with contractions. A contraction needs an apostrophe because it's an abbreviation for two words. A possessive pronoun is just one word and doesn't need an apostrophe.

Possessive Pronouns	Contractions
its	it's → it is
their	they're → they are
your	you're → you are
whose	who's → who is

Using Other Pronouns

The following six guidelines will help you use other (non-personal) pronouns.

1 Know the difference between reflexive and intensive pronouns.

A reflexive pronoun adds information to a sentence. An intensive pronoun emphasizes its antecedent and can be left out without changing the meaning of a sentence.

Reflexive pronoun
*Toby bought **himself** a box of popcorn.*

Intensive pronoun
*I **myself** would never talk during a film.*

2 Don't use a -self pronoun by itself.

A *-self* pronoun should always have an antecedent in the same sentence.

No
*Alex and **myself** loved watching Lizard Lips.*
Reflexive alone

Yes
*Alex and **I** loved watching Lizard Lips.*
Use personal pronoun

Yes
*I found **myself** terrified by Lizard Lips.*

3 Don't add here or there to demonstrative pronouns.

Avoid using the expressions *this here* and *that there*. The demonstrative pronoun *this* already means "here," and *that* already means "there."

No
*This **here** is my seat, isn't it?*

Yes
This is my seat, isn't it?

4 Know the difference between who's and the interrogative pronoun whose.

Who's is the contraction for who is; it is not an interrogative pronoun.

No
***Who's** are these ticket stubs?*

Yes
***Whose** are these ticket stubs?*

5 Make personal pronouns agree with indefinite pronouns.

Indefinite pronouns can be antecedents of personal pronouns. Make the personal pronoun agree in number and gender with the indefinite pronoun to which it refers.

No
***Everyone** on the girls' team has **their** uniform.*
↑ singular   ↑ plural

Yes
***Everyone** on the girls' team has **her** uniform.*
↑ singular   ↑ singular

6 Think about the gender of indefinite pronouns.

In the past, the pronouns *he, him,* or *his* were used to refer to both males and females as a group. Today, most people avoid using a masculine pronoun to refer to people in general, unless the group is specifically male.

Avoid
*Every **person** must find **his** own way in life.*

Yes
*Everyone** must find **his** or **her** own seat.*
***All** must find **their** own seats.*
*Everyone on the **boys'** team had **his** own locker.*

Let's Edit Pronouns!

Here are some pronoun mistakes. Read about why they are errors and how to correct them. You can use them to help you fix your own pronoun errors.

Keep an eye on the case of personal pronouns.

DRAFT ***Me and my family*** *went to the cinema Saturday afternoon.*
Subject or object pronoun?

WHAT'S WRONG? *Me and my family* is the subject, but *me* is an object pronoun. Use the subject pronoun *I*. Also, *I* is part of a compound; it should always come last.

EDIT IT *My family and I went to the cinema Saturday afternoon.*

Make sure your pronouns have clear antecedents.

DRAFT *... so naturally we couldn't miss the double feature* **they** *were showing.*
Who is meant by *they*?

WHAT'S WRONG? The reader can't tell who *they* is. Instead of an unclear or vague pronoun, use a noun.

EDIT IT *... so naturally we couldn't miss the double feature* **the cinema** *was showing.*

Don't switch the pronoun to you unless there's a reason.

DRAFT *I like horror shows because* **you** *can actually feel the suspense.*
Stick to one person.

WHAT'S WRONG? Why did Toby change from *I* to *you*? It was not necessary. Stick with the same personal pronoun unless you actually change person.

EDIT IT *I like horror shows because* **I** *can actually feel the suspense.*

Make a pronoun match or agree with its antecedent.

DRAFT *...* ***everybody*** *screamed* ***their*** *lungs out during the concert.*   Match the antecedent.

WHAT'S WRONG? *Their* refers to *everybody*, but *everybody* is singular and *their* is plural. When you're referring to a group that includes males and females, use *his* or *her*, or, even better, make the antecedent plural.

EDIT IT *...* ***all the viewers*** *screamed* ***their*** *lungs out during the concert.*

Know the difference between possessive pronouns and contractions.

DRAFT ***Your*** *going to love that one when you see it!*   Pronoun or contraction?

WHAT'S WRONG? *Your* should be a contraction of *you are*, not a possessive pronoun. Use an apostrophe.

EDIT IT ***You're*** *going to love that one when you see it!*

Adjectives

Adjectives describe. They tell what the things named by nouns and pronouns are like. Adjectives can show which or what kind of thing you're talking about. Examples: the *tiny* one, the *awesome* one, *that* one, *no* one.

Types of Adjectives

Adjectives fall into different groups, depending on what job they perform and how they're written.

Descriptive Adjectives

Descriptive adjectives **add details. They answer these questions: What kind? What's it like?**

long	red
squishy	strong
hilarious	rainy
round	box-shaped
faithful	Canadian

Compound Adjectives

Compound adjectives are made up of more than one word. They can be written as one word, as hyphenated words, or as separate words. Check your dictionary to find the correct form.

lightweight jacket
wide-eyed fans
Nova Scotia salmon
hair-raising stories

Find out more about hyphenating compound adjectives on page 340.

Proper Adjectives

Proper adjectives are formed from proper nouns and begin with a capital letter. Sometimes proper adjectives look just like proper nouns. At other times they have special forms.

Newfoundland coast – adjective is same as noun
Vietnamese culture – adjective has a special form

Turn to page 315 to learn more about capitalizing proper adjectives.

Articles

Articles are special adjectives that help you introduce nouns.

Definite article points out one of a certain group – the
Indefinite article refers to any one of a certain group — a, an

Limiting Adjectives

Limiting adjectives make nouns and pronouns more specific. They answer these questions: Which one? How many? How much?

this	that	those	my
our	your	his	its
their	first	right	left
one	ninety-six	many	few
both	no	more	less
which	what		

Features of Adjectives

Placement

In general, adjectives go before the nouns they describe. You can also put them after a noun and after a linking verb.

Before a noun
*My **orange** kite flies wonderfully.*

After a noun
*My kite, **orange** as a pumpkin, flies wonderfully.*

After a linking verb
*My kite is **orange** and flies wonderfully.*

Endings

Probably you have often noticed these word endings: *-able, -ful, -ic, -is, -less, -like, -ous.* Add an ending like this to a word root or word, and what do you get?

Base word		Ending		Noun
move	+	able	=	movable

Let's Practise

By using endings such as *-able* or *-ful*, make a list of at least ten adjectives.

Comparisons

Adjectives have three different forms for making comparisons. Which form you use depends on how many things you're comparing, how many syllables the word has, and whether the adjective is regular or irregular.

Positive Form
When there's no comparison

Comparative Form
When two things are compared

Superlative Form
When three or more things are compared

Regular Adjectives

You can form most comparisons by adding either *-er* or *-est* to the adjective or by using *more* or *most* with it. For one-syllable words, add *-er* or *-est*. For some two-syllable words, add *-er* or *-est*. Others require *more* or *most*. For three-syllable or longer words, use *more* or *most*.

One syllable

clear	clearer	clearest

Two syllables

pretty	prettier	prettiest
careful	more careful	most careful

Three syllables

difficult	more difficult	most difficult

Irregular Adjectives

Some adjectives that you use often have irregular forms. They don't follow the rules above, so you just have to learn them.

good	better	best
bad	worse	worst
little	less	least
much, many	more	most

Using Adjectives

Here are a few tips for using adjectives correctly.

1 Know how to use less and least.

Sometimes a comparison has to do with less of something, not more. Then, instead of *more* or *most*, you use *less* or *least*, no matter how many syllables the adjective has.

One Syllable

That hill is **steep**.	Positive
That hill is **less steep** than this one.	Comparative
That hill is the **least steep** of all.	Superlative

Three Syllables

My sister was **excited**.	Positive
My sister was **less excited** than I was.	Comparative
She was the **least excited** family member.	Superlative

2 Know the difference between fewer and less.

The adjectives *fewer* and *less* mean just about the same thing. However, *fewer* counts separate items, and *less* measures the amount of a substance. Use *fewer* with plural nouns. Use *less* with singular nouns.

Plural
Which class has **fewer students**?

Singular
Which bread has **less sugar**?

Let's Edit Adjectives!

Here are some adjective errors. Read about why they're errors and how to fix them. Use what you learn to help you do a better job of editing your own adjectives.

Count the things compared.

DRAFT	... *I don't know who's **happiest**, Mom or I.*
WHAT'S WRONG?	Only two people are being compared—*Mom* and *I*. The comparative form is needed, not the superlative.
EDIT IT	... *I don't know who's **happier**, Mom or I.*

Put a cap on proper adjectives.

DRAFT	My ***scottish*** *aunt is thirty-five years old.*
WHAT'S WRONG?	*Scottish* comes from the proper noun *Scotland*, so it needs a capital letter.
EDIT IT	My ***Scottish*** *aunt is thirty-five years old.*

Know the difference between a and an.

DRAFT	*Last time she brought me **a** orange kite with blue stripes.*
WHAT'S WRONG?	*Orange* begins with a vowel sound, so the article before it should be *an*, not *a*.
EDIT IT	*Last time she brought me **an** orange kite with blue stripes.*

Know whether to use -er/-est or more/most.

DRAFT	*Aunt Daphne seemed **more sad** than usual.*
WHAT'S WRONG?	*Sad* has only one syllable, so it forms the comparative with *-er*, not more.
EDIT IT	*Aunt Daphne seemed **sadder** than usual.*

Fewer and less go with different nouns.

DRAFT	*She brought us **less** presents, too.*
WHAT'S WRONG?	*Less* is used with singular nouns, but *presents* is plural. Use *fewer* with plural nouns.
EDIT IT	*She brought us **fewer** presents, too.*

Know the irregular forms for comparing.

DRAFT	*... it was **worser** than we thought.*
WHAT'S WRONG?	The comparative form of *bad* is *worse*, not *worser*.
EDIT IT	*... it was **worse** than we thought.*

Let's Practise

Rewrite the following sentences, using the correct comparative.

1. After he had finished rewriting his assignment, Ahmad was a more sad but more wise student.

2. My father thought that the less suitcases we took on the trip the more easy time we would have.

3. Jane was jealous because, when we compared our two coin collections, mine was best.

4. Jody was not much of a soccer player; she was the worse I knew.

5. Zena wanted to be a pilot, but she realized that she would need more high math marks.

Verbs

Verbs make other words move. Without them, there wouldn't be any action in your sentences. Nothing would dance or laugh or worry or roar. You need verbs to tell what nouns or pronouns can do, be, and feel.

Types of Verbs

There are three types of verbs. Action and linking verbs work with nouns and pronouns. Helping verbs work with other verbs.

Action Verbs

Action verbs tell what someone or something does. An action isn't always physical. An action can be mental, too.

cook	compose	paint
run	realize	think
write	draw	take
make	dream	

Linking Verbs

Linking verbs link or join a noun or pronoun to another word that tells something about the noun or pronoun. Forms of the verb *to be* are the most common linking verbs.

be	being	been
am	are	is
was	were	appear
become	feel	grow
look	remain	seem
smell	sound	stay
taste		

Helping Verbs

Helping verbs do just what their name suggests. They help the **main verb** do its job. Together the helping verb and the main verb make a **verb phrase**. Forms of the verb *to be* are common helping verbs.

be	being	been
am	are	is
was	were	has
have	had	does
do	did	can
could	will	would
shall	should	may
might	must	

Using Action, Linking, and Helping Verbs

The following six guidelines will help you use verbs.

1 *Know the difference between transitive and intransitive verbs.*

A **transitive verb** directs its action to another word, the direct object. An **intransitive verb** doesn't need a direct object to complete its meaning. **(For more on direct objects, see page 327.)**

Transitive
Tina **found** the **cave**.   Direct object

Intransitive
They all **rested**.

Some verbs can be used as both transitive and intransitive verbs.

Transitive
*Kevin is afraid they **forgot him**.*   Direct object

Intransitive
*Oh, no! They **forgot**.*

2 Know the difference between the active and the passive voice.

Action verbs tell whether the subject of the sentence carries out the action or receives it.

Active voice
***Tina found** the cave.*   Subject acts.

Passive voice
*The **cave was found** by Tina.*   Subject receives.

3 Watch out for verbs that can be used as both linking and action verbs.

A verb is a linking verb if a form of *to be* can be substituted for the verb. A verb is an action verb if it is followed by a direct object.

Linking verb
*The cave **smelled** musty. → The cave **is** musty.*

Action verb
*Ben **smelled** the **flower**.*   Direct object

4 Remember that other words can come between helping verbs and a main verb.

Two or more verbs can combine to help a main verb. Other words can come between the parts of the verb phrase, especially when you form questions.

Verb phrase together
*Kevin **will be rescued** by someone.*

Verb phrase separated
***Will** Kevin **be rescued** by someone?*

5 Remember the apostrophe in a contraction.

Helping verbs can hide in contractions. Use an apostrophe to replace left-out letters in contractions.

Helping verbs
*She **is** going. She **will** go.*

Contractions
***She's** going.*
***She'll** go.*

The contraction *n't* is different. It means "not" and isn't part of the verb. (**See adverbs, page 291.**)

Helping verb
*I **do** not know.*

Contraction
*I **don't** know.*

6 Know the difference between have and of.

When you say *could have gone,* you're using *could* and *have* as helping verbs for *gone.* Don't use *of* instead of the helping verb *have.*

No

could of	would of	should of

Yes

could have	would have	should have

Verb Tenses

Want to know **when** something happened? Ask the verb. Verbs have different forms, called **tenses**. Tenses tell when something happened.

There are six tenses in English—three **simple tenses** and three **perfect tenses**—that help place an event in time. The six tenses are formed by using the helping verbs *has, had,* and *will,* plus verb forms called **principal parts**.

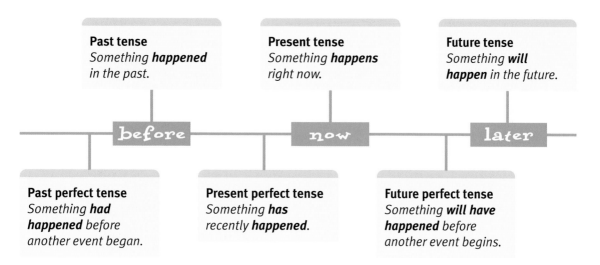

Past tense
*Something **happened** in the past.*

Present tense
*Something **happens** right now.*

Future tense
*Something **will happen** in the future.*

before · now · later

Past perfect tense
*Something **had happened** before another event began.*

Present perfect tense
*Something **has** recently **happened**.*

Future perfect tense
*Something **will have happened** before another event begins.*

Principal Parts of Verbs

Every verb has four forms called **principal parts**. Present and past participles are made with helping verbs. (Participles can also work as adjectives and nouns. **To learn more about participles, see page 329.**)

Regular Verbs

These verbs form the past and past participle by adding *-ed* or *-d*. Most verbs follow this pattern.

Present	Present Participle	Past	Past Participle
Basic form of the verb	Basic form + *-ing*. Used with forms of *to be*	Basic form + *-ed*	Basic form + *-ed*. Used with forms of *to have*
walk	is walking	walked	has walked

Irregular Verbs

These verbs form the past and past participle in different ways. You can either memorize the different parts or look them up in the dictionary in the entry for the main verb. **See Dictionary, page 318.** Here are some of the patterns of irregular verbs.

Present	Present Participle	Past	Past Participle
Basic form of the verb	Basic form + *-ing*. Used with forms of *to be*	Basic form + *-ed*	Basic form + *-ed*. Used with forms of *to have*
hurt	is hurting	hurt	has hurt
bring	is bringing	brought	has brought
become	is becoming	became	has become
break	is breaking	broke	has broken
eat	is eating	ate	has eaten
begin	is beginning	began	has begun
lie	is lying	lay	has lain
be	is being	was, were	has been

Here's How to

Form Verb Tenses

Here are the correct ways to form all six tenses of the verb *to check*. You can use this model to form the tenses of other regular verbs.

1. For the simple present, use the basic verb form.
   *I **check** my watch.*

2. For the simple past, use the past form.
   *I **checked** my watch.*

3. For the simple future, use *will* + the basic verb form.
   *I **will check** my watch.*

4. For the present perfect, use *have* or *has* + the past participle.
   *I **have checked** my watch. Tina **has checked** her watch.*

5. For the past perfect, use *had* + the past participle.
   *I **had checked** my watch.*

6. For the future perfect, use *will have* + the past participle.
   *I **will have checked** my watch fifty times by sunset.*

Using Verb Tenses

The following guidelines will help you use verb tenses.

1 Use progressive verb forms to show continuing action.

Make the progressive by adding a form of the verb *to be* to the present participle.

Present possessive

*Kayley **is waiting** for you.*

Past progressive

*Kayley **was waiting** for you.*

Future perfect progressive

*By noon, Kayley **will have been waiting** for you for two hours.*

2 Change tense only when the time changes.

When you're talking about two events in the past, use the past perfect tense for the first event and the past tense for the second.

past perfect
↓
*Tina **had returned** by the time the rescuers arrived.*
↑
past

When you're talking about two events in the future, use the future perfect tense for the first event and the present tense for the second.

future perfect
↓
*Tina **will have returned** by the time the rescuers arrive.*
↑
present

Singular and Plural Verbs

Whether a verb is singular or plural depends on whether its subject is singular or plural. The subject is the noun or pronoun that performs the action. A singular noun takes a singular verb, and a plural noun takes a plural verb.

- **Present tense**

Singular
*The tree **looks** like an oak.*   Add -s to the verb.

Plural
*The trees **look** like oaks.*   Don't add -s to the verb.

- **Present perfect tense**

Singular
*The tree **has lost** its leaves.*   Use *has* with the verb.

Plural
*The trees **have lost** their leaves.*
Use *have* with the verb.

Verb Conjugation

A *verb conjugation* shows all the forms of a verb. Here are the conjugations of the regular verb *to wait*, and the irregular verb *to be*. These charts show verbs with pronoun subjects only. If you're using a noun subject, just substitute it for a third person singular or third person plural pronoun.

substitute "the girls" for "they":

they will wait, the girls will wait.

Conjugation of the Regular Verb *to Wait*

Tense	Person	Number	
		Singular	Plural
Present tense	first person	I wait	we wait
	second person	you wait	you wait
	third person	he, she, it waits	they wait
Past tense	first person	I waited	we waited
	second person	you waited	you waited
	third person	he, she, it waited	they waited
Future tense	first person	I will wait	we will wait
	second person	you will wait	you will wait
	third person	he, she, it will wait	they will wait
Present perfect tense	first person	I have waited	we have waited
	second person	you have waited	you have waited
	third person	he, she, it has waited	they have waited
Past perfect tense	first person	I had waited	we had waited
	second person	you had waited	you had waited
	third person	he, she, it had waited	they had waited
Future perfect tense	first person	I will have waited	we will have waited
	second person	you will have waited	you will have waited
	third person	he, she, it will have waited	they will have waited
	third person	he, she, it will have been	they will have been

Conjugation of the Regular Verb *to Be*

Tense	Person	Number	
		Singular	**Plural**
Present tense	first person	I am	we are
	second person	you are	you are
	third person	he, she, it is	they are
Past tense	first person	I was	we were
	second person	you were	you were
	third person	he, she, it was	they were
Future tense	first person	I will be	we will be
	second person	you will be	you will be
	third person	he, she, it will be	they will be
Present perfect tense	first person	I have been	we have been
	second person	you have been	you have been
	third person	he, she, it has been	they have been
Past perfect tense	first person	I had been	we had been
	second person	you had been	you had been
	third person	he, she, it had been	they had been
Future perfect tense	first person	I will have been	we will have been
	second person	you will have been	you will have been
	third person	he, she, it will have been	they will have been

Verb Know-how

There's a lot to know about how verbs work. The following reminders can make using verbs a little easier.

1 Remember to make a verb agree with its subject.

A singular subject requires a singular verb, just as a plural subject needs a plural verb.

Think about this, especially when you use the present and present perfect tenses. Tip: If a sentence has one or more helping verbs, it's the first helping verb that must agree with the subject.

Singular
A smart hiker **rests** *every hour.*
↑
Present

Plural
Smart hikers **rest** *every hour.*
↑
Present

Singular
*The smart hiker **has rested**.*
↑
Present perfect

Plural
*The smart hikers **have rested**.*
↑
Present perfect

2 Make a verb agree with its subject, not with a noun that comes between verb and subject.

Be sure the verb agrees with its subject, not just the nearest noun.

No
*The smell of the pine **trees are** wonderful.*

Yes
*The **smell** of the pine trees **is** wonderful.*

3 Make verbs agree with indefinite pronouns.

Some indefinite pronouns are always singular. Some are always plural. Some can be either singular or plural, depending on the words they refer to. **(For more on indefinite pronouns, see page 272.)**

Singular
***Everybody is** here at last.*

Plural
*Only a **few have** left.*

Either
***All** of the **water has** been poured.*
***All** of the **peanuts have** been eaten.*

4 Make a linking verb agree with its subject.

Don't let a noun that follows a linking verb confuse you. The verb always agrees with its subject, not with any other noun.

No
*Our only weapon **were cans** of bug spray.*

Yes
*Our only **weapon was** cans of bug spray.*

5 Remember, the subject doesn't always come first.

Some sentences are *inverted.* This means the subject comes *after* the verb, not before it. Find the subject and make the verb agree with it. **(See Word Order, page 332.)**

Verb + subject
*Where **does** that **trail** take us?*

Verb + subject
*There **are bats** in that cave.*

Verb + subject
*Here **comes one** of the hikers.*

6 Watch out for compound subjects.

A *compound subject* has two or more parts. When the parts are joined by *and,* the subject is plural and takes a plural verb.

Plural
*Tina **and** Leo **have** just made some sandwiches.*

When the parts are joined by *or,* the verb agrees with the last part.

Singular
*Tina **or** the other **hikers** have dropped a flashlight.*

Plural
*The other hikers **or** Tina **has** dropped a flashlight.*

When *each* or *every* is part of a compound, the subject is singular.

Singular
***Each** boy and girl **has** a backpack.*

Some compounds are used together so much that they're thought of as one thing. They even take singular verbs.

Singular

*Bread and butter **was** served for breakfast.*
*Rock-and-roll **is** my favourite music.*

7 Recognize collective nouns.

A collective noun names a group—*class, team, club.* **(See Nouns, page 267.)** It's considered singular when it refers to the group as a whole. However, it's considered plural when it refers to the members as individuals.

Singular

*The group **is arriving** at ten o'clock.*

Plural

*The group **are signing** their permission forms now.*

8 Look out for amounts.

Amounts, times, and measurements are singular when they're considered as a single unit. Otherwise they're considered plural.

Singular

*Ten dollars **is** too much for that.*
        ↑
     Single amount

Plural

*Ten dollars **were** lying on the floor.*
        ↑
   Individual coins

9 Use the active voice most of the time.

The active voice is just what the name says—active. It's stronger and more direct than the passive voice, which is often a more roundabout way of saying something.

Active

Kevin's dad made the first aid kits for the hikers.

Passive

The first aid kits for the hikers were made by Kevin's dad.

10 Know the difference between commonly confused verbs.

To lay means "to put or set something down." It is followed by a direct object. *To lie* means "to rest or recline." It is not followed by a direct object.

Lay

***Lay** the **flashlight** next to you.*
              ↑
        Direct object

Lie

***Lie** on the grass and rest awhile.*

To raise means "to lift up." It is usually followed by a direct object. *To rise* means "to move upward." It is not followed by a direct object.

Raise

*Please **raise** your **hand**.*
              ↑
        Direct object

Rise

*The sun will **rise** at 6:00 a.m.*

Let's Edit Verbs!

Keep a special eye on verbs when you edit. Here are some verb problems. Find out why they are problems and how to fix them. Keep what you learn in mind when you edit your own verbs.

Remember the difference between lie and lay.

DRAFT	*Kevin is **laying** on the grass outside the cave.*
WHAT'S WRONG?	*To lay* means "to put or set down." It's *to lie* that means "to rest or recline."
EDIT IT	*Kevin is **lying** on the grass outside the cave.*

Know which verb forms don't follow the regular rules.

DRAFT	*He sure hopes he hasn't **breaked** it.*
WHAT'S WRONG?	The forms of *to break* are irregular.
EDIT IT	*He sure hopes he hasn't **broken** it.*

Make verbs agree with indefinite pronouns.

DRAFT	*Now everybody else **are** off exploring the cave.*
WHAT'S WRONG?	*Everybody* is the subject and it's singular, but *are* is plural. Use *is*, the singular form.
EDIT IT	*Now everybody else **is** off exploring the cave.*

Use the plural for subjects with and.

DRAFT	*Leo and Ben **is** supposed to come back to keep him company.*
WHAT'S WRONG?	Subjects joined with *and* are plural, but *is* is singular. Use *are*, the plural form.
EDIT IT	*Leo and Ben **are** supposed to come back to keep him company.*

Use have, not of.

DRAFT	*And Tina should **of** gotten help by now.*
WHAT'S WRONG?	The main verb *gotten* needs the helping verb *have*. *Of* isn't a helping verb.
EDIT IT	*And Tina should **have** gotten help by now.*

Don't switch the tense unless there's a reason.

DRAFT	*Kevin **checked** his watch.*
WHAT'S WRONG?	*Checked* is past tense, but the rest of the paragraph is in the present tense. Use *checks*.
EDIT IT	*Kevin **checks** his watch.*

Adverbs

Adverbs describe and modify or change other words, just as adjectives do. Instead of describing *things*, however, they describe *actions* and *qualities*. Rather than modifying nouns and pronouns, adverbs qualify the meanings of verbs, adjectives, and other adverbs. How did the runner run? How deep was the snow? How well did the singer sing? Adverbs will tell you.

Types of Adverbs

Adverbs describe or modify verbs, adjectives, and other adverbs. The four types of adverbs answer different questions about the words they modify.

Adverbs of Manner

Adverbs of manner tell how an action was performed.

badly	carefully	easily
fast	innocently	loudly
quietly	well	

Adverbs of Place

Adverbs of place tell where an action took place.

anywhere	down	everywhere
far	here	nowhere
outside	up	

Adverbs of Time

Adverbs of time tell when or how often an action was done.

always	anytime	immediately
later	now	often
sometimes	yesterday	

Adverbs of Degree

Adverbs of degree tell to what extent—how much or how little—an action was performed.

almost	extremely	less
nearly	not	really
too	very	

Negative Adverbs

Negative adverbs counter the meaning of the words they modify. The word *not* and the contraction *-n't* that you attach to the ends of verbs are adverbs. There are other negative words that are adverbs, too.

not	-n't	nowhere
never	hardly	scarcely

Features of Adverbs

Learn what an adverb looks like, what it can modify, and where it goes in a sentence. Knowing these things will help you recognize an adverb when you see one—or want to use one.

Many Adverbs End in *-ly*

Many adverbs are formed by adding *-ly* to an adjective. Be careful, though. The *-ly* ending doesn't guarantee a word is an adverb. *Lovely* and *ugly*, for example, are adjectives.

Adjective		*-ly* Ending		Adverb
quiet	+	ly	=	quietly

sadly, happily, briefly, easily, truly

Adverbs Modify

When you use an adverb, you modify or change the meaning of a verb, an adjective, or another adverb.

Modify verb
*Good drivers turn that corner **slowly**.*

Modify adjective
***Really** good drivers turn that corner slowly.*

Modify adverb
*Good drivers turn that corner **very** slowly.*

Placement of Adverbs

Adverbs modifying verbs can usually be moved around in a sentence without changing the meaning.

Before verb
*The car **immediately** stopped.*

After verb
*The car stopped **immediately**.*

Adverbs that modify adjectives or other adverbs belong right in front of the words they modify.

Before adjective
*That's an **extremely** dangerous corner for bicycle riders.*

Before adverb
*The car turned the corner **really** quickly.*

Adverbs and Comparisons

Adverbs, like adjectives, have positive, comparative, and superlative forms that let you make comparisons. Which form you use depends on how many things you're comparing and how many syllables the adverb has. It also depends on whether the adverb is regular or irregular. (**See page 278 for more about regular and irregular comparisons.**)

Regular adverbs

Positive	Comparative	Superlative
One syllable		
fast	faster	fastest
Two syllables		
early	earlier	earliest
rapidly	more rapidly	most rapidly
Three syllables		
easily	more easily	most easily

Irregular adverbs

Positive	Comparative	Superlative
badly	worse	worst
far	farther	farthest
well	better	best

Watch out for these confusing adverb-adjective pairs.

Adverb	well	badly	really	surely
Adjective	good	bad	real	sure

Example:

Her test results were good.
(adjective linked to *results*)

She did well on her test.
(adverb modifying verb *did*)

Let's Edit Adverbs!

Find out why the following mistakes are problems and how to fix them. This will help you edit your own adverbs.

Know the difference between adjectives and adverbs.

DRAFT	*We feel **badly** about the bike accident at Judge's Corner...*
WHAT'S WRONG?	*Feel* is used as a linking verb. Use the adjective *bad*, not the adverb *badly*.
EDIT IT	*We feel **bad** about the bike accident at Judge's Corner...*

Use only one negative word for each negative idea.

DRAFT	*Everybody complains, but **nobody** does **nothing** about it.*
WHAT'S WRONG?	*Nobody* and *nothing* are both negative words. Only one is needed.
EDIT IT	*Everybody complains, but **nobody** does **anything** about it.*

Count the things being compared.

DRAFT	*Maybe the mayor could do things **fastest**.*
WHAT'S WRONG?	The mayor is compared with the school board. Use *-er*, not *-est*, when comparing two things.
EDIT IT	*Maybe the mayor could do things **faster**.*

Let's Practise

Rewrite the following sentences, using adverbs correctly.

1. Opening the door of the old house, I sensed that something felt wrongly.

2. Tracy felt well about her track time.

3. Jeanne thought that Harry didn't really know nothing about computers.

4. "Never tell nobody your innermost thoughts. They'll gossip," Lesley advised.

5. The boss said she needed the job done as good as possible.

6. The racing greyhound was running less quick than usual.

Prepositions

Prepositions show relationships between things. Consider the relationship between a cat and a mouse, for instance. The mouse might be *near* the cat, *behind* the cat, *in front of* the cat, or even *inside* the cat. All the italicized words in the preceding sentence are prepositions. They show different relationships.

Following is a student's draft in which some prepositions need editing. As you work through this section, think about how you would edit them. **For more on editing Natalie's draft, see page 94.**

"What's for Dinner?"

by Mitzy the Cat (as told to Natalie Padia)

Meow ... it's dinnertime again at the Padia house, but where is everybody (at?) Isn't anybody hungry (beside) me? Nobody's in the room, so I think I'll just hop on this chair and take a peek. Mmmm. Two platters of fried chicken! And what's in the bowl (among) the two platters? Chopped liver! My favourite!

Oops! Here's Mrs. Padia with another dish of food. I'd better jump off (of) this chair or she'll ... Thump! Oh, well, maybe I'll hang out under the table until somebody gets the hint and FEEDS ME!

No extra prepositions

Beside or besides?

Among or between?

No extra prepositions

Types of Prepositions

Prepositions show the relationship of a noun or a pronoun to some other word in the sentence. They also introduce phrases. **For more about phrases, see page 328.** Here are some common prepositions:

Single-word Prepositions

Single-word prepositions consist of one word.

about	above	across
against	among	around
at	before	behind
beneath	beside	besides
between	by	down
except	for	from
in	into	like
near	of	off
outside	through	to
under	up	with

Multiple-word Prepositions

Multiple-word prepositions are compound. They are made up of more than one word.

according to	along with
because of	in addition to
in front of	in regard to
in spite of	in view of
instead of	next to
on account of	

Using Prepositions

The following guidelines will help you use prepositions.

1 Identify the object of the preposition.

If you look at the first few words that follow a preposition, you'll always find a noun or a pronoun. This noun or pronoun is called the *object of the preposition.* The preposition's job is to relate its object to another word in the sentence.

Preposition
↓
*Rachel sat **near** her **friend**.*
↑
Object of the preposition

2 Know which preposition is which.

Use *between* when you talk about two things. Use *among* for three or more.

Two things
*Mitzy passed silently **between** two chairs.*

Three things
*We split the dishwashing **among** the three of us.*

Beside means "next to." *Besides* means "in addition to."
***Besides** Mr. Padia, who else sat **beside** Natalie?*

In means "inside." *Into* means "moving from the outside in."
*Mitzy crept **into** the kitchen once food was **in** there.*

Let's Edit Prepositions!

Here are the preposition errors from Natalie's draft. Find out why they are errors and how she can fix them. Use what you learn to edit your own prepositions.

Don't add prepositions that aren't needed.

DRAFT	*... where is everybody **at**?*
WHAT'S WRONG?	The preposition *at* doesn't make the sentence any clearer. It does, however, make the sentence wordier. Leave it out.
EDIT IT	*... where is everybody?*

DRAFT	*I'd better jump off **of** this chair...*
WHAT'S WRONG?	*Off* should be used by itself as a preposition. Delete *of*.
EDIT IT	*I'd better jump off this chair...*

Know which preposition is which.

DRAFT	*Isn't anybody hungry **beside** me?*	*Beside* or *besides*?
WHAT'S WRONG?	*Beside* means "next to," not "in addition to." Change *beside* to *besides*.	
EDIT IT	*Isn't anybody hungry **besides** me?*	

DRAFT	*And what's in the bowl **among** the two platters?*	*Among* or *between*?
WHAT'S WRONG?	With two things, use *between*. Change *among* to *between*.	
EDIT IT	*And what's in the bowl **between** the two platters?*	

Let's Practise

1. Rewrite the following sentences to take out unneeded prepositions.
   a) Blair needed to get up on top of the truck's cab.
   b) Tara thought she should try to carry the trunk down from out of the attic by herself.

2. Rewrite the following sentences using the correct preposition.
   a) Ahmed found the light bulbs in the cupboard besides the stairs.
   b) Jannah and Govinda divided the leftover cake among themselves.

Conjunctions

Conjunctions connect words and groups of words. They don't hook up just any old words and phrases, though. They join two or more parts of a sentence—words, phrases, or clauses—that work in the same way or in a closely related way. Following is a student's draft in which some conjunctions need editing. As you work through this section, think about how you would edit them. **For more on editing Keesha's draft, see page 94.**

A Book Report on Harriet's Daughter

by Keesha Mondesir

Harriet's Daughter by Marlene Nourbese Philip is a great book. I liked not only the story, but I also liked the characters. — Equal parts

Margaret is my favourite character. Margaret is strong. Margaret always does what she thinks is right. — Combine sentences

Margaret's father loves her, although he complains that she's rude. He often threatens to send her to the West Indies to learn discipline, manners, proper respect. — Connect a series

For fun Margaret thinks up the Underground Railroad game, which is based on the life of black leader Harriet Tubman. Neither Margaret or Harriet could be stopped — Two parts of a unit

from doing what she thought was right.

Types of Conjunctions

There are three different kinds of conjunctions, and each has a different job.

Co-ordinating Conjunctions

Co-ordinating conjunctions connect words or groups of words used in the same way. They can link a subject with another subject, a verb with another verb, or an independent clause with another independent clause. **Learn about verb agreement with co-ordinating conjunctions on page 288.**

*Margaret **and** Zulma were friends.*

and	but	for
or	so	yet

Subordinating Conjunctions

Subordinating conjunctions connect two clauses, making one dependent on the other. **For more about clauses, see page 330.**

*Zulma moved to Toronto **because** her mother lived there.*

after	although	as
because	before	if
since	than	unless
until	when	whenever
where	while	

Correlative Conjunctions

Correlative conjunctions work in pairs to connect words or groups of words used in the same way.

***Neither** Zulma's mother **nor** her stepfather understood her feelings.*

both—and	either—or
neither—nor	not only—but also

Using Conjunctions

The following three guidelines will help you use conjunctions.

1 Connect things in a series.

When three or more words or word groups go together, you can use a co-ordinating conjunction to link the last two.

No
Zulma got dressed, braided her hair, dashed out the door.

Yes
*Zulma got dressed, braided her hair, **and** dashed out the door.*

2 Join equal parts.

Co-ordinating and correlative conjunctions connect matching parts. Correlatives can be tricky because they have two parts themselves.

No
Margaret both respected and she admired Harriet Tubman.

Yes
*Margaret **both** respected **and** admired Harriet Tubman.*

3 Use conjunctions to combine sentences.

Look for sentences that belong together, and combine them with conjunctions. That way you show your reader just how your ideas are related. (**Find out how to punctuate conjunctions on page 337.**)

Two sentences
Margaret wanted to watch TV. Zulma wanted to go to the park.

Combined sentence
*Margaret wanted to watch TV, **but** Zulma wanted to go to the park.*

Let's Edit Conjunctions!

See how Keesha Mondesir improved the conjunctions in her book report draft. Use what you learn to edit your own conjunctions.

Make sure the joined parts match.

DRAFT *I liked not only the story, but I also liked the characters.*

WHAT'S WRONG? *Not only … but also* joins unequal parts. Change the second part of the sentence to a noun, to match the first part.

EDIT IT *I liked not only the **story but also the characters**.*

Combine sentences that belong together.

DRAFT *Margaret is my favourite character. Margaret is strong. Margaret always does what she thinks is right.*

WHAT'S WRONG? The connection between the sentences isn't clear, and repeating Margaret's name is awkward. Combine the ideas with conjunctions.

EDIT IT *Margaret is my favourite character **because** she is strong **and** always does what she thinks is right.*

Connect a series with a conjunction.

DRAFT *He often threatens to send her to the West Indies to learn discipline, manners, proper respect.*

WHAT'S WRONG? More than two joined items need a conjunction. Add *and*.

EDIT IT *He often threatens to send her to the West Indies to learn discipline, manners, **and** proper respect.*

Be sure the parts of the correlative conjunction go together.

DRAFT ***Neither** Margaret or Harriet could be stopped from doing what she thought was right.*

WHAT'S WRONG? *Neither* should be paired with *nor*, not *or*.

EDIT IT ***Neither** Margaret **nor** Harriet could be stopped from doing what she thought was right.*

Interjections

Interjections are exclamations or brief remarks. Often they appear at the beginning of sentences to get attention or to show strong feeling. An interjection can also make a statement all by itself. Everyday conversation is full of interjections.

Following is a student's draft in which some interjections need editing. As you work through this section, think about how you would edit them. **For more on editing Max's draft, see page 94.**

Ah ha	All right	Hey	Hurrah
Mmmm	Oh	Oh boy	O.K.
Oops	Ouch	Phew	Ugh
Well	Whew	Wow	

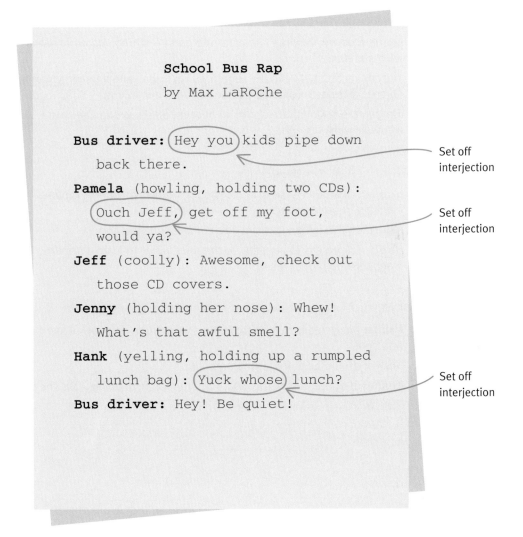

School Bus Rap

by Max LaRoche

Bus driver: (Hey you) kids pipe down back there. — Set off interjection

Pamela (howling, holding two CDs): (Ouch Jeff,) get off my foot, would ya? — Set off interjection

Jeff (coolly): Awesome, check out those CD covers.

Jenny (holding her nose): Whew! What's that awful smell?

Hank (yelling, holding up a rumpled lunch bag): (Yuck whose) lunch? — Set off interjection

Bus driver: Hey! Be quiet!

Interjection Info

Interjections usually appear at the beginning of the sentence. In that case, they are followed by either a comma or an exclamation mark. They may also stand alone—unattached to a sentence. Either way, interjections need to be accompanied by punctuation.

Using Interjections

Separate an interjection from the rest of the sentence. Use an **exclamation point** if the interjection is really strong. Capitalize the word that follows.

Capitalize
Ugh! I hate that song.
Great! We're getting a new driver!
Phew! That was a close call.

Use a **comma** if the interjection is not very strong. Don't capitalize the word that follows.

Don't Capitalize
Uh oh, here comes trouble.
O.K., that's enough for now.
Oh, he must be the new kid.

Let's Edit Interjections!

Here are some problems Max LaRoche had with interjections in his script draft. Find out how Max can fix his errors. Keep in mind what you can learn when you fix your own interjections.

Use punctuation to set off interjections.

DRAFT	**Hey you** *kids pipe down back there.*
WHAT'S WRONG?	Interjections should be set off from the sentence. Either add a comma after the interjection, or add an exclamation point and capitalize the next word.
EDIT IT	**Hey, you** *kids pipe down back there.*
	OR
	Hey! You *kids pipe down back there.*

DRAFT	**Ouch Jeff**, *get off my foot, would ya?*
EDIT IT	**Ouch! Jeff**, *get off my foot, would ya?*

DRAFT	**Yuck whose** *lunch?*
EDIT IT	**Yuck, whose** *lunch?*
	OR
	Yuck! Whose *lunch?*

Spelling

A few centuries ago, writers could spell words almost any way they liked. In those days, few people could read. There weren't many books available anyway. It was only after the printing press was invented—in the late 1400s—that large numbers of people learned how to read and write. Spelling became standardized when dictionaries were published.

Standardized spelling makes words instantly recognizable. If you want your words to look be easily understood, you have to spell them the standard way.

Knowing standardized spelling is more easily said than done, however. There are thousands of words in the English language, and many ways to spell many sounds. For example, here's one vowel sound that can be spelled ten different ways: b**oo**t, bl**ue**, r**u**by, thr**ew**, wh**o**, thr**ough**, s**ou**p, fr**ui**t, sh**oe**, ne**u**tral. No wonder people have such trouble spelling!

Sound and spelling don't always match in English. But if you look beyond the sound to language history and word meanings, you'll find English spellings make more sense. To become a better speller, what you need is some language know-how and a few smart strategies. This section on spelling is intended to help you develop them.

Following is a student's draft in which some words are incorrectly spelled. As you work through this section, think about how you would correct them. **For more on editing Susan's draft, see page 94.**

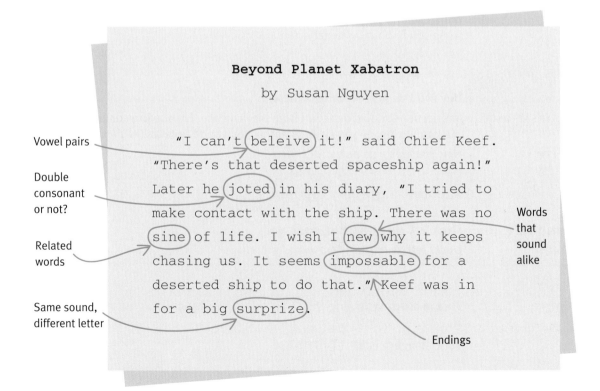

Vowel pairs

Double consonant or not?

Related words

Same sound, different letter

Beyond Planet Xabatron

by Susan Nguyen

"I can't beleive it!" said Chief Keef.
"There's that deserted spaceship again!"
Later he joted in his diary, "I tried to
make contact with the ship. There was no
sine of life. I wish I new why it keeps
chasing us. It seems impossable for a
deserted ship to do that." Keef was in
for a big surprize.

Words that sound alike

Endings

Language Know-how

You write words, not sounds. Think about the words—their parts, meanings, and history as well as their sounds—and you're more likely to spell them right.

Don't try to spell a word only by breaking it into individual sounds. This works to some extent, but not completely. Usually it's helpful to look also at the pattern of the word as a whole.

- A final *e* doesn't add an *e* sound. It changes the sound of the earlier vowel.

  No *e*
  bit   cut   not   rat

  Final *e*
  bite   cute   note   rate

- The letters *gh* have one sound at the beginning of a word and different sounds at the end.

  Beginning of word
  ghost

  End of word
  rou**gh**   throu**gh**   bou**gh**

Spelling Strategies

Combine your language know-how with some smart tips, and watch your spelling improve. Try the following six strategies.

1 Create a personal speller.

In your notebook or a separate booklet, keep a list of words that you tend to misspell. Circle the troublesome letters, and next to the word jot down any helpful hints. Study your list, and use it when you proofread.

February
Remember that first **r**!

misspell
You **miss** when you misspell.

2 Use the dictionary.

Give the dictionary a chance. It isn't always easy to find the word you need. Just the process of looking for it, however, can give you clues or help you remember how to spell it. **(See page 318 for more information about how to use the dictionary.)**

3 Use memory helpers.

A memory helper can be a rhyme, a phrase, a statement, or anything that helps you remember. In your personal speller, jot down the following memory helpers—and others you invent.

Rhyme
a fri**end** to the **end**
Use **i** before **e** except after **c**.

Phrase
a **pie**ce of *pie*

Statement
Station**e**ry is for letters.
A cell**ar** is d**ar**k.
Se**par**ate the word into **par**ts.

4 Pronounce right to spell right.

If you don't pronounce words carefully, you can end up adding letters that shouldn't be there. You may also leave out letters that should be there.

No
athaletic   suprise

Yes
athletic   surprise

Here's How to

Study Hard-to-Spell Words

1. Look at the word. Say it. Spell it out loud.
2. Shut your eyes and picture the word. Spell it out loud.
3. If you spelled the word correctly, try writing it in a sentence.
4. If you wrote the word correctly, good for you. Check it again tomorrow.

6 Have a proofreading plan.

Proofreading means looking at every letter of every word. Pay special attention to words that have the following features:

Double letters
mi**ss**pell, sto**pp**ed, ba**rr**el

Vowel pairs
bel**ie**ve, c**ei**ling

Letters that sound alike
cane, **k**ey; ca**s**e, ra**c**e

Words that sound alike
to, too, two; there, their, they're

Tricky endings
poss**i**ble, cap**a**ble

Silent letters
thum**b**, bus**i**ness, strai**gh**t

Spell Checkers: Pros and Cons

A spell checker in a word-processing program will highlight a misspelled word and let you use the built-in dictionary to correct it. Spell checkers are great at finding typing mistakes, but they won't find words that you *use* incorrectly.

Will find
thers instead of ***theirs***

Will not find
bear instead of ***bare*** or ***too*** instead of ***two***

Also be aware that not all spell checkers use Canadian spellings. If yours doesn't, the spell checker will unnecessarily suggest corrections (such as changing *humour* to *humor*). This can slow you down as you work.

Some word-processing programs include a spelling "on the fly" option. As you key in each word, the computer immediately identifies spelling errors. But don't rely on the spell checker alone. Dictionaries and your own good judgment are still important.

Roots, Prefixes, and Suffixes

Understanding spelling patterns can help you become a better speller. Many words are built from separate parts. As you spell and proofread them, you can follow these parts from beginning to end. The word *returnable*, for example, is made up of *re* + *turn* + *able*. The **root,** or base, of a word carries the main meaning. A **prefix** added at the beginning or a **suffix** added at the end can alter the meaning and form a new word. The following chart defines these three word parts and gives examples.

Root Words

A root, or base, is a word part to which prefixes and suffixes can be added to form new words, or derivatives.

Root	Meaning	Derivatives	Root	Meaning	Derivatives
-bio-	life	**bio**graphy **bio**logy micro**bio**logy	-phone-	sound; voice	micro**phone** **phono**graph tele**phone**
-lab-	to work	el**ab**orate **lab**our **lab**oratory **lab**orious	-port-	to carry	im**port** ex**port** **port**able trans**port**ation

Prefixes

A **prefix** consists of one or more syllables that can be added at the beginning of a word or word part to form a new word.

ad-	to; toward	**ad**join
anti-	opposed to	**anti**social
bi-	two	**bi**cycle
com-	together; with	**com**press
con-	together; with	**con**form
de-	opposite of	**de**forest
dis-	opposite of	**dis**agree
ex-	out of	**ex**port
im-	not; opposite of	**im**possible
in-	not; opposite of	**in**active
inter-	between	**inter**national
mis-	wrong	**mis**spell
post-	after	**post**date
pre-	before	**pre**school
re-	again	**re**read
sub-	under; below	**sub**marine
super-	over; more than	**super**human
trans-	across	**trans**mit
un-	not; opposite of	**un**load

Suffixes

A **suffix** consists of one or more syllables that can be added at the end of a word or word part to form a new word.

Adjective Suffixes

-able	capable of	port**able**
-ful	characterized by	beauti**ful**
-less	without	speech**less**
-ous	full of	envi**ous**

Noun Suffixes

-er, -or	one who does	paint**er**
-hood	condition or quality of	child**hood**
-ment	product of	enjoy**ment**
-ness	state of being	silli**ness**
-ship	quality or state of	friend**ship**
-tion	act of	construc**tion**
-ty	state of being	varie**ty**

Verb Suffixes

-ate	to make	alien**ate**
-en	to cause to be	fright**en**
-fy	to make	simpli**fy**
-ize	to cause to be	vapor**ize**

Adverb Suffix

-ly	in a certain way	proud**ly**

Attaching Prefixes

Prefixes don't change the spelling of words or roots to which they're added. Sometimes, though, the prefix itself changes to match the word.

No change
mis + lead = mislead
mis + spell = misspell

Prefix changes
in + logical = illogical
in + mature = immature

What other examples can you suggest? Watch for them in your reading. You could make a list to use as a reference when spelling such words.

Attaching Endings and Suffixes

Endings include **inflected endings,** which change the number, tense, or comparative form of a word. They also include **suffixes,** which change the meaning or part of speech of a word.

Inflected endings
-s, -es, -ed, -ing, -er

Suffixes
-ful, -ly, -ment, -ness, -y

In many cases, you just add the ending to the base word.

-s
play + s = play**s**

-ly
sincere + ly = sincere**ly**

-ed
happen + ed = happen**ed**

-ness
sudden + ness = sudden**ness**

-ing
repeat + ing = repeat**ing**

-y
rain + y = rain**y**

In other cases, however, you need to adjust the spelling. Following are some exceptions to the "just add the ending" rule.

1 Double *the consonant.*

If the word has one syllable, one vowel, and one final consonant, **double** the consonant before an ending that begins with a vowel. Don't double the consonant, however, when the word ends in *x*.

Double
grab+ing = gra**bb**ing
fit + est = fi**tt**est
shop + ed = sho**pp**ed
sun + y = su**nn**y

Don't double
wax + y = waxy
fix + ing = fixing

Suppose the final syllable is stressed and has one vowel and one final consonant. In that case, **double** the consonant before an ending beginning with a vowel. If the stress is not on the last syllable, do not double the final consonant. Exception: For words ending in a single vowel and the letter *l*, double the *l* before a suffix beginning with a vowel.

Double
begin + ing = begi**nn**ing
control + er = contro**ll**er
occur + ence = occu**rr**ence
permit + ed = permi**tt**ed

Don't double
benefit + ed = benefited
open + ing = opening

Exceptions
level + ing = leve**ll**ing
travel + er = trave**ll**er

2 **Drop the silent e.**

If the base word ends with a silent *e*, drop the *e* before adding any ending that begins with a vowel. The *e* is also dropped in certain words before endings that begin with a consonant.

Before a vowel
nerve + ous = nervous
value + able = valuable

Before some consonants
true + ly = truly
argue + ment = argument

3 **Keep the silent e.**

In words that end with *ce* or *ge*, the *e* stays before *-able* or *-ous*.

Before *-able*
change + able = chang**e**able
replace + able = replac**e**able

Before *-ous*
courage + ous = courag**e**ous

4 **Change y to i.**

If the base word ends with the consonant *y*, change the *y* to an *i* before endings except those that begin with *i*.

Change
try + ed = tried
pity + ful = pitiful
lazy + ly = lazily

Don't change
fly + ing = flying

Exceptions
shy + ness = shyness

5 **Drop the le at the end.**

If the base word ends in a consonant followed by *le*, drop the *le* before adding the *-ly* ending.

simple + ly = simply
gentle + ly = gently

6 **Watch out for these tricky endings.**

Is it *-able* or *-ible?* In general, add *-able* to words that can stand alone and *-ible* to word parts that cannot.

Can stand alone
drink + able = drinkable

Cannot stand alone
incred + ible = incredible

Is it *-ance* or *-ence?* You either have to memorize words with these endings or remember to check the dictionary.

-ance
assist**ance**
guid**ance**
perform**ance**

-ence
abs**ence**
differ**ence**
occurr**ence**

Is it *-cede, -ceed,* or *-sede?* These are a cinch to memorize:

Only one word ends in *-sede*.
super**sede**

Three words end in *-ceed*.
ex**ceed,** pro**ceed,** suc**ceed**

All others end in *-cede*.
con**cede,** pre**cede,** re**cede**

Some Words Vary in Spelling

Occasionally more than one spelling of a word is correct. Examples: Either *good-bye* or *good-by* is correct. Either *Halloween* or *Hallowe'en* is correct. Usually, one spelling is preferred. If in doubt, check a standard Canadian dictionary. The dictionary will give the preferred spelling first, like this: *centre* or *center*. In this case, *centre* is the preferred spelling.

In some ways, Canadian spelling is similar to British spelling (for example, *colour*, not *color*). In other ways, it is similar to American spelling (for example, *tire*, not *tyre*). When in doubt, consult an up-to-date Canadian dictionary. Following are seven word types to watch. Spellings given here are those generally preferred by Canadians.

1. **-*our* words** neighbour; labour; humour; valour; honour; favour; colour; odour
   Exceptions: humorous; glamorous

2. **double-consonant words** travelling, traveller; marvellous; worshipped; jewellery

3. **single-consonant words** fulfil, fulfilment; enrol, enrolment; extol

4. ***c* noun, *s* verb words** a licence, to license; a practice, to practise; a device, to devise

5. **-*ize* words** organize; recognize; serialize

6. **-*re* words** centre; metre; theatre; manoeuvre

7. **other words** *mould; cheque; defence; medieval; encyclopedia; plough; grey; catalogue*

Let's Practise

Identify the incorrectly spelled words in each sentence. Rewrite the sentence, substituting the correct spelling.

1. In the 1930s the annual arrival of the Eaton's Catalog was an important event in households across Canada.

2. Tessa knew when her Mom's rent check had bounced because the landlord would come to cheque up on them.

3. Mayor Singh considered it an honor to open the new community center.

4. The lawyer insisted that his client had acted in self-defense.

5. Kwosi decided to enroll in a computer course to improve his job prospects.

6. The odor from the meat packing plant offended the neighbors.

7. The government refused to licence another meat packing plant in that town.

Let's Edit Spelling!

Susan found and fixed these spelling errors when she proofread her draft. Watch for errors like these in your work, too.

Know the difference between ei and ie.

DRAFT	*"I can't **beleive** it!" said Chief Keef.*
WHAT'S WRONG?	The vowel letters *e* and *i* are reversed.
EDIT IT	*"I can't **believe** it!" said Chief Keef.*

Know when to double a final consonant.

DRAFT	*Later he **joted** in his diary...*
WHAT'S WRONG?	*Jot* is a one-syllable word ending in a consonant, so the final *t* should be doubled before *-ed*.
EDIT IT	*Later he **jotted** in his diary...*

Think about related words.

DRAFT	*There was no **sine** of life.*
WHAT'S WRONG?	The word that Susan intends, *sign*, has a silent *g*, which can be heard in the related word *signal*.
EDIT IT	*There was no **sign** of life.*

Know the difference between easily confused words.

DRAFT	*"I wish I **new** why it keeps chasing us."*
WHAT'S WRONG?	*New* means "not old." The word needed here is *knew*, the past tense of *know*.
EDIT IT	*"I wish I **knew** why it keeps chasing us."*

Watch out for tricky endings.

DRAFT	*"It seems **impossable** for a deserted ship to do that."*
WHAT'S WRONG?	The ending should be *-ible*, not *-able*.
EDIT IT	*"It seems **impossible** for a deserted ship to do that."*

Remember that different letters can sound alike.

DRAFT	*Keef was in for a big **surprize**.*
WHAT'S WRONG?	The sound *z* is spelled *s* here, not *z*.
EDIT IT	*Keef was in for a big **surprise**.*

Spelling Stumpers

Following are tricky spellings that stump many people.
Look at the words, study them, and learn them.
Try learning a few each week, until none of them will ever stump you again!

A
accept, except
accidentally
ache
address
advice, advise
affect, effect
allowed, aloud
all ready, already
all right
although
answer
appearance
argument
athlete
awful
awhile

B
balloon
beginning
believe
bibliography
biography
bough, bow
bought
brake, break
busy, business
buy, by, bye

C
calendar
careful
ceiling, sealing
cent, scent, sent
centre
cereal, serial

chews, choose
close, clothes
committee
cough
council, counsel
country

D
decide, decision
definitely
desert, dessert
doctor

E
early
embarrass
emigrate, immigrate
enough
environment
excellent
exercise
exhibit
explanation

F
favourite
February

G
government
grammar
guarantee
guess

H
half, have, of
hear, here
heard, herd
height
here, hear
hoarse, horse
hole, whole
hospital
hour, our

I
I'll, aisle, isle
immediately
impossible
incredible
interesting
it's, its

K
knew, new

L
loose, lose

M
machine
marry, merry
maybe
meant
minute

N
necessary
neither

O

occasionally
occur
o'clock
often
opportunity

P

parallel
passed, past
peace, piece
pleasant
pneumonia
possess
possible
practice, practise
principal, principle
privilege
probably
procedure

Q

quarter

R

raise, rays, raze
receive
recommend

remember
restaurant
rhythm
ridiculous
right, rite, write
root, route

S

sandwich
separate
several
similar
sincerely
souvenir
stationary, stationery
straight, strait
succeed
sugar
suppose
surprise
surrounded
syllable

T

terrible
their, there, they're
thorough
though

thought
threw, through
tomorrow
tonight
truly
Tuesday

U

usually

V

vacation
vacuum

W

waist, waste
wait, weight
way, weigh
weather, whether
Wednesday
weird
which, witch
who's, whose

Y

yore, your, you're

Let's Practise

Check 10 of the pairs of words in the above list. Prepare a mini-lesson to teach another student how to differentiate between these words. **See How to Teach a Mini-Lesson on page 222.**

Capitalization

What's the difference between *red cross* and *Red Cross*? Just some capital letters, you may say, but those capitals are important signals. They tell you the words name something specific. Without them, you wouldn't be able to tell the difference between a cross that happens to be red and the worldwide organization called the Red Cross.

Like most language rules, capitalization rules have a purpose. They make meanings clearer for the reader. Do your reader a favour. Use the following information to put capital letters in their proper places.

The Pronoun "I"

Capitalize the pronoun *I*.
I know where I'm going!

First Word in a Sentence

Capitalize the first word in a sentence. For most forms of poetry, capitalize the first word in a line. Also capitalize the first word in a direct quotation.

Sentence
Who wrote this limerick?

Poetry
There was an old man with a beard,
Who said, "**I**t is just as I feared!"

Quotation
William Van Horne said, "**A**ll I can say is that the work has been done well in every way."

You do **not** need to capitalize the continuation of a quotation unless it begins a new sentence.

Continuation
Every day," he replied, "**she** walks two kilometres."

New sentence
"That's true," Eva agreed. "**She** walks the dog."

Proper Nouns

1 Capitalize names and initials of people and animals.

Michael **J**. **F**ox
Laura **S**ecord
Snoopy
Jumbo

2 Capitalize titles used with names, including *titles that are abbreviated.*

Ms. **R**osa **Q**uintero
Mr. **I**ra **R**oss, **J**r.
Dr. **M**ohammed **W**asey
Rev. **J**uan **C**ereceda
Prime **M**inister **W**ilfrid **L**aurier
Premier **R**honda **M**c**A**rthur
Mayor **T**ammy **M**into
Col. **Q**uigley

3 Capitalize family titles when used as names or parts of names.

Where are you going, **M**om?
Here comes **U**ncle Ezra now.

You do **not** need to capitalize a family title if it comes after a possessive pronoun or article.

No
My Mom works in a bank.

Yes
My **mom** works in a bank.

4 Capitalize names of specific places.

Planets
Mars
Earth
Pluto

Heavenly bodies
Milky Way
North Star

Continents
Africa
South America
Europe

Countries
Jamaica
Belgium
El Salvador
Iran

Regions
the Maritimes
the Prairies
the Middle East

Canadian provinces
British Columbia
Alberta
Ontario
Nova Scotia

American states
New Mexico
Minnesota
Florida

Cities and towns
New Delhi
St. Louis
Vancouver
La Paz

Bodies of water
Pacific Ocean
Lake Winnipeg
Hudson Bay
Fraser River

Mountains
Mount Logan
Canadian Rockies

Deserts
Gobi Desert
Sahara Desert

Parks
Banff National Park
Wood Buffalo National Park

Forests
Sherwood Forest
Black Forest

Buildings and monuments
Peace Tower
Saddledome
Bellevue House

Highways and streets
Trans-Canada Highway
Route 1A
Jasper Avenue

You do **not** need to capitalize words such as *city, desert, park,* and *street* unless they are part of a name.

No
The City of Rome is ancient.

Yes
The **city** of Rome is ancient.

You do **not** need to capitalize directions unless they name specific regions.

No
Do you prefer living East or North of the city?

Yes
Do you prefer living **east** or **north** of the city?

Yes
I lived in the West before I moved to the North.

5 Capitalize names of ships, trains, planes, and spacecraft.

Bluenose
HMCS Haida
Orient **E**xpress
Concorde
Voyager

6 Capitalize languages, nationalities, and religions.

Languages
Cree
Hindi
French
Vietnamese
Arabic

Nationalities
a **S**paniard
an **I**sraeli
a **C**anadian

Religions
Roman **C**atholicism
Protestantism
Islam
Judaism
Hinduism
Buddhism

7 Capitalize names of specific groups and businesses.

Organizations
Math **C**lub
National **H**ockey **L**eague

Institutions
St. **P**aul's **G**eneral **H**ospital
Concord **H**igh **S**chool

Government bodies
Canadian **S**enate
British **P**arliament

Businesses
Ford **M**otor **C**ompany
Mc**C**ain's

8 Capitalize names of historical events, periods, and documents.

Events
World **W**ar II
Industrial **R**evolution

Periods
Middle **A**ges
Renaissance
Eighteenth **D**ynasty

Documents
Canadian **C**harter of **R**ights and **F**reedoms

9 Capitalize names of special events, days, months, and holidays.

Special events
Stanley **C**up
World **S**eries

Days
Monday
Saturday

Months
January
November

Holidays
Victoria **D**ay
New **Y**ear's **D**ay
Canada **D**ay

You do **not** need to capitalize the names of the seasons: spring, summer, winter, fall.

No
Uncle Jon visits Regina every **Summer**.

Yes
Uncle Jon visits Regina every **summer**.

10 Capitalize names of brands, awards, language courses, and numbered courses. You do not need to capitalize a noun that follows a brand name.

Brands
Bata shoes
Macintosh computers
Wheaties cereal

Awards
Grammy
Governor **G**eneral's **A**ward
Genie **A**ward

Courses
French
English
History 2
Woodworking 101

Proper Adjectives

Capitalize adjectives formed from proper nouns.

Proper noun
Italy
Shakespeare

Proper adjective
Italian bread
Shakespearean plays

Titles of Works

Capitalize the first word, last word, and all other important words in titles. You do *not* need to capitalize articles, conjunctions, or short prepositions unless they're the first or last words in a title. You may, however, capitalize these parts of speech if they contain five or more characters. Remember, when *copying* titles of works, you should capitalize the words as they appear in the titles.

(Titles like those that follow can be either underlined or *italicized*.) If you're writing by hand or typewriter, underlining is usually easier. If you're using a computer, italicizing is usually easier.)

Books
West to Cattle Country

Magazines
Maclean's
Owl

Newspapers
The Globe and Mail

Short stories
To Build a Fire

Films
Star Wars

Plays
That Scatterbrain Booky

TV programs
The National
Royal Canadian Air Farce
Due South

Musical works
the opera *Madame Butterfly*
the song *Early Morning Rain*

Works of art
the painting *The Habitant Farm*

Letters, Faxes, and E-mail

Capitalize the words in the greeting of a letter, fax, e-mail, or other correspondence.
Dear **M**s. **C**hang:
Dear **S**ir or **M**adam:
Dear **J**anet,
Dear **D**ad,

Capitalize only the first word in the closing.
Sincerely yours,
Yours truly,
Your friend,

Word Building

Origins of English

Words are your basic language tools. If you know where they come from, you're better able to work with them, play with them, and maybe even make up some of your own. In a language that is being used every day, words are always coming, going, and changing.

The history of a word is called its *etymology*. **For more on etymology, see the Dictionary section beginning on page 318.** Etymology can tell you something about the history of people who use a language. We know, for instance, that ancient Latin borrowed words from Greek. The Romans first introduced Latin (along with Greek borrowings) to Britain almost 2 000 years ago. Then Germanic tribes—Angles, Jutes, and Saxons—came to Britain and introduced a language now known as Old English. This early version of English contained familiar words such as *and, eat, go,* and *the.*

More Latin words, such as *candle,* were added to the English language as Christianity spread throughout the Roman Empire. Later, Viking settlers, who spoke Old Norse, and then Norman conquerors, who spoke French, added words.

English spread to North America with European explorers and kept on changing. A major reason for the continual change was that travel and immigration kept introducing new words from around the world.

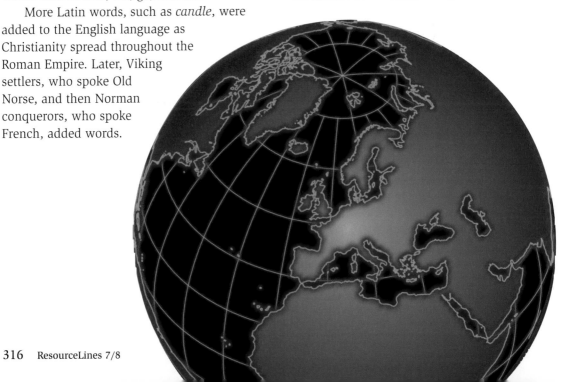

Borrowed Words

Africa
banana, banjo, cola, tote, yam

Arabia
algebra, checkmate, sherbet, zero

China
ketchup, mandarin, silk, tea, typhoon

France
art, beauty, beef, court, dessert, feast, gown, marry, music

India
bungalow, calico, jungle, orange, pyjamas

1. Popular culture and the media—videos, movies, TV, radio, advertising, music, plays, books, newspapers, and magazines. Example: If a popular media character says *hoser*, other people may start saying it, too. In time the term may become so common that it becomes part of standard English, and dictionaries list it.

2. A country's units of measure, symbols, coins, and so on. Examples: *Click* refers to more than using a computer mouse. It also refers to *speed*, as in *We were only doing forty clicks.* The Canadian dollar coin is called a *loonie* (or *loony*) because it has a loon picture on it. Based on that term, the Canadian two-dollar coin is a *toonie* (or *toony*). In time such words will (or have) become part of standard Canadian English.

3. Science and technology—research, new discoveries, exploration, inventions, computers. Examples: The plant variety *Canola*™ was developed by Canadian researchers. *Bombardier*™ is a snowmobile made for travelling on snow and ice which is named after its Canadian inventor, Armand Bombardier. Computer-related terms such as *input, on-line, joystick,* and *crash* are also new or have new meanings.

4. Travel, immigration, and other contacts with people from many cultures. Examples: A Vancouver teenager may say, *"Throw a chicken on the bar-bee"* because he heard it on a visit to Australia. A Calgary teenager may say, *"You have a lot of chutzpah"* because she read it in a novel by a Jewish writer. In time words such as *bar-bee* (meaning *barbecue*) and *chutzpah* (meaning *nerve*) will (or have) become part of standard English.

Borrowed Words

Italy
cello, concert, spaghetti, stanza, violin

The Netherlands
drill, sleigh, smuggle, pickle

North American Aboriginal Groups
moccasin, moose, muskrat, parka, pecan, skunk, squash, toboggan

Scandinavia
die, egg, freckle, get, skin, sky, window, wrong

Spain
alligator, breeze, plaza

English Is Still Changing

New words are still coming from many sources. New words, and new uses for old words, enter the language through influences that include the following.

Dictionary

A dictionary, as you probably know, is a reference tool that lists words in alphabetical order. It gives information about the meaning, pronunciation, and history of each word it lists. You can use a dictionary to learn more about words you already know, and to learn about words you have yet to discover.

Dictionary Features: Examples

bookstall   176   **boot²**

Guide words

[i]	m*ee*k, b*e*, pr*e*tty, mar*i*ne		[ʌu]	l*ou*t, h*ou*se
[ɪ]	*i*t, p*i*n		[ə]	*a*bove, penc*i*l, lem*o*n, circ*u*s
[ei]	*a*ge, f*a*ce		[ər]	wat*er*, adv*er*tise
[ɛ]	l*e*t, b*e*d		[ɜr]	t*er*m, l*ear*n
[æ]	h*a*t, c*a*b		[ɒ]	h*o*t, r*o*d
[ɑ]	c*ar*t, b*ar*n		[ɔ]	*or*der, d*oo*r
[aɪ]	f*i*ve, h*i*gh		[ɔɪ]	*oi*l, v*oi*ce
[aʊ]	l*ou*d, c*ow*		[ou]	c*oa*t, r*o*de, g*o*
[ʌ]	b*u*n, b*u*tter		[ʊ]	f*u*ll, p*u*t
[əi]	*i*ce, b*i*te		[u]	r*u*le, r*oo*t

Pronunciation key

Part-of-speech label

Entry word

Definition

boon¹ [bun] *n.* **1** a blessing; great benefit. **2** *Archaic.* something asked or granted as a favour. (ME < ON *bón* petition)

Example phrase

boon² [bun] *adj.* **1** jolly; merry: *a boon companion.* **2** *Poetic.* kindly; pleasant. (ME < OF *bon* good < L *bonus*)

Etymology

boon·docks ['bundɒks] *n.pl. Slang.* Rough backwoods; bush country. (< Tagalog *bundók* mountain)

Inflected forms

boon·dog·gle ['bun,dɒgəl] *v.* **-gled, -gling;** *n.* –*v. Informal.* do trivial, unnecessary, or pointless work. -*n.* **1** Informal. trivial, unnecessary, or pointless work or its product, often at public expense. **2** *Cdn.* a device used to take up the slack in a chin strap, such as a large wooden bead. (origin uncertain) – **'boon·dog·gler,** *n.*

Restrictive label

From *Gage Canadian Dictionary*, 1997

Dictionary Features: Explanations

Guide words. The guide words name the first and last entries on a page. Compare the word you're looking up with the guide words to see if you're on the right page.

Pronunciation key. The pronunciation key shows how to pronounce the sounds indicated. A short pronunciation key can sometimes be found at the bottom of each page. A full pronunciation key is often on the inside front and back covers of the dictionary.

Entry word. The entry word shows the spelling of the word. If the word is longer than one syllable, it is divided into syllables, as in *boondocks* or *boondoggle*. Dots are placed where the word may be hyphenated.

boon • docks

Part-of-speech label. The part-of-speech label shows how the word can be used in a sentence. The following labels are often used:

n. = noun
pron. = pronoun
adj. = adjective
v.i. = intransitive verb
v.t. = transitive verb
adv. = adverb
prep. = preposition
conj. = conjunction
interj. = interjection

For more on parts of speech, see pages 266–301.

Pronunciation Key. This feature shows how the word is pronounced. The letters and symbols indicate specific sounds. Look at the pronunciation key at the front of the dictionary to find out what sounds the letters and symbols represent.

Inflected forms. The inflected forms include the principal parts of verbs **(see page 283)**, the plurals of nouns **(see page 268)**, and the comparatives and superlatives of adjectives and adverbs **(see pages 278 and 292)**.

Definitions. The definitions, or meanings, of the word are grouped by part of speech. Definitions are numbered, showing the most common meaning first.

Example phrase. An example phrase or sentence shows how the word can be used in speech or writing.

Etymology. The etymology is the origin and historical development of the word. Following are some symbols and abbreviations you may find in etymologies. The arrow sign (<) means "from" or "taken from." F–French, Sp–Spanish, L–Latin, LL–Late Latin, OE–Old English, ME–Middle English, Gk–Greek, OF–Old French, ON–Old Norse, ult.–ultimately.

(ME < OF *bon* good < L *bonus*)

This means that *boon* is a Middle English word, which was taken from the Old French word *bon*, which means "good," which came from the Latin word *bonus*.

Restrictive label. A restrictive label identifies a word or particular meaning as being special or different from typical usage. It usually appears in italic type before the definition to which it applies. For example, the abbreviation ***Cdn.*** indicates that the meaning is Canadian in origin or usage.

Find a Word You Don't Know How to Spell

1. **Say the word to yourself, thinking about its beginning sounds.** Decide what the likely spellings are for those sounds. There may be more than one possibility. For example, the *far* sound could be spelled *far* as in *farmer*, or *phar* as in *pharmacist*. **See page 302 to learn more about spelling.**

2. **Open the dictionary to words beginning with the likely letters.** Run your finger down the entries. You may need to do this for several pages.

3. **Find the word.** Then check the pronunciation and meaning to make sure it's the word you want.

4. **Copy the word into your spelling list for future reference.**

Use a Computer to Check Spelling

1. Click Tools, then Spell Check, from the menu at the top of your screen. (Since software programs vary, you may have to do it slightly differently.)

2. Review all spelling corrections as the computer offers them. Computer spell checkers can be useful. Keep in mind, however, that they aren't completely flexible or correct. Sometimes, a word that is spelled correctly may appear as a misspelled word. For example, say you write freewrite. Your computer spell checker may not know this word. So it may show it as a misspelling when, of course, it is not.

3. Use your judgment and check new spellings. Technology alone is not enough! You may wish to check your new spellings with a dictionary or peer editor.

Thesaurus

A thesaurus is a reference tool that you can use to find new and livelier words that have meanings similar to those of the words you use all the time. A thesaurus can help you broaden your vocabulary and make your writing more interesting.

Thesauri come in different forms. Some thesauri list entries alphabetically, while others list them by category or key word. Still others, like the one below, use a format that lists categories of words alphabetically. Most thesauri contain indexes to help you quickly locate the word you want.

Thesaurus Features: Examples

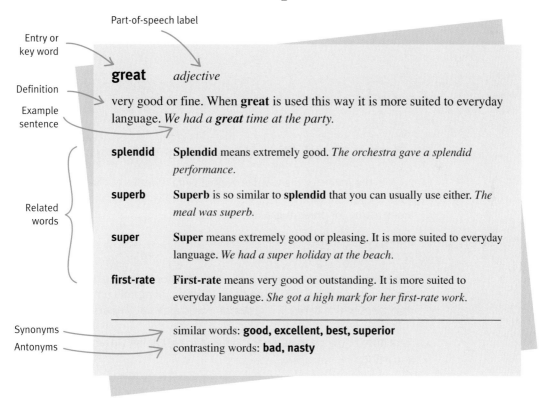

Part-of-speech label

Entry or key word

Definition

Example sentence

great   *adjective*

very good or fine. When **great** is used this way it is more suited to everyday language. *We had a **great** time at the party.*

Related words

splendid   **Splendid** means extremely good. *The orchestra gave a splendid performance.*

superb   **Superb** is so similar to **splendid** that you can usually use either. *The meal was superb.*

super   **Super** means extremely good or pleasing. It is more suited to everyday language. *We had a super holiday at the beach.*

first-rate   **First-rate** means very good or outstanding. It is more suited to everyday language. *She got a high mark for her first-rate work.*

Synonyms

Antonyms

similar words: **good, excellent, best, superior**
contrasting words: **bad, nasty**

From *Young Canada Thesaurus*, 1988

Thesaurus Features

1. **Entry or key word.** The entry or key word is the word you look for if you want to find other words that express the same idea.

2. **Part-of-speech label.** The part-of-speech label tells you how the word can be used in a sentence: as a noun, pronoun, adjective, verb, adverb, preposition, conjunction, or interjection.

3. **Definition.** The definition shows what the word means. It can help you choose a word that conveys precisely the meaning you want.

4. **Example sentence.** An example sentence shows how a word is used in speech or writing.

5. **Related words.** These are the synonyms or words that are related in meaning to the entry word.

6. **Synonyms.** Synonyms are words that mean the same or nearly the same as the entry word.

7. **Antonyms.** Antonyms are words that have a meaning opposite to the meaning of the entry word.

Here's How to

Find the Word You Want in a Thesaurus

1. Look in the index for the word you would like to replace. There are guide words to help you locate the word quickly. For example, the index listing for *great* might look like this:

great	*adjective*	182	
great	*adjective*	**important**	205

   The **bold** type tells you *great* is the key word for a group of words with the overall meaning *great*. The second listing, in normal type, indicates that *great* is also listed in a group of words meaning *important*.

2. Take note of the page number following the meaning closest to the one you want.

3. Go to that page in the body of the thesaurus and read through the entry for word suggestions.

4. Double-check the new word in the dictionary to make sure it really means what you think it does.

Here's How to

Use a Computer Thesaurus

Here's one way. Software varies, so you may need to do it slightly differently.

1. Click *Tools* at the top of your screen.

2. Click *Thesaurus* in the dropdown list.

3. You'll see a place to type. Type the word you'd like to replace; for example, *eat*. Then click *Look Up.* A list of synonyms and antonyms will appear; for example, *chew, devour, feast, dine.*

4. If you want more possibilities to consider, try double-clicking some of the synonyms and antonyms. In some cases, this will produce more synonyms and antonyms.

5. When you have finished using the computer thesaurus, click *Close* or *Replace. Replace* will insert the new or alternative word into your document.

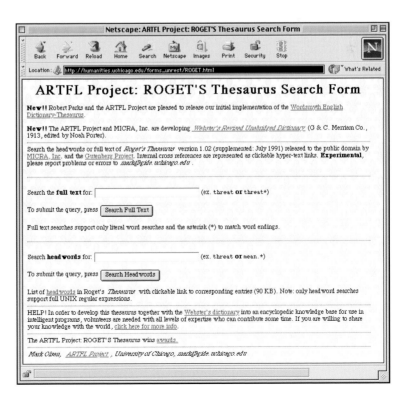

Constructing Sentences

A sentence is a group of words that expresses a complete thought. When you write, you signal sentences for readers by beginning each with a capital letter and ending each with closing punctuation, such as a period.

How are sentences made? You put them together, word by word. There are only a few basic patterns. However, by placing different words in different combinations, you can go on creating new sentences forever.

Following is a student's draft in which some sentences need editing. As you work through the sections on sentences, think about how you would edit Lara's sentences. **For more on editing her draft, see page 94.**

A Real Dragon

by Lara Haddad

You may think dragons don't exist, they do. ← Avoid run-ons

There is a real-life dragon. It lives on an island. The island is called Komodo. It is in Indonesia. The dragon of Komodo is a huge lizard The biggest lizard in the world, in fact. — Combine sentences / Avoid fragments

This is what the dragon looks like. It can grow to be three metres long and is covered with scales. It has a powerful body and a long, flat head with a mighty tail. A forked tongue shoots out of its mouth, which is lined with rows of sharp teeth. The only thing missing is that this dragon doesn't breathe fire. — Sentence types / Modifier placement

Types of Sentences

Sentences are grouped or classified according to their content. Statements of fact have a different form and meaning than questions. Questions have a different form and meaning from commands or exclamations. What do you want to say? The four different kinds of sentences—declarative, interrogative, imperative, and exclamatory—will help you say it.

Declarative sentences

Declarative sentences state facts or ideas and usually end with a period.

Apollo was a figure in ancient myths.

Interrogative sentences

Interrogative sentences ask questions. They end with a question mark.

Didn't he battle the dragon Python?

Imperative sentences

Imperative sentences make commands or requests. They usually end with a period but can also end with an exclamation point when the command is really strong.

Tell me more, please.

Please hurry!

Any declarative, interrogative, or imperative sentence spoken with strong emotion can be followed by an exclamation point.

Exclamatory sentences

Exclamatory sentences express strong feeling and end with an exclamation point.

What an amazing story that was!

I loved that story!

Let's Practise

1. Write a sentence of each type.

2. Exchange with a partner.

3. Identify the types of sentences written by your partner.

Sentence Structures

Sentences are also classified according to their structures.
Following are the four basic sentence structures.

Simple Sentences

Simple sentences are made up of one independent clause, which may have compound parts and added phrases. **See Independent Clauses, page 330.** Examples:

Apollo slew a dragon.

Apollo and Hercules, two figures in mythology, fought with dragons and won.

Complex Sentences

Complex sentences are made up of one independent clause and one or more subordinate clauses. **See Subordinate Clauses, page 330.** Examples:

Although some dragons had many heads, most had only one.

As you can see, artists who draw dragons can be very creative.

Compound Sentences

Compound sentences are made up of two or more independent clauses joined by a co-ordinating conjunction: *and, but, for, or, so, yet*. Example:

Some dragons had many heads, but most had only one.

Compound-Complex Sentences

Compound-complex sentences are made up of two or more independent clauses and one or more subordinate clauses. Example:

Some dragons guarded treasures, and anyone who slew the beast won the treasure.

Let's Practise

In your reading, find one example of each type of sentence structure.

Parts of the Sentence

Tripped over a dragon lying in its cave isn't a sentence, but *I tripped* is. A sentence doesn't have to have a lot of words. What does it have to have? Most sentences have two basic parts, a **subject** and a **predicate.** Each part can be expanded. Some sentences also have **objects** and **complements** that complete the meaning of the verb or the subject. Following are definitions and examples.

1 Subject

The subject names what the sentence is about. The **complete subject** is made up of all the words that tell what the sentence is about. It always contains the **simple subject**—a noun or pronoun that actually names the subject.

2 Predicate

The predicate tells about the subject. The **complete predicate** is made up of all the words that tell what the subject is or does. Its key part is always a verb, called the **simple predicate**.

An **object** is a word that completes the meaning of the verb. Without it, the sentence would be meaningless. Transitive verbs always require an object.

The noun or pronoun that receives the action of the verb is called the **direct object.** To find the direct object, locate the verb. Ask a question about the verb that ends with "whom or what."

The **indirect object** is a noun or pronoun that answers the questions "To whom or for whom?" or "To what or for what?" about the verb. The words *to* and *for* are often implied.

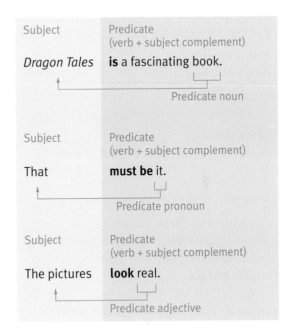

Objects are used with action verbs. **Subject complements** are used with linking verbs. A subject complement can be a noun, a pronoun, or an adjective. It comes after a linking verb and says something about the subject.

Adding to the Basic Sentence Parts

All a sentence usually needs is a subject and a predicate, as in *Dragons fly* or *Earl drew*. But such plain sentences can be boring. What's more important, they don't say much. Fortunately, sentence-making can be a lot more creative. You can take the basic sentence and keep adding parts—words, phrases, and clauses.

Phrases

A phrase is a group of words, but not just any group. A phrase acts as a single word and doesn't have a subject and verb. You can liven up a basic sentence by adding a phrase to it.

Basic sentence
Earl drew a dragon.

Phrase added
*Earl drew a dragon **with wings.***

Phrase added
*Earl drew a dragon **flying through the air.***

Prepositional Phrases

A prepositional phrase begins with a preposition and ends with a noun or pronoun. The noun or pronoun is called the **object of the preposition**.

A prepositional phrase is usually one or two words long, though it can be longer. If there are any words modifying the noun or pronoun, they're part of the phrase too.

Preposition
↓
*Earl drew a dragon **with wings**.*
↑
Object of preposition

Preposition
↓
*It was a dragon **with huge, batlike wings**.*
↑
Object of preposition

A preposition can have more than one object in a phrase.

*The dragon flew over **land** and **sea**.*

One sentence can have lots of prepositional phrases.

According to some legends,** dragons **with huge wings** would fly **over ships on the sea.

See page 295 for a list of commonly used prepositions.

Appositives and Appositive Phrases

An appositive is a noun or pronoun that goes next to another noun or pronoun to identify or explain it. If it has any modifying words, the appositive becomes an appositive phrase.

The appositive *Hercules* identifies the noun *hero*. No commas are necessary because it is an essential part of the sentence. The appositive Hercules is essential because it tells which of many heroes the sentence is about.
*The hero **Hercules** killed a dragon.*

In the example below, the appositive phrase *a hero of great strength* gives extra detail about the noun *Hercules*. Commas are necessary to set off the phrase from the rest of the sentence because the phrase is not essential information.
*Hercules, **a hero of great strength,** killed a dragon.*

Verbals and Verbal Phrases

A verbal is a verb form that's used as a noun, an adverb, or an adjective. Add a modifier or object to the verbal, and it becomes a verbal phrase.

Verb
*The dragon **was roaring** like thunder.*

Verbal
*The **roaring** dragon crashed out of its cave.*

Verbal phrase
***Roaring like thunder,** the dragon crashed out of its cave.*

Participles and Participial Phrases

A participle is an *-ing* or *-ed* verb form that is used as an adjective. **See verbs on page 281.**

It becomes a participial phrase when you add modifying words. A participial phrase, like a participle, can be used as an adjective to modify a noun or pronoun.

Present participle
*a **sleeping** dragon*

Past participle
*an **excited** dragon*

Participial phrase
*Is that dragon **sleeping in the sun?***

Participial phrase
***Excited by the noise,** the dragon swished its mighty tail.*

Gerunds and Gerund Phrases

A gerund is an *-ing* verb form that is used as a noun. It becomes a gerund phrase when you add modifying words.

Verb
*Some dragons **fly** easily.*

Gerund
***Flying** was easy for some dragons.*

Gerund phrase
***Breathing fire** was another dragon pastime.*
↑
Subject

Gerund phrase
*Dragons enjoyed **frightening people.***
↑
Direct object

Gerund phrase
*They did not excel at **being affectionate.***
↑
Indirect object

Gerund phrase
*They scared people by **breathing fire**.*
↑
Object of preposition

Gerund phrase
*A favourite hobby was **battling knights**.*
↑
Predicate noun

Gerund phrase
*Dragons loved one thing, **battling knights**.*
↑
Appositive

Infinitives and Infinitive Phrases

An infinitive is a verb form (*to* + basic form of verb) that is used as a noun, an adjective, or an adverb. Add words to an infinitive to make an infinitive phrase.

Verb
*Dragons usually liked **to roar**.*

Infinitive phrase
***To breathe fire** was easy for them.*
↑
Noun/Subject

Infinitive phrase
*Dragons liked **to destroy things**.*
↑
Noun/Direct object

Infinitive phrase
*Now is the time **to read about dragons**.*
↑
Adjective

Infinitive phrase
*Some dragons were able **to fly**.*
↑
Adverb

Clauses

A clause, like a phrase, is a group of words. Unlike a phrase, however, a clause has both a subject and a verb. Following are some definitions and examples of clauses.

Independent clauses can stand alone. They are complete thoughts, with a subject and a verb. Independent clauses can be sentences themselves, or can work with other clauses.

As a complete sentence
The dragon lashed its tail.

With a subordinate clause
The dragon lashed its tail because it was angry.

Two independent clauses
The dragon lashed its tail, and everyone trembled.

Subordinate clauses, also called **dependent clauses**, can't stand alone. They are incomplete and always need to be connected to an independent clause. Subordinate clauses begin with words such as *because* or *although*. These words connect the subordinate clause to the independent clause. There are three types of subordinate clauses: adjective, adverb, and noun.

An **adjective clause** is used as an adjective to modify a noun or pronoun in the independent clause. It usually begins with a relative pronoun. **See Types of Pronouns, page 272.**

*The dragon, **which was angry,** lashed its tail.*
↑
Modifies noun *dragon*

*There once were many people **who believed in dragons.***
↑
Modifies noun *people*

*A dragon **that is angry** may lash its tail.*
↑
Modifies noun *dragon*

An **adverb clause** is used as an adverb to modify a verb, adjective, or adverb in the independent clause. It begins with a subordinating conjunction. **See Types of Conjunctions, page 298.**

*Dragon stories were told **before people could write**.*
↑
Modifies verb *were told*

*People grew frightened **when they heard the tales**.*
↑
Modifies adjective *frightened*

*Made-up things can scare people more **than real things do**.*
↑
Modifies adverb *more*

A **noun clause** is used as a noun within an independent clause. It can act in the same way as a noun in a sentence.

***How legends begin** is an interesting topic.*
↑
Subject

*Did you know **that dragons never existed?***
↑
Direct object

*Give **whoever asks** the book about dragons.*
↑
Indirect object

*Information about dragons is **what they want**.*
↑
Predicate noun

Sentence Know-how

There's a lot to know about how sentences work. This section will help you tell the difference between a sentence fragment and a run-on sentence. It will help you distinguish between natural word order and inverted word order. You'll also learn about combining sentences, adding variety to them, and fixing modifiers that aren't quite right.

Sentence Fragments

You can't take a bunch of words, add a capital letter and a period, and say it's a sentence. A sentence has to express a complete thought. A sentence fragment expresses only part of a thought. Something's missing—perhaps a subject, a verb, or both.

No subject
Never saw a dragon.

Add subject
Ancient people *never saw a dragon.*

Run-on Sentences

While a sentence fragment expresses too little, a run-on tries to express too much. A run-on sentence consists of two or more complete thoughts written as one sentence. The thoughts are connected without showing where one ends and the other begins.

Sometimes two independent clauses—two complete thoughts—are run together with all the punctuation missing except the period at the end. Or, a comma is stuck in the middle even though it doesn't really belong there.

No punctuation
Our library is great we go there a lot.

Comma fault
Our library is great, we go there a lot.

Long run-on sentence
Earl drew a dragon, but the dragon was so big it didn't all fit on one page so Earl needed more paper, by the time he was done drawing he'd used six pieces of paper!

Here's How to

Fix a Run-on Sentence

There are a number of ways: Which one you use depends on the situation.

1. Separate the run-on into two sentences.
    Our library is great. **We** *go there a lot.*

2. Connect the sentences in a run-on with a comma and a co-ordinating conjunction.
    Our library is great, **and** *we go there a lot.*

3. Use a semicolon to connect the sentences in a run-on.
    Our library is great; we go there a lot.

4. Add a subordinating conjunction to make one of the clauses dependent on the other.
    Because *our library is great, we go there a lot.*

Word Order

The positions of the subject and the verb in a sentence determine the sentence's word order. There are two kinds of word order in English: natural and inverted.

Natural Word Order

Sentences that name their subject and then say something about it are in natural word order. Most statements follow this pattern. Even commands in which the subject is unstated are in natural word order.

Subject + verb—Statement
Indonesia is in Asia.
I've seen that book before.
The creature is very big.

Subject + verb—Command
(You) Watch out for that dragon!
(You) Lend me your book about dragons.

Inverted Word Order

Sometimes the complete predicate, or part of it, comes first. Then the word order is inverted, or turned around, so that the verb is followed by its subject. Most questions and most sentences that start with *here* or *there* follow this pattern. Following are examples of inverted word order:

Verb + subject—Question
Is Indonesia in Asia?
Have you ever seen this book?
How big is the creature?

Verb + subject—Statement
Here is a book of dragon myths.
There are many stories about dragons.

Here's How to

Find the Subject in an Inverted Sentence

Finding the subject in an inverted sentence can be tricky. Does it matter where the subject is? It certainly does. You have to find the subject so that you can make the verb agree with it. **(For more on verb agreement, see page 287.)** Follow these steps:

1. First find the verb or verb phrase.

   *Through the forest **raced** a Komodo dragon.*
   ***Is** the creature **coming** toward us?*
   *There **are** people on the island.*

   Don't be fooled by *here* or *there*. They are never the verb or subject.

2. Then ask *who* or *what* about the verb. The answer will be the subject of the sentence.

*What **raced** through the forest?*	a Komodo dragon
*What **is coming** toward us?*	the creature
*Who **are** on the island?*	people

3. Double-check your answer by putting the sentence in natural word order: subject + verb.

A **Komodo dragon raced** through the forest.
The **creature is coming** toward us.
People are on the island.

Combining Sentences

How do you get rid of short, choppy sentences? Combine separate sentences with related content into longer, smoother ones. There are lots of possible combinations. Let your ear help you choose one.

Choppy
Dragons had snake bodies. They had bat wings. They also had lion claws.

Smooth
*Dragons had snake bodies, **bat wings, and lion claws**.*

Sentence Variety

You can vary the rhythm of your sentences by moving certain parts around—as long as you're careful where you place them. You don't need to arrange every sentence the same way. Keep your reader involved and interested in your writing by using sentence variety. Following are two suggestions.

1 You can use a variety of sentence types.

Declarative sentence
Many people parade as dragons on the Chinese New Year.

Interrogative sentence
Did you know that many people parade as dragons on the Chinese New Year?

Imperative sentence
Let me tell you about the people who parade as dragons on the Chinese New Year.

Exclamatory sentence
What a tremendous sight it was to see people parading as dragons on the Chinese New Year!

2 Experiment with different kinds of phrases and clauses.

Prepositional phrase
On the Chinese New Year, many people parade as dragons.

Adverb clause
When the Chinese New Year comes, many people parade as dragons.

Using Phrases and Clauses

You already know how to use phrases and clauses. You use them all the time when you write and talk. There are a few tips you can follow, though, when you want to consciously use them to make your writing clearer. Use the following three guidelines:

1 Watch out for misplaced and dangling modifiers.

A modifying phrase should go with the word it modifies. Be sure to double-check the modifiers in your sentences so you don't say something that sounds strange or confusing.

Basic sentence
People wind through the streets,

Modifying phrase
wearing dragon costumes.

A modifier is called "misplaced" when it's put next to the wrong word in a sentence. Do the streets wear dragon costumes or do people? The phrase *wearing dragon costumes* is in the wrong place.

Corrected sentence
People wearing dragon costumes wind through the streets.

Basic sentence
The streets are crowded,

Modifying phrase
making lots of noise.

A modifier is called "dangling" when it doesn't have a word to modify in the sentence. The phrase *making lots of noise* is dangling because there's no noun for it to modify. Streets can't make noise; people can.

Corrected sentence
People making lots of noise crowd the streets.

2 Know the difference between who and whom.

You can use *who* if it is the subject of its own clause. You can use *whom* if it is the object in its own clause. Look at the clause by itself to find its subject, verb, and object.

No
I wonder whom wrote it.

Yes
*I wonder **who** wrote it.*
↑
Subject of clause

No
I wonder who I can ask.

Yes
*I wonder **whom** I can ask.*
↑
Object in clause

3 Know the difference between an essential clause and a non-essential clause.

Is the clause needed to identify the noun, or does it just add extra information? A clause that identifies a noun is considered **essential** to the sentence and isn't set off with commas. A clause that provides extra information is considered **non-essential** and does need to be set off with commas.

Essential
Dragons that breathe fire are common in ancient legends.

Non-essential
Dragons, which often breathe fire, are imaginary monsters.

Let's Edit Sentences!

Lara Haddad had some sentence problems in her draft report. Read about how she changed them. Use what you learn to revise your own sentences.

Don't let your sentences run on.

DRAFT   *You may think dragons don't exist, they do.*   Avoid run-ons.

WHAT'S WRONG?   Two complete thoughts, or independent clauses, need to be separated by more than just a comma. Add *but* after the comma.

EDIT IT   *You may think dragons don't exist,* **but** *they do.*

Combine sentences that can go together.

DRAFT   *There is a real-life dragon. It lives on an island. The island is called Komodo. It is in Indonesia.*   Combine sentences

WHAT'S WRONG?   Many short sentences in a row can sound choppy and child-like. Combine them by using a subordinate clause or a participial phrase.

EDIT IT   *There is a real-life dragon* **that lives on the island of Komodo in Indonesia.**
Subordinate clause

Write complete thoughts.

DRAFT   *The biggest lizard in the world, in fact.*   Avoid fragments

WHAT'S WRONG?   It's only a fragment; it has no subject or verb. Add *It is* as subject and verb.

EDIT IT   **It is** *the biggest lizard in the world, in fact.*

Use different kinds of sentences.

DRAFT   *This is what the dragon looks like.*   Sentence types

WHAT'S WRONG?   Declarative sentences are the sentences that we use the most. For variety, try sprinkling different kinds of sentences—interrogative, imperative, and exclamatory—throughout your writing.

EDIT IT   *What amazing features belong to the Komodo dragon!*

Watch for misplaced modifiers.

DRAFT   *It has a powerful body and a long, flat head with a mighty tail.*

WHAT'S WRONG?   It's not the head that has a mighty tail. Move the phrase next to the word *body*, which it modifies.

EDIT IT   *It has a powerful body* **with a mighty tail and a long, flat head.**

Punctuation

Punctuation marks are standard symbols used in writing. They help the reader by showing where sentences end and where pauses occur. Your writing will be clearer and more polished if you know what the marks of punctuation mean and how to use them.

Periods

1 A period signals that a statement, a mild command, an indirect question, or a polite request has ended.

Statement
Nadia is in grade eight this year.

Mild command
Remember to shut the door after you leave.

Indirect question
I asked if I could go to the library.

Polite request
Would you please send me your latest catalogue.

2 A period after initials and many abbreviations shows that letters have been left out.

Initials
T. S. Eliot
L. M. Montgomery

Abbreviations

Mr.	Ms.	R.N.	Prof.
Rd.	Ave.		
a.m.	Thurs.	Feb.	

3 Some abbreviations do not require periods. Examples:

CBC   (**C**anadian **B**roadcasting **C**orporation)
RCMP (**R**oyal **C**anadian **M**ounted **P**olice)
km   (**ki**lo**me**tres)
g   (**g**rams)

4 Acronyms—words formed from the initial letters of a series of words—are usually written without periods.

radar   (stands for **ra**dio **d**etecting **a**nd **r**anging)
UNICEF (stands for **U**nited **N**ations **I**nternational **C**hildren's **E**mergency **F**und)
scuba   (stands for **s**elf-**c**ontained **u**nderwater **b**reathing **a**pparatus)

Question Marks

A question mark signals the completion of a direct question, an incomplete question, or a statement intended as a question.

Question
Where did Kim Wan-soo get her cats?

Incomplete questions
When? How many? What kind?

Intended question
Kim has four cats?

Exclamation Points

An exclamation point shows that an exclamatory statement, a strong command, or an interjection expressing strong emotion has ended.

Exclamatory statement
What a wonderful surprise!

Strong command
Get out of that street!

Interjections
Hey! Phew! Unbelievable! Wow!

Sometimes an interjection can appear before a short exclamatory sentence or a question. You can use either a comma or an exclamation point after the interjection.

With comma
Phew, whose socks are these?

With exclamation point
Phew! Whose socks are these?

Commas

1 Commas separate items in a series.

A series consists of three or more items of the same kind: words, phrases, clauses, or numbers.

Words
My morning classes are art, English, and science.

Phrases
Run over the bridge, around the tree, and up the hill.

Clauses
I saw a green T-shirt, I liked it, and I bought it.

Numbers
The answers in order are 3, 119, and 647.

2 Commas separate adjectives that come before a noun.

Try saying the word *and* between the adjectives. If *and* makes sense, then the words should be separated by a comma.
We live in a small, cosy house.

3 A comma separates clauses in a compound sentence. Put a comma before the joining word, or conjunction.

*I received ice skates three years ago, **and** they still fit.*

A comma isn't necessary if two verbs share one subject.

No
I own ice skates, and use them almost daily.

Yes
I own ice skates and use them almost daily.

4 A comma sets off a phrase or clause that introduces a sentence.

Phrase
***Instead of a steering wheel**, the first car had a stick.*

Clause
***Although it is over a hundred years old**, the car still runs.*

5 A comma sets off an interrupter.

An interrupter is a word or phrase that breaks into the main thought of a sentence. It supplies extra information and can be put almost anywhere in the sentence.
*The Vikings, **incidentally**, came ashore to dry their fish.*
***Incidentally**, the Vikings came ashore to dry their fish.*
*The Vikings came ashore, **incidentally**, to dry their fish.*

Common Interrupters

after all	by the way
for example	furthermore

however	in fact
in my opinion	incidentally
nevertheless	of course
on the other hand	therefore

6 A comma sets off the speaker from a quotation.

The comma falls inside the quotation marks when it comes at the end of the quotation.

Sara said, "I can't type."
"I'll type it for you," Eva replied.

7 Commas can set off words, phrases, and clauses not essential to the basic idea of the sentence.

A word, phrase, or clause is non-essential—not necessary—if it adds information that can be left out without changing the main idea of the sentence.

Main sentence
Canada's coastline is one of the world's longest.

Added information
*Canada's coastline, **which stretches for more than 243 797 kilometres,** is one of the world's longest.*

You do **not** use commas around words, phrases, and clauses that **are** essential to the basic idea of the sentence. A word, phrase, or clause is necessary if it clarifies or identifies a noun.

Noun unidentified
My sister plays on the hockey team.

Noun identified
*My sister **Miranda** plays on the hockey team.*

("Miranda" is essential to the sentence since it identifies which sister is being referred to.)

If the speaker has only one sister, set off the name with commas. It is additional information, but not essential to know.

*My sister, **Miranda,** plays on the hockey team.*

8 Use commas to set off dates, places, addresses, and titles.

Dates
On Friday, March 3, 2000, Ms. Lee bought a boat.

Places
Jane was born in Vancouver, British Columbia.

Addresses
We live at 12 Gary Road West, Saskatoon, Saskatchewan.

Titles
My father's name is Alan Oates, Esquire.

You do **not** need a comma between month and year.

No
We drove to Thunder Bay in January, 1993.

Yes
We drove to Thunder Bay in January 1993.

You do **not** need a comma before a postal code. Just leave two spaces.

No
Coquitlam, BC, V3K 3H8

Yes
Coquitlam, BC V3K 3H8

Semicolons

A semicolon joins independent clauses in a compound sentence when the words *and*, *but*, or *or* are not used.

New Brunswick joined Confederation in 1867; Newfoundland didn't join Confederation until 1949.

1 Semicolons are used in a series to separate items that already contain commas.

On our last vacation, we stopped at Nelson, British Columbia; Banff, Alberta; Regina, Saskatchewan; and Winnipeg, Manitoba.

2 Use a semicolon between independent clauses connected by transition words.

Our vacation was terrific; however, I was glad to get home after being on the road for two weeks.

Transition Words

consequently	furthermore	however
instead	moreover	nevertheless
otherwise	therefore	thus

Colons

1 A colon can introduce a list, especially after words such as *the following* or *these*.

My favourite fish include the following: sockeye salmon, halibut, and red snapper.
***These** are my favourite fish: sockeye salmon, halibut, and red snapper.*

2 A colon can introduce a long or formal quotation.

As Shakespeare said in As You Like It: *"All the world's a stage, /And all the men and women merely players."*

3 You can use a colon after the introductory salutation in a formal letter.

Dear Ms. Feld: Dear Sir or Madam:

4 You can use a colon between numbers to indicate hours and minutes.

7:18 p.m.   12:01 a.m.

Parentheses

You can use parentheses to set off added information.

Punctuation that belongs to the parenthetical material goes **inside** the parentheses. Punctuation that belongs to the whole sentence goes **outside** the parentheses.

Inside
Jared drove us to the store (Uncle Pete had said, "I can't drive,") and then took us home.

Outside
Coast-to-coast service was provided in 1886 by the Canadian Pacific Railway (later called CP Rail).

Hyphens

1 A hyphen is a short horizontal mark used in some compound nouns and with certain prefixes and suffixes.

sister-in-law	ex-mayor
self-control	all-star

Most compound nouns, however, are **not** connected by hyphens.
recording studio, governor general.

Check your dictionary to be sure.

2 A hyphen connects compound adjectives that precede nouns.

You do **not** need to use hyphens in most compound adjectives that follow nouns. Also you do **not** need to use hyphens with adverbs ending in -ly.

Hyphen
It is a **25-year-old** house.

No hyphen
The house is 25 years old.

No hyphen
It's a carefully constructed house.

3 You use hyphens when spelling out numbers from twenty-one through ninety-nine.

twenty-three   eighty-seven   ninety-two

4 You can use a hyphen to break a word at the end of a line.

Be sure to break a work at one of its natural syllable breaks.

No
pun-ctu-ate

Yes
punc-tu-ate

Hint: Use your dictionary to double-check where a word should be hyphenated.

Dashes

A dash (—) is a horizontal mark twice as long as a hyphen (-).

It is used to set off words that break into the main idea.

Large numbers of immigrants from Great Britain—England, Ireland, Scotland, and Wales—came to Canada after the War of 1812.

Apostrophes

1 You can use an apostrophe and s to form possessive nouns.

See page 270 for more about possessive nouns.

Keiko's first date, Mr. Jones's book

2 You can use an apostrophe and s to form the plural of a letter, a number, a symbol, or a word.

several A's   some 9's
no #'s   too many the's

3 An apostrophe stands for the missing letters in a contraction.

don't = do n**ot**
he'll = he **wi**ll
it's = it **is**

Underlining and Italics

1 Underline or italicize the titles of long works.

Use underlining if you're writing by hand or using a typewriter. Use italics if you're using a computer or word processor. Long works include books, plays, long poems, newspapers, magazines, films, radio and TV series, operas, tapes and CDs, and the names of ships, spacecraft, and trains.

Book
<u>Invitation to the Game</u> or *Invitation to the Game*

Magazine
<u>Canadian Geographic</u> magazine or *Canadian Geographic* magazine

Film
<u>The Loon's Necklace</u> or *The Loon's Necklace*

TV series
<u>This Hour Has 22 Minutes</u> or *This Hour Has 22 Minutes*

CD
<u>Arctic Rose</u> or *Arctic Rose*
<u>On a Day Like Today</u> or *On a Day Like Today*

Ship
<u>HMCS Fredericton</u> or *HMCS Fredericton*

Find out how to capitalize titles on page 315.

2 Underline or italicize letters used as letters, words used as words, and words from languages other than English.

Letters as letters
Is that a <u>T</u> or an <u>F</u>? Is that a *T* or an *F*?

Words as words
Your report overuses <u>therefore.</u> Your report overuses *therefore.*

Non-English words
<u>Dix</u> means "ten" in French. *Dix* means "ten" in French.

Quotation Marks

1 Quotation marks can set off a person's exact words.

Quotation marks indicate where a speaker's exact words begin and end.

Meera said, "Pollution is ruining our planet."

You do **not** need to set off words that aren't the speaker's exact words.

No
Roy said that "Electricity changed life for the better."

Yes
Roy said that electricity changed life for the better.

2 A quotation within another quotation requires single quotation marks.

Frank asked, "Who wrote, 'Life is a fragile dewdrop'?"

3 Quotation marks enclose titles of short works.

A work is generally considered short when it is part of a longer work such as a book, an audiotape, or a television series. Short works include short stories, articles, poems, songs, and radio or TV episodes.

Short story
"The Hockey Sweater"

Magazine article
"Today's Hottest T-shirts"

Poem
"The Song My Paddle Sings"

Song
"O Canada"

4 Quotation marks can distinguish words within sentences.

I always have to check the spelling of "pneumonia" in the dictionary.

Punctuate with Quotation Marks

1. Always put commas inside quotation marks.

   "Cars are a mixed blessing," said Moira.

2. When a quotation mark ends a sentence, the period falls inside the quotation marks.

   Moira said, "Cars are a mixed blessing."

3. Exclamation points and question marks fall inside only if they are part of the quotation.

   Zhura asked, "Is that what you think?"

   Did Moira say, "Cars are a mixed blessing"?

4. Colons and semicolons go outside the quotation marks unless they are part of the quotation.

   Zhura said, "I agree"; however, he changed his mind later.

5. Remember to begin a new paragraph for each new speaker's words.

   "I believe," said Moira, "that cars are a mixed blessing."

   "I disagree," replied Zhura.

   "What?" Moira asked sharply. "Look at what they've done to the environment."

Ellipsis

Ellipsis points are used to indicate that a word or words have been left out. For example, in a quotation, you may wish to leave out words that are unnecessary or irrelevant to your writing purpose. You use ellipsis points to show where you've left out words. Ellipsis points look like periods. The following guidelines will help you use ellipsis points correctly.

1. Use three ellipsis points where part of a sentence has been left out.

   "Life ... bowl ... cherries."

2. Use four ellipsis points where the end of a sentence is missing (three ellipsis points plus the period).

   "The grass is always greener ...."

3. Use four ellipsis points when leaving out a sentence or more.

   "Peter Piper picked .... Where's the peck of pickled peppers Peter Piper picked?"

4. If what you are writing would normally have punctuation on either side of the ellipsis points, you may omit this punctuation unless it is necessary to make the meaning clear.

   One, two, three ... ten.

Glossary

A

acronym A word made from the first letters of a series of words, as in *radar* (radio detecting and ranging) or *UNICEF* (United Nations International Children's Emergency Fund).

action verb A word that expresses physical or mental action.

ad lib To speak or perform on the spur of the moment, without preparation.

adjective A word that describes or modifies a noun or pronoun.

adverb A word that describes or modifies a verb, adjective, or other adverb.

agreement When words match each other in number, person, and case.

alliteration The repetition of sounds at the beginning of words, as in *wind whispering in the weeds*.

almanac A book that contains lists, charts, and tables of information on many topics.

anecdote A short retelling of a funny or interesting incident.

animation The technique of filming a series of pictures so quickly that the images seem to move.

article Any of the adjectives *a, an,* or *the,* used to introduce a noun.

autobiography A true story written by a person about his or her own life.

B

ballad A poem or song that tells a story and follows a traditional form.

bias An opinion that affects your understanding of certain events or people.

bibliography An alphabetical list of books, articles, and other sources used in a report, placed at the end of that report.

biography A true story written by an author about the life of another person.

blackout To darken a film or video scene to black.

body The middle of an essay, article, or letter, in which you explain the points you want to make.

brainstorm To search for ideas by writing down every word that comes to your mind.

C

call number A number used by a library to classify a nonfiction book and to organize books on the shelves.

camera angle The position from which a camera takes pictures: from above, at eye level, from below, and so forth.

case The grammatical feature of nouns and pronouns showing how they are used in a sentence.

catalogue A library's listing of the subject, author, and title for each book in the library.

CD-ROM An acronym for *compact disk read-only memory*; a disk that holds information that a computer can read but cannot usually change.

characterization A writer's description of a character.

characters The people whose actions create a story.

choral reading A group reading a poem aloud in unison.

classification The grouping of items into categories.

clause A group of words containing a subject and a verb and forming part of a compound or complex sentence.

climax The dramatic turning point in a story.

clustering Searching for ideas or organizing a topic by writing down a word and surrounding it with related words. Each related word is then surrounded with words related to it—forming a cluster.

coherence A clear, logical flow in writing, with smooth transitions from sentence to sentence and paragraph to paragraph.

collage An arrangement of materials and objects attached to a surface.

complex sentence A sentence made up of one independent clause and one or more subordinate clauses.

compound sentence A sentence made up of two or more independent clauses joined by a co-ordinating conjunction.

compound-complex sentence A sentence made up of two or more independent clauses and one or more subordinate clauses.

conclusion The end of an essay or article, in which you summarize your ideas and leave your readers with something to think about.

conferencing Discussing a draft with other people and looking for ways to improve it.

conflict The problem in a story that the characters have to work out, making up the main part of the story's plot.

conjunction A word used to connect words or groups of words in a sentence.

connotation The attitudes, feelings, and opinions suggested by a word, apart from its dictionary definition.

contraction The shortened form of two words, which uses an apostrophe to replace the letters that were left out.

copyright date The date following the © symbol on a written work, usually showing when the writer completed the work and became the legal owner of it.

critical response Your reaction to the quality and effectiveness of something you see, hear, or read.

critique A review or commentary which reflects on the strengths and weaknesses of an artistic work.

D

database A large amount of information organized logically and stored electronically, which you can open, search, and read, using a computer.

debate Presentation of opposite sides of an issue by two people or teams before an audience or judge.

descriptive essay A piece of writing in which you use your senses, memory, and imagination to bring an experience to life.

Dewey decimal system A system of organizing library books into ten major categories and many subcategories, developed by Melvil Dewey (1851–1931).

dialogue A quoted conversation between two or more people.

dialogue journal A journal for written conversations with friends about opinions, thoughts, and feelings.

documentary A television show or film that presents and analyses events, the natural world, people, or issues in a factual way.

draft The stage of the writing process in which you turn ideas and plans into sentences and paragraphs.

E

edit A part of the writing process in which you check for wording, punctuation, or organization that is incorrect or confusing. *Or*, to arrange film or video shots and scenes, during or after shooting, in order to create a desired effect.

editor Someone who helps you revise your draft by reading it and looking for errors and unclear writing.

either/or fallacy A claim that there are only two options when there are actually more.

essay A written paper on a single topic that includes an introduction, body, and conclusion.

evidence Facts used in a debate or in persuasive writing to support an argument.

F

faulty cause and effect A claim that one event is caused by another event without having proof.

feature article An essay that informs and entertains readers, usually published in newspapers and magazines.

figurative language Writing that contains words or phrases, called figures of speech, that are not literally true but make you see something in a new way.

flash-back The insertion of an earlier event into the time order of a story.

font The size and style of a typeface. See *typeface*.

foreshadowing Creating suspense by hinting at things to come.

form In art, a three-dimensional shape; in literature, a type of written work, such as a poem, novel, or essay.

format A plan for organizing words and/or images on a page.

frame One photograph on a reel of film.

free verse A poetic form that does not have a set pattern of rhyme or metre.

freewrite To search for or explore ideas by setting your mind free and writing about topics as they come to mind, without worrying about correctness.

G

gender The grammatical division of nouns and pronouns into masculine, feminine, and neuter.

gender-inclusive Use of language that includes both genders, such as terms like *firefighter* and *chairperson*, and phrases like *Every student should bring his or her coat.*

genre A category of literature, such as mystery, romance, or science fiction.

H

haiku An unrhymed, seventeen-syllable poem of Japanese origin, arranged in three lines, often describing a single sound or sight and showing a mood or impression inspired by nature.

hypertext Highlighted words in any electronic document (such as a web site) that lead you to related information when you click on them.

I

illustration Drawings or photographs that accompany and add to a piece of writing.

imagery Vivid descriptions, figures of speech, or objects used to create mental pictures or to appeal to the senses and emotions.

improvise To do something without having prepared or planned ahead.

independent clause A group of words that can stand alone as a simple sentence.

index An alphabetical listing of names, places, and subjects, with their page numbers, at the end of a book.

inference Conclusions based on your own interpretation or understanding of a story.

infinitive A verb form (*to* + basic form of verb) used as a noun, adjective, or adverb, such as *to give*.

interjection A word used to get attention or express strong feeling; can be treated as an entire sentence.

interview To talk with someone in order to learn something from him or her, while taking notes or recording the conversation so you can refer back to it.

introduction The beginning of an essay or article, where you first present the main idea and interest your readers.

J

jigsaw A discussion among three to five people, who share with each other what they have learned separately.

journal A place for writing your opinions, thoughts, and feelings.

juxtaposition Placing side by side to create a particular effect.

K

keyword The word or phrase you enter when you are conducting a computerized search for a particular subject.

KWL plan An acronym which stands for a reading strategy in which you consider what you Know about a topic, what you Want to know, and what you Learned about a topic.

L

lead The opening sentence or sentences you write to grab a reader's attention.

legend A traditional story about a heroic person or event.

literary circle A discussion among three to eight people with the goal of critically responding to literature.

literary device A tool, such as alliteration or imagery, used in narratives or poetry to appeal to the senses and emotions.

logic Reasoning that makes sense.

logical order Organizing information and details in a written work in a way that makes sense.

looping Looking for an angle on a topic by freewriting on index cards, choosing the most interesting phrases, and then freewriting about those phrases.

M

media Means of expression or types of communication, such as visual art, print material, music, television, radio, etc.

metaphor A figure of speech that speaks of one thing as if it were another thing in order to show a connection between the two, as in *The wind is a dancer*.

metre The pattern of stressed and unstressed syllables in a poem.

microfiche, microfilm Film used in libraries, containing miniature photographs of printed information, which can be read with a special viewing machine.

monologue A speech by one person.

multimedia Using several media in one production or work.

myth A traditional story that explains natural happenings (such as the sun disappearing at night) or tells of heroes or superhuman beings.

N

narrative A fiction or nonfiction story that has a beginning, a middle, and an end.

narrator Someone who tells a story.

notes A numbered list of references or extra information printed at the bottom of the page (footnotes) or the end of a book or document (endnotes).

noun A word or words that name a person, place, thing, or idea.

O

omniscient narrator An all-knowing narrator, who may tell a story from the point of view of any, all, or none of the characters.

on-line Hooked up to a computer network, such as the Internet, and able to share information with other computers.

onomatopoeia A figure of speech in which a word sounds like what it means, such as *buzz, clank,* and *splash.*

overgeneralization A claim that goes beyond what the evidence supports.

P

pan To move a film or video camera horizontally to follow an action or show a wide view of a scene.

panel discussion A group of people invited to speak about their ideas on a certain subject and to respond to one another's comments.

paraphrase To explain someone else's ideas in your own words.

peer conferencing Discussing a draft with other students and looking for ways to improve it.

periodical A printed work that is published at regular intervals, such as a magazine or newspaper.

personal narrative A true story written about something that happened to the narrator.

personal response Reacting to something you see, read, or hear by expressing your feelings and thoughts about it.

personification A figure of speech in which human qualities are given to animals or objects, as in *Flowers danced about the yard.*

phrase A group of words that does not contain both a subject and a verb.

pitch The highness or lowness of a sound.

plot The series of actions and conflicts that make up a story.

point of view The position of a story's narrator; how much the narrator knows about the characters' thoughts and the story's outcome. In film and video, abbreviated *POV*; the narrator is the camera.

predicate A verb, or a group of words including a verb, that tells something about the subject of a sentence.

predraft The stage of the writing process in which you search for ideas and plan your writing.

prefix A word part added to the beginning of a root or word to change its meaning.

prejudice A judgment based on opinions or feelings about someone or something rather than on facts.

preposition A word that relates a noun or pronoun to another word in the sentence.

prepositional phrase A phrase that begins with a preposition and ends with a noun or pronoun that is the object of the preposition.

preview To glance through something you are about to read so you can prepare to think about the material.

pronoun A word that takes the place of a noun.

proofread A stage of the writing process in which you check for errors in grammar, usage, spelling, and punctuation.

propaganda Manipulative communication that tries to influence what people think, often by presenting only those facts that are favourable to the conclusion.

publish The final stage of the writing process, when you present your final draft to others.

publisher A person or company that produces a book, periodical, or other form of communication.

purpose What you hope to accomplish when you begin a task.

Q

quotation The direct use of someone else's words, with credit given to that person.

R

rap A kind of talk-singing that began in West Africa and the Caribbean and that uses many literary devices, like alliteration.

Readers' Theatre A presentation of a script or text by a group of people who use only their voices to create dramatic effects.

rebuttal A short speech in a debate in which you try to disprove your opponents' points.

redundant Needlessly using several words or phrases that mean the same thing, as in *a long and lengthy speech.*

reference section The area of a library that holds collections of factual sources like encyclopedias, almanacs, and dictionaries.

refrain A phrase or verse repeated throughout a poem or song, often at the end of each stanza.

research Careful study of a topic, which involves reading and interviewing various sources and taking notes on the information.

resolution The final working out of the problems or conflicts in a story.

response journal A journal for writing your opinions, thoughts, and feelings about what you read or experience.

revise The stage of the writing process in which you look critically at what you have written and make improvements.

revising checklist A list of problems to look for when revising your writing.

rhetorical question A question you ask without expecting an answer.

rhyme Matching word sounds; often used in poetry.

rhyme scheme A pattern formed by the rhymes, often in a poem.

rhythm The pattern of beats or stresses in spoken or written language.

root The word part that carries the main meaning of a word; also called the *base.*

run-on sentence Two or more sentences punctuated as if they were one sentence.

S

scan To glance through written material in an effort to find something; *or,* in a poem, reading to find the rhythm pattern.

score To write performance directions for a poem to prepare it for a choral reading; *or,* a copy of the poem with directions marked.

script A story made up of dialogue and stage directions, written to be acted out.

sculpture A three-dimensional work of art, usually made of stone, wood, clay, or metal.

sensory language Wording that brings to mind sights, sounds, smells, feelings, and tastes.

sentence A group of words that expresses a complete thought.

sentence fragment Part of a sentence punctuated as if it were an entire sentence.

setting The place and time in which the action of a story takes place.

shooting script The complete text used to create a film or video, containing the dialogue and a description of the action and props.

simile A figure of speech in which seemingly unlike things are compared using the word *like* or *as*, as in *He's as light as a feather.*

skim To read quickly through written material for a general idea of the contents.

slant The opinion, perspective, or bias that affects how information is presented or what aspects of a story are emphasized.

sonnet A fourteen-line poem that follows a particular rhyme scheme and metre.

sound effects Recorded or made-up sounds that add to a performance or a video.

spatial order Organizing a description according to where objects are located in relation to others.

special effects Sounds or images that are added to film or video scenes; abbreviated *sfx*.

SQ3R plan An acronym which stands for a reading strategy in which you Survey what you are about to read, ask yourself Questions about it, Read it to answer the questions, Rephrase (or Recite) the answers in your own words, and Review the main headings.

stanza A group of lines in a poem that stand together, separated from other stanzas by a blank line.

stereotype A fixed, often incorrect, idea about certain people or things.

storyboard An outline of a story or advertisement to be filmed, usually containing descriptions, dialogue, and illustrations for each major shot.

stress Emphasis you give to certain words to bring out the rhythm of a poem or the drama in a reading.

subject The word or words, always including a noun or pronoun, that name who or what a sentence is about.

subordinate clause A clause that depends on another independent clause in a sentence.

suffix A word part added to the end of a root or word to change its meaning.

summarize To restate in a few words or sentences the main points of a longer work.

symbol A simple object or picture that stands for a more complicated or abstract idea.

symbolism Using an object in your writing to represent an idea or feeling.

T

tempo The speed or pace of the beat.

tense The feature of a verb that shows time.

theme The message or point of a piece of writing.

Think-Write plan A reading strategy in which you make notes on what is going through your mind as you read.

thumbnail A small sketch you draw to show what a final product might look like.

tilt To move a film or video camera vertically in order to follow an action or to show an unusual point of view.

time order Organizing the events in a story in the order in which they happened.

tone The attitude you communicate when you speak or write.

topic sentence The sentence in a paragraph that states the main idea of the paragraph.

track To follow a moving object while you film it with a film or video camera.

transition A change; transition words and sentences prepare readers for changes in topic so they don't get lost or confused.

typeface A set of type with a particular style and design, such as Times Roman or Helvetica. (See also *font*.)

unity A quality of writing in which all the sentences and paragraphs support one main idea.

verb A word that expresses action or a state of being.

vertical files Library files containing newspaper and magazine clippings.

web site A group of linked documents on the World Wide Web.

writing process A series of stages involved in creating a written work, from thinking about it to showing the final product to others.

z

zoom To adjust the lens on a camera in order to show a section close up or far away.

Index

R

radio
  citing, 264
  mass media, 172
  plays, 161–163
  research, 103, 258
  titles of series, 340
raise/rise difference, 289
rap, scores, 156
Readers' Guide to Periodical Literature, 249, 252
readers' theatre, 163
reading, 12–66
  See also critical reading
  between the lines, 53
  in depth, 25–27
  dramatic, 154, 163
  log, 17
  personalizing, 16–17
  plans, 21–23
  purposes, 13–14, 15
  questions, 43–45
  Recommended Reading lists, 253
  responding to, 17–20
  scores, 155, 156
  speed, 15, 25
reading aloud
  See also reciting
  performance, 152–156, 163
  personalizing reading, 17
  poetry, 58, 59
  publishing your work, 96
reciting, 23, 27
  See also reading aloud
reflecting, writing, 96–97
reflexive pronouns, 272, 275
regular adjectives, 278
regular verbs, 283
relative pronouns, 272
repetition, 143, 149, 156
rephrasing, reading strategy, 24
reports
  oral, 137–138
  research, 74, 113–116
  summary paragraphs in, 90
representing, 205–237
research, 238–265
  See also resources, research
  choosing sources, 253–257
  drafting, 115

field trips, 258
interviews, 132, 259–260
notes, 261–264
persuasive writing, 103
reports, 74, 113–116
using libraries for, 241–252
resolution, story, 51, 52, 109
resources, research
  audiovisual, 255
  computer, 254–255
  gathering, 239
  library, 244–246
  previewing, 253
restrictive labels, 318, 319
reviewing
  books, 55
  film, television, or video, 199
  notes, 5
  reading strategies, 23, 27–29
revising, 92–93, 98, 110
rhetorical questions, 149
rhyme
  free verse, 63
  memory aid, 9, 303
  patterns, 63, 118, 156
  schemes, 60, 64
  sounds of, 60, 61
rhythm
  memory aid, 9, 56
  pattern, 59, 63, 118
  performance, 154, 162
  sounds of, 59, 61
rising action, 51
role play, 166
roots, grammar, 304–305
run-on sentences, 331, 335

S

sans-serif typefaces, 225
scanning
  newspaper articles, 46
  reading, 14–15, 23, 59
  research planning, 239
  visual images, 171
schedules
  managing time, 6, 8
  print, 176
  research, 243
  study, 10
science fiction, 48, 51
script typefaces, 225

sculptures, 174, 210–211, 213
secondary colours, 188
-self pronouns, 275
semicolons, 338–339, 342
sensory language, 54
sentences, 331–335
  See also exclamatory statements or sentences; topic sentences
  capitalization, 312
  closing, 83, 91
  combining, 298, 299, 333, 335
  compound, 235, 337, 338
  constructing, 324–327
  example, 321, 322
  fragments, 331
  opening, 88
  parts, 327
  structures, 326
  subjects, 327, 332
  supporting, 83, 115
  types of, 325
series
  commas, 337
  conjunctions, 298, 299
  semicolons, 339
serif typefaces, 225
settings
  bias and, 40
  media codes, 172
  story elements, 49, 52, 108, 109
short-answer questions, 43–44
short stories, 108–110
  critical reading of, 37
  planning, 74
  titles, 82, 315, 341
  writing tips, 78, 81
silent *e*, 307
silk-screening, 212
similes, 62, 87
simple predicate, 327
simple sentences, 325
simple subjects, 327
simple to complex order, 84
single-word prepositions, 295
singular
  nouns, 268, 269, 270, 289
  pronouns, 272, 273
  verbs, 285
sitcoms, 197
sketches, 45, 115, 236

Credits

Literary Credits

Every reasonable effort has been made to obtain permissions for all articles and data used in this edition. If errors or omissions have occurred, they will be corrected in future editions provided written notification has been received.

p.57 Appeared in *The Moon Is Like a Silver Sickle: A Celebration of Poetry by Russian Children* collected and translated by Miriam Morton. Copyright © 1972 Miriam Morton. Published by Simon & Schuster. Reprinted by permission of Miriam Morton's estate; **p.57** From *Collected Poems* by Langston Hughes. Copyright © 1994 by the Estate of Langston Hughes. Reprinted by permission of Alfred A. Knopf Inc.; **p.59** "The sun that brief December day..." by John Greenleaf Whittier; **p.60** "Dust of Snow" from *The Poetry of Robert Frost* edited by EDWARD CONNERY LATHEM. Copyright © 1951 by Robert Frost. Copyright 1923, © 1969 by Henry Holt and Company. Reprinted by permission of Henry Holt and Company, Inc.; **p.61** "Poetry" by Eleanor Farjeon from *The Children's Bells* edited by Eleanor Farjeon. Published by Oxford University Press; **p.61** "Rush Hour in the Rain" by Tiffany Stone. First appeared in *Do Whales Jump at Night?* edited by Florence McNeil. Copyright © 1990 by Douglas & McIntyre Ltd. Reprinted by permission of the author; **p.62** From *The Wandering Moon and Other Poems* by James Reeves. Copyright © James Reeves. Reprinted by permission of the James Reeves Estate; **p.62** From *The Collected Poems of F.R. Scott* by F.R. Scott. Used by permission of the Canadian publishers McClelland & Stewart, Toronto; **p.63** © Bruce Meyer by permission of the author; **p.63** "Elephants" from *Elephants, Mothers, and Others*

by John Newlove. Copyright © 1963 by John Newlove; **p.64** From *Collected Poems of Edna St. Vincent Millay*. Copyright © 1917, 1945 by Edna St. Vincent Millay. Published by HarperCollins; **p.64** "Annabel Lee" by Edgar Allan Poe; **p.87** Richard Thomas Wright, Maclean Hunter; **p.88** Excerpt by Al Clouston, Dicks and Co.; **p.88** From *Canadian Internet New User's Handbook* by Jim Carroll and Rick Broadhead; **p.118** From *The New Oxford Book of Canadian Verse in English*, edited by Margaret Atwood. Reprinted by permission of University of Toronto Press Incorporated; **p.155** "Dream Dust" by Langston Hughes. Alfred A. Knopf, Inc.; **p.156** "Our Time Has Now Come" Hal Leonard Corporation; **p.262** From "Dialects in the Language of the Bees" by Karl von Frisch. SCIENTIFIC AMERICAN, August 1962, W.H. Freeman and Co. **p.318** Gage Educational Publishing Company, 1997.

Visual Credits

Every reasonable effort has been made to obtain permissions for all articles and data used in this edition. If errors or omissions have occurred, they will be corrected in future editions provided written notification has been received.

p.22 From *Citizenship: Rights and Responsibilities*. Left (top and bottom): Canapress; Right: The Toronto Sun; **p.41** Library of Congress; **p.48** Book cover from *Spirit of the Dragon: The Story of Jean Lumb* by Arlene Chan. Reproduced with permission of Umbrella Press; **p.49** Stoddart Kids; **p.49** PHC Archives; **p.50** PHC Archives; **p.153** Ray Boudreau; **p.157** Helen Mason; **p.175** *Junior Jays Magazine*, Fall 1998; **p.179** R.C.M.P.; **p.184** National Gallery of Canada, Ottawa; **p.185** Bomani Gallery; **p.186** Giraudon/Art Resource, NY; **p.187** Kollwitz,